IMAGES OF WOMEN IN THE FOLK SONGS OF GARHWAL HIMALAYAS

About the Author

Anjali Capila is presently Reader and Head of the Post-graduate Department of Community Resource Management and Extention at the Lady Irwin College, University of Delhi. She teaches Development Communication and is actively involved with the Planning and Organisation of the field work of the department in rural and semi-urban communities. She has been a consultant to UNICEF on a number of projects, namely, "Images of Girls on Television : Perceptions of viewers in Delhi (1988)"; "Training of field functionaries of ICDS (1991)"; "Health and sanitation kit for rural motivators - a study in Jammu and Kashmir (1992)." She co-ordinated a research project "Women leaders in Panchayati Raj" in five States of north India in collaboration with All India Womens' Education Fund Association (1996). She has edited a book entitled *Studies in Communication* which is a compilation of abstracts of the research in Communication and Extension conducted at the Department. This book is based on her doctoral thesis entitled *Socio-cultural images of women in the folk songs of Garhwal Himalayas.*

Address : 4, Doctor's Lane, New Delhi - 110 001 (India) Tel. : 3364529.
E-mail : ladyirwin@vsnl.com.

Concept's Discovering Himalayas Series No . 6

IMAGES OF WOMEN IN THE FOLK SONGS OF GARHWAL HIMALAYAS

A Participatory Research

ANJALI CAPILA

CONCEPT PUBLISHING COMPANY, NEW DELHI-110059

ISBN : 81-7022-896-4

First Published 2002

Published and Printed by
Ashok Kumar Mittal
Concept Publishing Company
A/15-16, Commercial Block, Mohan Garden,
NEW DELHI-110059

Phones : 5648039, 5649024
Fax : 091-11-5648053
E-mail : publishing@conceptpub.com

DEDICATED TO THE WOMEN OF THE GARHWAL HIMALAYAS

PREFACE

The present book looks at folk songs as a source material for understanding women's lives in a society, since women are the active bearers of expressive traditions which are linked to all aspects of life in a community. Here songs have been seen as a process, not as mere descriptive entities of some peripheral, entertainment situations. A holistic image of the women of Garhwal is drawn up by looking at their relationship with the natural environment, their work roles, and their social relationships. Songs describing the beauty — aesthetics — of a woman as well as various life cycle events, and those incorporating aspects of social change related to women's lives also form an integral part of this research.

The conceptual-theoretical framework provides a background, in order to state that folk songs are to be understood as a matter of actual experience; through participation and observation. It is at this experiential-participatory level that folk songs are able to provide a great cohesiveness to the community.

The introduction chapter sets forth the problem, discusses the importance of oral traditions in the context of Indian civilization, with special emphasis on folk songs. It looks at various definitions of folk songs, locating these songs as entry points to a culture. It goes on to examine the crucial theme of folk songs as a source material for understanding women's lives among the communities of Garhwal.

The second chapter gives the profile of the area; the physical, geographical features as well as briefly the history and culture of Garhwal. The dress, food habits, caste structure of the people of Garhwal are described in general as background material. The district of Tehri Garhwal where this research was conducted is discussed in greater detail, particularly the two blocks of Bilangana and Chamba where the songs were collected from.

The third chapter entitled the approach deals with the theoretical aspects of the research and focuses on the notion of participation as an integral aspect of all stages of the study.

The fourth chapter is the analysis and discussion chapter, which is divided into six sections. The first section deals with songs relating to nature and ecology in the context of women's lives. In the second section songs describing the life-cycle events, viz. birth of a child, *mundan* ceremony and all aspects of the wedding ceremony are analysed with special reference to the images of women as reflected in them. The third section focuses on various dimensions of the social relations of the women of Garhwal as reflected in the songs. The fourth section highlights the work roles of the women of Garhwal. Her daily routine and her position in the family in the context of her contribution to the community life are also emphasised. In the fifth section songs describing the beauty of the woman of Garhwal have been analysed. The sixth section highlights the aspects of dissent, protest and social change as reflected in the songs on issues related to women's lives.

The summary and conclusion chapter reiterates the important contribution of this research, followed by the epilogue.

In the presentation of this book visuals form a very integral aspect. The content of the songs and the context in which they are sung create visual images which are presented here in the form of line drawings. Every word creates a picture, an image. Transcreating this image on to paper, as well as the songs from their local Garhwali dialect, was indeed a challenge to me.

In addition, the photographic evidence of this study adds further to the visual aspect of the environment of Garhwal.

Appendix I contains all the 150 songs collected from the area in the original Garhwali script. These have been translated into English by me and some of these appear in the text.

Appendix II contains all the transcribed recorded interviews with various persons in Garhwal as well as interviews with some women. These are presented in Hindi.

Appendix III is a compilation of the socio-economic cultural background of the people of Garhwal as narrated to me by the women and several resource persons, during their intensive group discussions. These describe the physical features, rivers, ceremonies, food-habits, methods of agricultural practices, life of women in particular, family relationships, etc. This forms the contextual background of the canvas against which the songs are set. They are presented in Hindi.

ANJALI CAPILA

ACKNOWLEDGEMENTS

How does one begin to acknowledge and thank so many individuals on a journey like the one I undertook, from New Delhi to the Garhwal Himalayas in pursuit of understanding a culture and transforming this experience into a construct for knowledge.

I gratefully acknowledge :

* Dr. Geeta Katarya, Reader in the Department of Child Develoment, Lady Irwin College, under whose supervision this research was conducted.
* Dr. Satinder Bajaj, Director, Lady Irwin College, for encouraging me to pursue a Ph.D. programme.
* The women of Tehri Garhwal, whom I interacted with, over a period of three years. Their warmth, enthusiasm and joy at participating in all the stages of the research was indeed a special experience. The hospitality and affection I received cannot be described in words. The voices of the women reverberate in my ears, and our 'dialogue' still continues at many levels.
* Dr. M. L. Dewan, Director for 'Trees for Life India', who initiated me into the Tehri Garhwal region where his projects are located. Dr. Dewan's insights, knowledge of the region, and wide network of contacts with NGOs in the area helped tremendously in my field work. I also thank Rakesh Bahuguna and Shanti Bahuguna who work for 'Trees for Life' in Ranichauri Garhwal, for their help.
* Shri Bihari Lal, Secretary 'Lok Jeevan Vikas Bharati', Budakedar; Shri Pratap Shekhar, Director, 'Uttarakhand Jan Jagriti Sansthan', Khadi Jajal; and Shri Ganga Prasad Bahuguna, NGO Representative, "Parvatiya Jan Kalyan Samiti", Ranichauri, Chamba; who spent several hours of their valuable time drawing up the contextual framework of the society in Garhwal. Their vast experience and knowledge of the culture of the region added richness to the research.
* Smt. Shashi and Vipin Raturi of 'Mahila Nav Jagran Samiti Chamba' for providing me a home to stay in on my various field visits to Garhwal; it was a home where I could meet several resource persons involved with development work in the region of Tehri Garhwal. After a hard

day's work and walking 12 to 15 kilometers, coming home to a hot-meal, and warmth and affection was a great support.

* Dr. Rajan and Reena Sharma, Chief Medical Officers, Hill Campus, Ranichauri; Dr. Veer Singh and Dr. Kedial, Professors of Animal Husbandry and Agricultural Extension respectively for their valuable suggestions and insights on the status of women in the Hill areas.
* Shri Narayan Bisht from Tehri Garhwal who helped with writing the Appendices.
* Shri Murari Lal, from village Pata in Tehri Garhwal who worked pains-takingly on transcribing the 15 audio-cassettes of 90 minutes duration each.
* Shri Manoj Pande, Secretary, 'Himalaya Seva Sangh', New Delhi; Ms. Radha Bhatt from Lakshmi Ashram, Kausani; Shri Vishveshwar Dutt Saklani who got the Indira Gandhi Vriksh Mitra Puruskar; Shri Bhawani Bhai, Secretary, Remand Home for Boys in Tehri; and Smt. Ramabehn in-charge of the Mahila Samakhya Project Tehri, for their support and help in understanding so many aspects of the socio-cultural environment of the Garhwal Himalayas.
* Dr. Kapila Vatsyayan, Academic Director, Indira Gandhi National Centre for the Arts, New Delhi, for the opportunity to interact with scholars in various disciplines. The excellent collection in the library of IGNCA was a great help, along with the facilities of the computer centre and the staff.
* Also at IGNCA, Shri P. T. Deshpande, the cartographer who prepared the maps.
* Dr. S. C. Malik, UGC Professorial Scientist, Nehru Memorial Museum and Library for introducing me to a wide reading on 'Integral Listening' and the 'Participatory Universe'; and, his other valuable theoretical and editorial inputs, that went into several drafts.
* Mr. Vijay Chandhok from Pittsburgh, U.S.A. who has taken and composed the photographs with great sensitivity.
* Pranav Capila, my younger son, for his editorial comments, and insights into the analysis of the songs; and my elder son, Ishan Capila and his wife Priya for their interest in my work.
* The love, warmth and support of 'Appanji' my mother-in-law throughout the Ph.D. programme, who looked after the home in my long absences during and after my field work. And my husband Vinay Capila for his quiet support.
* All my colleagues in the Department of Community Resource Management and Extension, Lady Irwin College, for their support and

encouragement.

* The grace of 'Thakur' Sri Ramkrishna and Sharada 'Ma' without which the journey to the Himalayas and this enriching experience would not have been a reality.

CONTENTS

LIST OF PLATES

LIST OF MAPS AND FIGURES

MAPS

FIGURES

LIST OF SKETCHES

The Garhwal Mountains — A View

PROLOGUE

In the summer of 1992, I visited Garhwal for a pilgrimage to Kedarnath and Badrinath. Besides the grandeur of the Himalayas, the waterfalls, the thick forests and the temples, I was fascinated by the people, their myths, and the beliefs associated with the river Ganga. Every little stream had a history, a reason for its existence. The myths seemed to permeate the very fabric of the life of the people across the length and breadth of the region.

At one confluence, on our way to Badrinath, I asked the local guide why the stream joining the Alaknanda was called the 'Birahi Ganga'. According to him, Lord Vishnu asked his consort Goddess Laxmi to leave him at that point, so that he could move alone into the Himalayas. This was for the attainment of salvation and the ultimate merging with the Universal Consciousness. The Goddess Laxmi wept and wept for days at the separation from her 'lord' and hence the name 'Birahi Ganga'. The imagery stayed with me for a long time creating within me a need to know more about these myths and narratives.

Beyond Badrinath, at a distance of about 4 km. is a quaint village called Mana, which they say is the last village on the border of India. At Mana we met a local man, about 90 years old, who told us that the Saraswati river has its origin in a gorge there. It is believed that when Vyas muni was dictating the Mahabharat in a cave near by, the noise of the Saraswati river disturbed him and he asked the river to keep quiet. The belief is that the Saraswati river disappears underground at this point and only re-appears at the Triveni at Allahabad.

The old man looked at me and said, "If you have any desire to study more, drink some water of the Saraswati, or touch it to your forehead". I was surprised to hear him say something about my plans to register for a Ph.D. and doing some meaningful work! I walked a few yards to the gorge where the Saraswati river falls about a 100 feet down and felt its spray on my face. There were no thoughts at that moment, only Silence........

On coming back to Delhi, many things fell into place. Garhwal had left a lasting impression and I was determined to come and work here.

Since 1986, a major focus of research in Communication at the Department of Community Resource Management and Extension in Lady Irwin College, New Delhi, had been documenting the life styles of women as reflected in the folk songs of an area. We had collected folksongs of Haryana, Himachal Pradesh(Palampur), Rajasthan (Sikar districts), and analysed them with special reference to the images of women as reflected in them. Modification of folk songs with the participation of the women had formed a significant aspect of these researches.

Keeping in mind the multi-disciplinary and integrated methodologies of social anthropology and communication which are a part and parcel of social science research, and a consequence of the on going work stated above, I was motivated to continue the work in the area of the Garhwal Himalayas.

In the context of the above experience, some significant questions began to emerge in my mind. Is a song the soul of a society? Does it mirror a culture in its entirety? Are songs an expression of a woman's lived experience? Does she breathe life and meaning into them? Do they in turn provide valuable insights into her life? This study attempts to answer some of these questions in the following chapters, i.e. several aspects are looked at in terms of the context in which the songs are sung. The focus is thus on songs as a source material for reflecting various socio-cultural images of the women of the Garhwal Himalayas. What is significant and relevant in this research is that it is not simply a documentation of the songs and an analysis of their contents, but it includes the world view of the women, their feelings, and the perception of their songs. Most important of all it is the method and approach which is significant since it involves the participation of the researcher and the women at all stages of the research, thus forming an integral part of the study.

The Journey Begins — on the way from Rishikesh to Chamba

THE PROCESS

The thesis on which this book is based "Images of Women in the Folk Songs of Garhwal Himalayas — A Participatory Research" was undertaken to examine the following objectivies :

1. To examine the potential of folk songs as a source material for understanding women's lives.
2. To study the relationship, if any between the life-patterns of the women of Garhwal and the content of the folk songs.
3. To analyse the content of the folk songs with special reference to women in terms of the following aspects :

   (a) Women and enviornment.
   (b) Life-cycle events.
   (c) Social relations.
   (d) Work roles/activities performed.
   (e) Aesthetic depiction.
   (f) Contemporary issues.

Methodology of field work : Collection of songs

Locale of Investigation

Garhwal comprises the five hill districts of Dehradun, Uttarkashi, Tehri Garhwal, Pauri Garhwal and Chamoli. The present study was conducted in the Tehri Garhwal region of the Garhwal Himalayas :

For entering any region or community for the purpose of research certain factors act as guidelines for investigation.

(a) Either the researcher belongs to the area.
(b) Personally knows people working in the region.

Dr. Madan Dewan, Director Himalayan Consortium for Trees for Life, (an NGO, located at Ranichauri, Tehri Garhwal) was known to me for a while in the context of sharing his work and ideas. Several discussion were held with him and other NGOs, including Manoj Pande, Secretary Himalaya Seva Sangh. A decision was taken to make an exploratory visit to the field in March 1993.

While some degree of theoretical, ethnographic or linguistic preparation was undertaken prior to going into the field, it was decided to allow many of these issues to surface during work as one observed, experienced, and interacted with people on the exploratory visit.

The learning process began in the car itself as we covered the distance from Delhi to Gurukul Kangri (Haridwar), our first stage in the journey. The discussions focused on women's participation in agriculture in the hill communities of Tehri Garhwal, the absence of the male for occupational reasons, the relationship of women to the environment, formal institutions in the area, viz. primary schools, secondary schools and the role of NGOs.

At Gurukul Kangri we interacted with a number of teachers working on different projects in the Garhwal region — ranging from aquaculture/ fisheries and bee-keeping, to compilation of work on Vedic philosophy as related to the Himalayan eco-system. The discussions were enriching, creating visual images about the area where I was to work. Such experiential sharing is indeed a richer source of knowledge rather than the mere reading of texts. One is in no way trying to denigrate the latter which is so necessary to develop a theoretical background. The intention here is to focus on the value of experiencing, sharing of ideas and interaction as constructs for anthropological knowledge.

The contextual framework was being drawn up every moment. It can be argued that such wide ranging discussions have no direct bearing on the research being undertaken, viz. 'Women and folk songs'. The focus of this research, is not to look at songs as entities as such in isolation, but as a process; and, to understand this process, an understanding of the context in its multi-layered manifestations becomes significant. Hence, the need to evolve a new methodological approach.

At Rishikesh we stopped to meet Yogesh Bahugana, Founder-member of an NGO — Parvitya Jankalyan Samiti, working with women's groups in various villages at Tehri Garhwal. Interestingly we walked into a meeting of women representatives of Mahila-Mandals from Tehri Garhwal, and they were discussing the issue of 33 per cent reservation for women in the Gram Panchayats. The women present there waited patiently to be introduced to me, one could sense their eagerness. Dr. Dewan's brief one line introduction, "Anjalibehn teaches at Lady Irwin College and has come to Tehri Garhwal to understand and collect your songs.."created warm ripples in the group. The refrain went around , "our voice, our songs, our voice.." and I knew that I was accepted. The expressions on their faces, the feedback was indeed special, I already felt included in their inner space, a very significant aspect of participatory research.

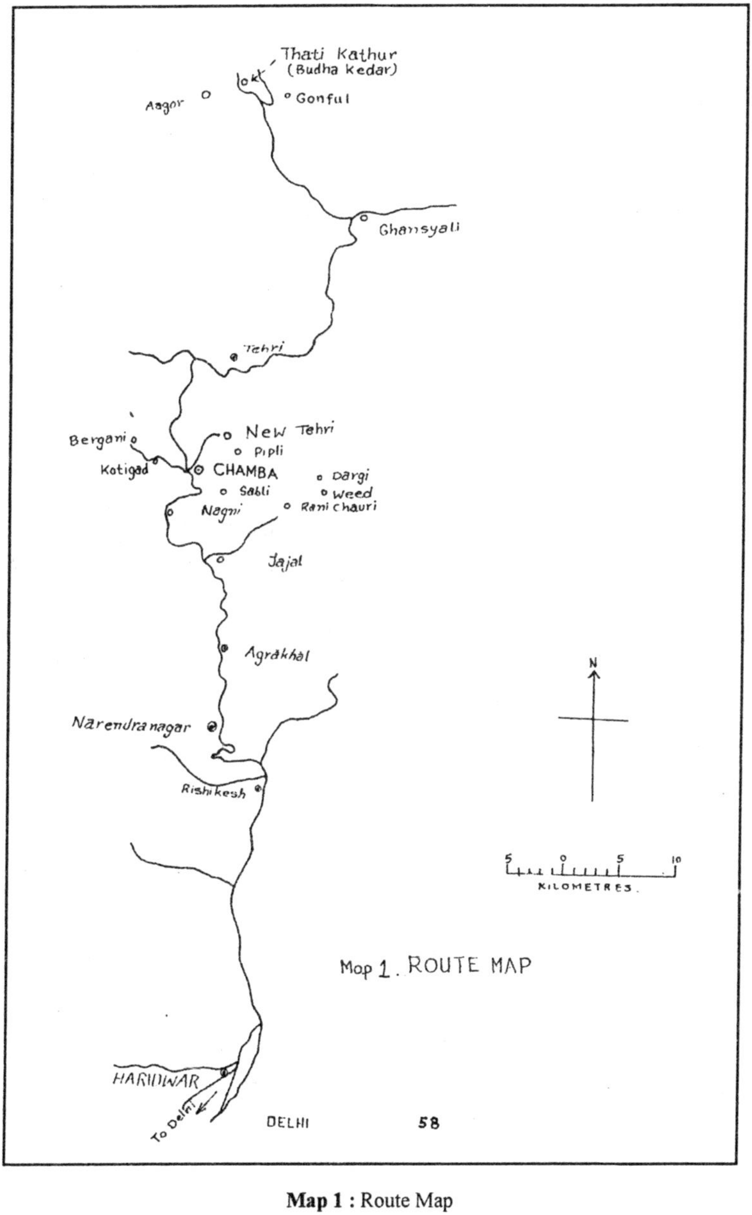

Map 1 : Route Map

The networking of NGOs working in the areas began to take shape as we moved up from Rishikesh, beyond Narendernagar, (the district headquarter for Tehri Garhwal), on to Khadi Jajal, situated on the banks of the Himal river at a height of 3,000 ft. At Khadi Jajal is located the NGO — Uttarakhand Jan Jagriti Sansthan, run by Pratap Shekhar and his wife Dularibehn, who had both worked with Chandi Prasad Bhatt in the *Chipko Andolan.*

A folk song collected later at the Hadamb village in Chamba block, sung by Vimlabehn outlines the journey from Rishikesh to Chamba, and makes a reference to all the places enroute describing their distinct characteristics.

Uttarakhand Jan Jagriti Sansthan was founded by Pratap Shekhar and its activities focus mainly on Mahila Mandals for women, environmental issues, and setting up Balwadis for children. At Khadi, Pratapbhai introduced me to Ryal Guruji, music teacher in the schools run by the organisation and to his eighty year old mother. Ryal Guruji quickly went and got his harmonium and sang a few songs which were recorded. Interestingly all the three songs he sung were about women, he said that he had learnt them from Pratapbhai's mother — who was beaming with joy at her songs being sung. Gonadevi the mother talked about women's lives, their work roles, their age of marriage, their participation in agricultural tasks, and their special relationship with the environment. I was being soaked with experiential knowledge, not just mere objective information.

Already NGO's as an entry point for the research was becoming an established methodological approach on this exploratory visit.

After a two hour halt at Khadi Jajal, we moved towards Ranichauri, at a height of about 6,000 ft. above sea level, and a distance of 6 km from Chamba. At Ranichauri Dr. Dewan had organised a meeting of representatives of the two NGOs — Trees for Life and Parvatiya Jan Kalyan Samiti, as well as resource persons from the Hill Campus which included Dr. Veer Singh, Dr. Kedial, Dr. B.D. Nautyal and Dr. Rajesh Uppal. Women representatives of Mahila Mandals from three villages were also present.

The discussions were varied in nature, ranging from deforestation and its impact on women's lives, to starting income generating activities and small scale industries from local produce, in order to give employment to men who were migrating in large numbers to the plains and metropolitan cities, because of lack of opportunities in the hill state of Garhwal. The researcher's work on folk songs and women's lives was discussed at length. It generated great enthusiasm both from the academics, as well as representatives from the NGOs. "Women are the backbone of Garhwal", said Ganga Prasad Bahuguna representative of the NGO Parvitya Jan Kalyan Samiti, "Any work on their songs would indeed be truly representative of their lives".

The women representatives of the Mahila Mandal of village Ranichauri, Sabli, Dargi were also present at this meeting. It was Vimlabehn of village Dargi who said, in Hindi, "Didi, in these villages located near the town Chamba, the practice of singing is much less now because other

Plate 1 : Ganga Prasad Bahuguna — NGO Representative, Ranichauri Chamba

sources of entertainment are available here, like the TV. If you were to go into the interior regions and collect songs from villages located at a distance from the road, you would get a more realistic picture". What wisdom and clarity of thought; all the academics present there were quite stumped by Vimlabehn's profound intervention.

Another aspect of the methodological approach of participation of women at all stages of the research got strengthened and reaffirmed during the exploratory visit.

Visits were made to the above mentioned villages, Ranichauri, Sabli and Dargi, along with the Mahila Mandal representatives, in the next couple of days. The women in the villages were warm, enthusiastic and absolutely thrilled at the fact that somebody was making an attempt to listen to their songs and understand their lives.

"Nobody has focused their attention on the women of Garhwal. If you had merely talked to us and written your work it would not be so correct, but to look at our lives through our songs is indeed special", said Khushadevi of village Sabli.

Every utterance from the women in the villages was more profound than the other! How did these so called unlettered women, understand in seconds the significance of the research, its relationship to their lives? Where in our world of information technology do we include this level of communication, this kind of experiential knowledge? These questions perplexed me, while at the same time confirming that I was on the right track.

It was strange that coming from such different ethnographic and linguistic background the area of commonness was so great. These experiences dispel the much fragmented dichotomy of me vs. you, the observer from observed, and point to the integral wholeness of cultures when they are experienced from 'within'. The approach chapter refers to these aspects which are are strengthened by the method of work in this research (Malik 1995).

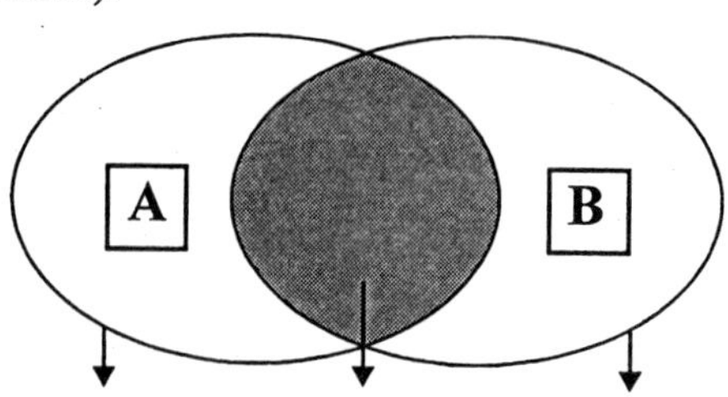

Fig. 0.1 : Field Experience of Researcher and Women

Each aspect emerging from the exploratory visit has a significant contribution to make to the methodology of field work for research studies in the areas of folk-lore, anthropology and communication; in fact in all social science research.

At Chamba, Dr. Dewan introduced me to Vipin Raturi and Shashi Raturi, founder members of the NGO, Mahila Nav Jagran Samiti (MNS), working with women in the forty villages of Chamba and Thaldar block. During the next three days visits were made to five villages; Kotigad, Pipli, Hadamb, Bergani and Manjyar, located at various distances from Chamba, accompanied by Shashibehn. This facilitated rapport formation with the women and the acceptance of myself, into their inner space. What emerged significantly during these visits was :

(a) that Mahila Mandal meetings were cohesive groups, where group interaction with women could happen with great ease;
(b) that women were constantly creating new songs, adding new content focusing on issues concerning their lives. For example, women sang songs on alcoholism, the Tehri dam, the changing image of Chamba town; and
(c) that the visit also helped me to get familiar with the activities of MNS, in these villages.

Since one of the objectives of this research was to look at this aspect of folk-songs and women's lives, it was decided to work in these villages for data collection related to these aspects.

Dr. Dewan also felt that the researcher should meet the District Magistrate of Tehri Garhwal, since work was being done in her area. Mrs. Deepa Singh Bagai, DM of Tehri Garhwal (1993) was very supportive and promised to provide facilities for lodging and travel, since these always posed a constraint in the remote areas.

There was a lot of deliberation on Vimlabehn's intervention about collecting songs from interior regions and hence the valley of Budakedar was selected where the NGO Lok Jeewan Vikas Bharati is situated. The high level of networking between all the NGOs working in Tehri Garhwal was evident.

I visited the valley of Budakedar along with Manoj Pande of Himalaya Seva Sangh. Budakedar is located at a distance of 80 km from Chamba in the Bilangana block of Tehri Garhwal. It is situated on the confluence of the two rivers, Dharam Ganga and Bal Ganga.

At Budakedar we met Behari Lalji, the founder director of Lok Jeewan Vikas Bharati, his wife Suman and other workers of the organisation, which is Gandhian in ideology. Behari Lalji invited women representatives of Mahila Mandals of three neighbouring villages and the local primary school teachers and health workers from the dispensary.

Discussions were held at length on the genesis of the organisation, its activities and outreach, the role of Mahila Mandal chiefs and the life patterns of women in these remote areas where electricity and other facilities like electric mills for grinding grain were not available.

I visited the villages of Aagor, Gonful, Budakedar, with the Mahila Mandal representatives. We also visited the 14th century Kedarnath temple called Budakedar, named so because apparently Lord Shiva had done *tapasya* here in his old age before attaining salvation. A Swaymbhu Shivling in the shape of a mountain had appeared at this site and is worshipped with as much reverence as the shrine at Kedarnath. The temple is looked after by priests of the family belonging to the Gorakhnath Panthi tradition.

The walk to Aagor was arduous, a steep climb through terraced hillsides. The housing structure was different here from the ones seen near Ranichauri/Chamba. The elderly women in the house still wore the traditional dress. Since Budakedar is not on the tourist track not too many people are seen here. It is quite untouched by urban culture in many ways. The women in the villages were eager to know who I was. Being with Dharamdevi the Mahila Mandal representative of village Thati, made interaction easy.

Again, what was significant was the joy and enthusiasm expressed by the women at the idea of the researcher documenting their songs in order to understand their lives. It seems as if I had somehow established an 'unsaid' deeper contact of communication. In the context of the women of Garhwal it seemed a very relevant source material for my study.

Highlights of the Exploratory Visit

1. The exploratory visit was helpful in giving an insight or unfolding the canvas of the area. It provided useful information about the village situation, the demographic profile, socio-economic structure and life patterns of the people. While observations helped, it was the interaction with various resource people, representatives of NGOs and village women that helped understand the contextual framework within which the 'Image of the Woman of Garhwal' is etched.
2. NGOs working in Tehri Garhwal emerged as a relevant entry point into the community :

(a) The NGOs have emerged from the grassroots level themselves, and their organisations are run by people belonging to the community itself;

(b) Their knowledge thus about the socio-cultural dynamics of life has strong foundations as it is not mere 'text-book knowledge but grounded on experiential first-hand knowledge';

(c) Since men in the community are away either in the army or employed in jobs in the plains, most of these organisations work hand in hand with the women of the community. This was very helpful since the focus of my research was the women of Garhwal; hence, the right entry point through these NGOs; and

(d) The NGOs co-ordinated their activities at the community level by the formation of Mahila Mandals. These were cohesive groups where women from different cross-sections of the population would gather at one venue. So, while the NGO itself became the entry point, it was the Mahila Mandal setup which was used by the researcher to interact with the village women.

Based on the highlights of the exploratory visit, three villages were

Fig. 0.2 : NGO's working in the area emerged as a significant entry point for the research.

selected near Chamba, and three villages from the interior valley of Budakedar. This was done bearing in mind the suggestions made by the NGOs, resource persons and village women, that different perspectives would be operational for those women living in the vicinity of town and roads, and those living in the interior regions of the hill state. This is important in the context of my emphasis on understanding oral traditions in general and folk songs in particular. Dr. Kusum Nautyal who documented the folk songs and literature of Garhwal with special reference to women for her doctoral thesis in 1982, also emphasised the significance of collecting material from the interior regions for the documentation of oral traditions, in a personal meeting with the researcher at her residence in Delhi.

The Map 2 indicates the geographical area in terms of location of

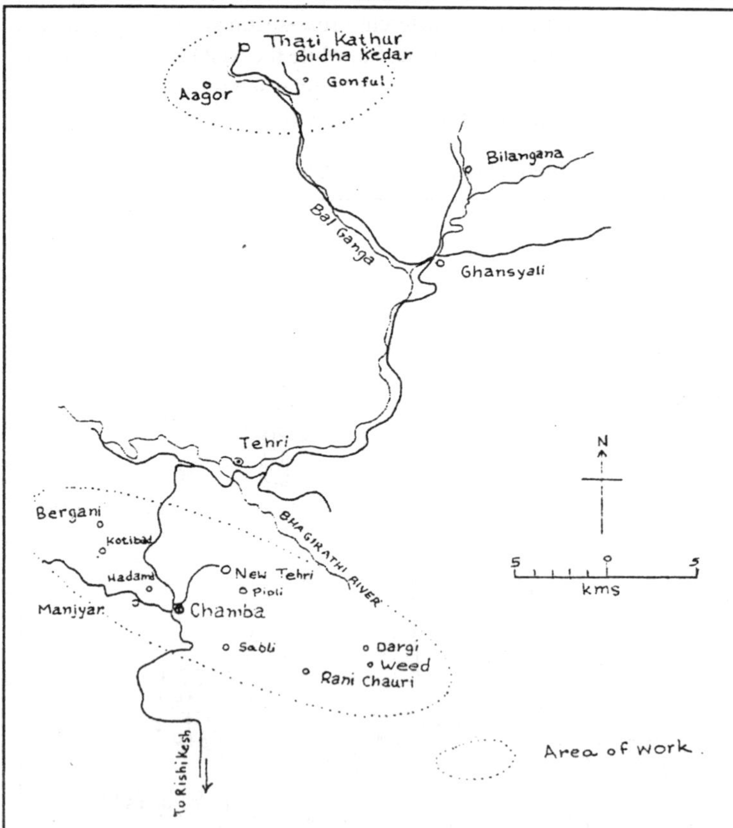

Map 2 : Detailed Area of Work in Chamba and Bilangana Block — District Tehri Garhwal

villages, in the two blocks of Chamba and Bilaganga in the district of Tehri Garhwal where the study was conducted.

I contacted and interacted with as many women as possible, depending upon their availability and convenience in each village. Two different approaches were used to do this.

The first approach was to meet women at a Mahila Mandal meeting in their village along with a representative of the NGO working in that particular village.

The second approach was to visit the house of a woman and she in turn would call out to the others from neighbouring households, again forming a cohesive group for interaction. Women from 3 to 4 houses would gather within a few minutes and one would be in the midst of a highly interactive vibrant group.

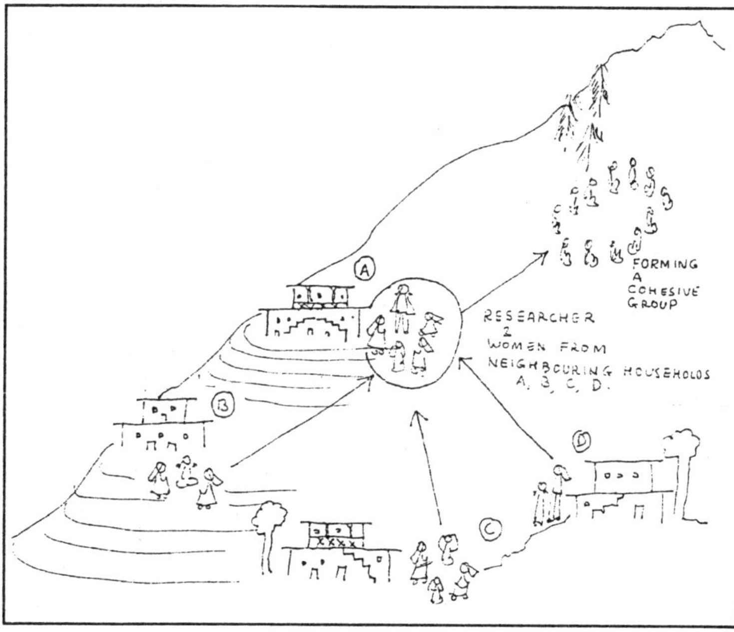

Fig. 0.3 : Processual Approach of Collecting Data

I also interacted with women from five villages, namely, Kotigad, Manjyar, Bergani, Pipli and Hadamb which had been adopted by the Mahila Nav Jagran Samiti for its activities in order to collect songs with new content on social issues concerned with women's lives.

Exploratory Visit

Contact with NGOs working in Chamba and Bilangana block

Visit to Mahila Mandal : Meeting with local NGO reps.

I. Mahila Mandals | Mahila Mandals | Mahila Mandals

* Group Discussions.
* Recording of Songs.
* Understanding Meanings of content from women.
* Understanding the context of the song in relation to actual life patterns. Women's Perception.

II. Individual Homes (Networking on the Hill Side)

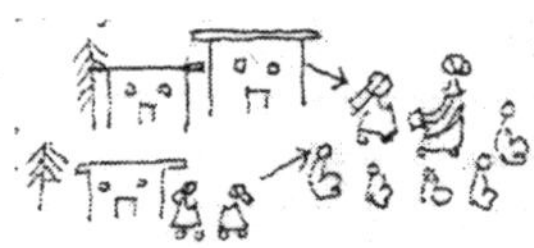

* Women from 2-3 households gather to form a small cohesive group.
* Recording of Songs.
* Understanding Meanings.
* Discussions with women.

III. Forests/Jungles

* Walking to forest with a group of women.
* Recording Songs in Natural Surroundings.
* Understanding Meanings.
* Discussions with women.

IV. Interaction with reps. of Local Institutions.
* Primary School Teachers.
* Secondary School Teachers.

* Village Pradhan.
* Mahila Mandal Chief.
* Reps. and Heads of NGOs.
* Academics from Universities.
* Adm. Personnel - DM/SDM/DFO.

Participation of women at every stage was a significant part of the research. The word data truly does not encompass the range of information and experiential knowledge being 'soaked' in. Since the canvas of the research was to include the 'hum behind the words' the sounds and visual images of the environment; and to link these contextually to the women's songs and her life; a lot more was happening than the mere collection of data. The word is limited in a way, yet in this research its wider usage is suggested. I have discussed about analogic and digital markers as indicators of development in the approach chapter. The word 'digital' represents, quantitative/objective information; whereas analogic represents or includes simultaneity. All events happening simultaneously in the culture which contribute to the holistic image of the woman as reflected in her song are of significance to the research. Hence, even though the tools may be conventional like recording, writing, interviewing, observing, they were used with a more intuitive, sensitive and empathetic presence. The recording of songs was supplemented by writing field notes and verbatim reports.

Since the methodological approach was more experiential in nature, observations were made on various aspects. The beauty of the natural environment, the home environment, the dress, and the jewellery worn by women, their participation in life in the community, their visibility. Observations were not restricted to places where women were contacted like Mahila Mandal meetings or individual home visits, but everywhere. Walking in the forest, in the market place, waiting at a bus-stop, in the fields, and so on.

A number of scholars (Bahulkar 1964, Chatak 1973, Nautyal 1992) have classified the Garhwali folk songs into various categories. However, before looking at the classifications presented by scholars it is essential to look at the way the folk songs have been classified by the local people. The following classification of Garhwali Lok Geet has been cited by Chatak (1973):

Jagar geet.
Mangal geet

Basanti, Chaiti geet
Khuder geet
Baju-Band geet
Laman geet
Chopti geet
Barahamasa geet
Holi geet
Chaufla geet
Tharya geet
Jhumalo geet

Based on the local categorisation Chatak (1973) classified Garhwali folk songs according to the essential elements inherent in them. His classification is as follows :

(a) Religous songs — Jagar,etc.
(b) Samskara songs — Mangal geet.
(c) Ritu geet — Barahmasa, Basanti, Chaiti.
(d) Nritya geet — Laman, Chopti, Chufla, Jhumalo.
(e) Love songs — Pranya geet.
(f) Miscellaneous songs.
(g) Folk tales.

Accordings to him all the categories in the classification by the local people can be assimilated in the above seven categories.

Govind Chatak's work (1973) focussed on documentation and analysis of Garhwali songs in order to draw up a complete picture of the life of the people of Garhwal. Many years later Kusum Nautyal (1982) worked on Garhwali folk songs and folk tales with special reference to the portrayal of women in them. She classified the folk songs as :

(a) Mangal songs.
(b) Love songs.
(c) Songs reflecting the emotional state of a woman (Khuder, Chaufla, Jhumalo)
(d) Songs reflecting the historical social context of women.
(e) Songs describing the beauty of a woman.

In the context of the recent research keeping in mind the objective of drawing up a holistic image of the women of Garhwal the songs collected were classified initially broadly into two categories :

1. The Natural Environment.
2. The Socio-Cultural Environment.

During group discussions with women in the village and interaction with various resource persons the integral relationship of the women of Garhwal with the environment came up for discussion. All of the songs have a poetic - descriptive - content and a social and emotional content, infact songs are multi-layered. Their classification therefore into categories is indeed difficult as they overlap.

A song was first placed into a category according to its predominant feature. In the context of the natural environment, four distinct categories emerged, as follows :

(a) Songs describing the land.
(b) Songs about forest/trees.
(c) Songs about water.
(d) Songs about seasons.

All these songs were then analysed in relation to women's lives. The portrayal of women with reference to the socio-cultural environment was studied in terms of the following categories :

Songs of celebration of life-cycle events.

(a) Birth of a child.
(b) Mundan .
(c) Marriage.

Social relations

These were explored in terms of the relationships in the parent's home and in the husband's home. The social interaction with friends and peer group as reflected in songs was also looked at in this category.

Work-roles

In order to understand the contribution of the women of Garhwal to the society, a study of their work-roles and, activities performed becomes essential. All songs reflecting or mirroring these aspects were put into this category.

Aesthetic depiction

Songs describing the beauty of the women of Garhwal, as well as her ornaments are analysed in this category.

Dissent, protest, social change

Songs are not static. They keep changing and reflect aspects of women's lives. In this category songs sung by women which reflect dissent or protest in some form are analysed. Songs of social issues related to her life which mirror a positive aspect are also looked at in this category.

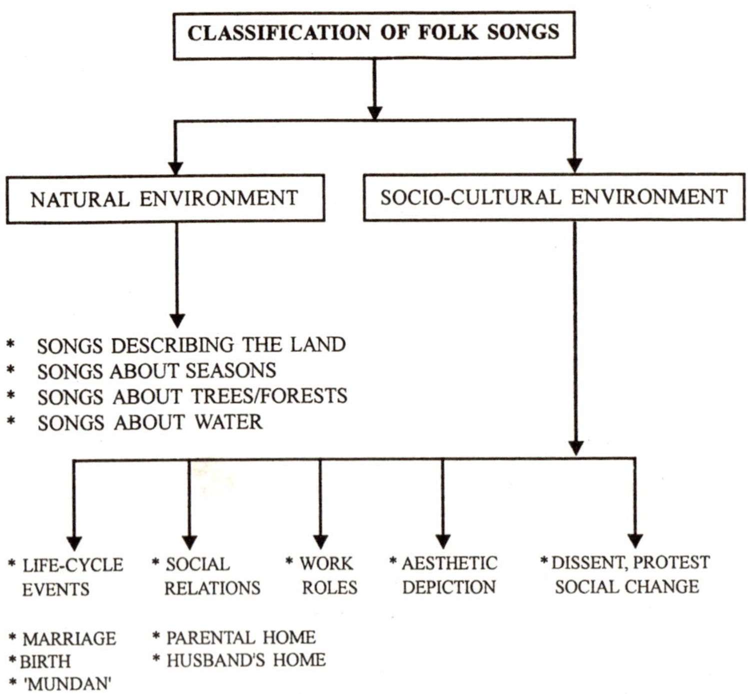

Fig. 0.4 : Diagramatic Representation of Classification of folk songs.

The following chapters based on the above classification present a detailed analysis and discussion of the songs in the context of the above categories. The English translation of some the songs is presented in the text, original Garhwali songs have been presented in the Appendix I.

What is significant here is that besides the analysis of the content of the song, the women's perception of the song as well as related commentary with various resource persons have also been integrated to enrich the analysis. The focus of the research is not merely on an analysis of the content of a song but understanding it in the context of women's lived experience. It is their words that enrich this source material.

A Garhwali Woman — Village Budakedar

1

INTRODUCTION

Oral Traditions in India

The transmission of culture in India may be seen within the totality of a communication system. Within this system an important subsystem is the oral means as for instance seen in the performance of myths, songs, dance, stories, and folk tales. These forms of audio-visual — non-verbal and verbal — expressions are all unwritten modes of human communication that have played an important role in the history of human civilizations. It was only about 6000 years ago, that the written word became an ingredient for the growth of culture. Today, against the background of the modern urban-industrial world, a study of the dynamics of oral traditions which are fast disappearing, requires a serious research endeavour.In recent years disciplines like anthropology and many others have recognised the significance of performance, memory, emotions, artistic actions, linguistic and other forms of literary unwritten texts. This is an area also of interest to oral historians for constructing historical fact, and for others to seek psychological and social constructions of past and present societies.

Today the modern world is in the midst of a revolution in information-technology, represented by the growth of computer-systems, radio and television networks, newspaper circulation and so on. These items are often taken to be indicators of the quality of life, representing 'development' and 'progress'. While at one level this may be an accurate statement, but do these indicators truly reflect an improvement in the quality of modern life ? There is a serious rethinking emerging in recent years about some of these modern concepts. These have tended to ignore other widely known cultural communication systems present amongst those communities which continue to follow their own indigenous — non-Western and non-industrial — world views. Here, cultural traditions are handed down by word of mouth. This is unlike modern man whose psyche is bombarded with messages — thoughts — that are so far removed from experiential reality that he is reduced to a passive recipient, and has become an 'object' of some one-sided monologue, minus the human face. Today when some researchers in the humanities and the sciences are re-formulating alternative paradigms, they are increasingly realising the importance of the experiential dimension of the transmission of tradition, especially amongst oral cultures. As is being emphasised throughout this book, this approach also allows one to take into account the many facets of human cultures; it partakes the idea of a dialogue which has been crucial for the continuation of this plurality of cultures, and their dynamics. This is what is intrinsic to Indian civilization.

In India, oral traditions cover a major area of human life, especially as it is tied up intricately with the written word. The oral and written interaction is part of a whole network of human communication system in which a number of different media and processes are involved. The notion of pure forms is practically and theoretically no longer true. In this process of studying oral traditions, new terms are emerging, such as 'discourse','text','narrative', 'performance', 'folk', etc. in order chiefly to bridge the old divide which made it difficult by and large to understand the long continuity of a civilization like the Indian one. It allows one to give attention on comparative questions about historical and cultural specific approaches to cultures local, regional and all-India ones.

My focus is thus on the multi-layered nature of the transmission of human expression — especially on audio-visual, verbal and artistic, excluding the literary ones. At the level of aesthetics and ethics, this perspective points towards some intrinsic commonness of creative cultural beings, beyond merely their socio-economic status. Now, for example, cultural continuity may be seen in terms of processes that are happening in the present, when verbal/written/oral divisions no longer stand in isolation. These processes represent a multiplicity of interpretive approaches that are not fixed within such clear cut binary divides, say, that of linguistic, textual and non-verbal symbols (Finnegan, 1992). Of the many areas included in this way of the transmission and communication of culture (viz. theatre, dance, music, pottery, sculpture and architecture) melodies as reflected in the songs of the non-industrial societies have also played a crucial role.

Folk Songs and Oral Traditions

Cultures in India may also be understood, besides sociologically, within the context of performing arts, particularly music and dance, located within the physio-geographical, ecological, linguistic and social environment. It is in this context that I have taken folk songs as an indicator of the larger civilizational phenomena which is characteristic of India. It is this urge to express, to communicate, to share something beautiful which has given birth to these many arts in general. It is this process of expressing the basic impulse of living, connected to the timeless universal which gets a coherent shape that is seen in these folk songs.

This fundamental framework of oral cultures — often labelled folklore — reflects the cultural unity of India, even though differences are apparent within the context of geographical, behaviouristic, magico-religious rites, customs and social institutions as seen in the different regions (Mahapatra, 1964). In fact it can be said that this is one of the factors responsible for maintaining cultural life and tradition in India. Folk songs have always formed a very significant and integral part of this heritage, especially because a large number of people participate in this activity. Nearly everyone in the community knows these songs, and sings them over generations, suiting the genius of the community (Gupta, 1964).

Oral Traditions — Definitions and Terminology

According to Finnegan, the dictionary definition of oral and orality is, "something uttered in spoken words, transacted word of mouth — spoken, verbal; folk lore is commonly defined as orally transmitted material. Hence, oral folklore life stories, songs or proverbs are distinguished from material culture. Oral tradition sometimes means any kind of unwritten tradition enunciated or transmitted through words". (Finnegan, 1992:11)

The word tradition is both common in everyday speech, and a term much used by social scientists, folklorists and oral historians. It has many different meanings however, namely, the processes of handing down practice, ideas or value. It has other overtones too; something called a tradition is often taken to belong to the whole community rather than to specific individuals or interest groups (Finnegan, 1992). The phrase 'oral tradition' conceals similar ambiguities. The addition of the word oral implies that the tradition in question is :

1. verbal,
2. non-written,
3. belonging to the 'people'or the 'folk,'and
4. fundamentally valued, often supposedly transmitted over generations by the community or folk rather than conscious individual action.

Henige (1982) defines oral tradition as strictly speaking "...those recollections of the past that are commonly or universally known in a culture...and have been handed down for at least a few generations...". Today the scope of folklore research has been broadened to include analysis of artistry and emotions; and, their manifestation in words and in action. Perhaps the most influential development has been the attention given to personal creativity and experience. The re-instatement of the individual as a thinking and feeling subject who is the creator of his society and culture is the most important aspect of folk-lore research which needs to be emphasized. Ruth Finnegan (1992) an eminent scholar in folk-lore research has formulated some crucial questions which are applicable to this research also. Some initial questions about language, speech and text, for example are :

"1. How far do human beings in particular situations express and clothe their ideas, emotions or actions in verbal forms and in what way are these traditional ways?
2. How far are interpretations imposed by the researcher ?
3. Can we separate verbal forms from other aspects of communication and action?
4. Can oral texts be divorced from those in writing?"

These questions are valid for all oral traditions or verbal art forms because the objectives are :

"1. To advance knowledge.
2. The recording, celebration, or better understanding of particular forms which are regarded as not widely know enough, or under threat of dying out.
3. The conservation or protection of the 'love of the folk'.
4. The documentation and dissemination of particular forms in order to assist some specific end, for example, developing material or group identity.
5. Indirect motivation like enhancing the researcher's career!;viz. this is relevant because some researchers treat people as 'samples' rather than as human beings. This is kept foremost in mind in the context of this thesis since only this humanistic role-allows one to be in touch with the community, unlike those who have a patronising attitude towards the informants who are used purely as sources for things — to be discarded when not wanted. Thus, if ever a researcher is tempted

to proceed on the assumption that she knows more about folk-lore than her informants do, she will lose their friendship and hence to the real nature of the sources (beliefs, glories, dreams, and so on values)."

We need new ways of conceptualizing the folk/classical continuity in India. One way suggested by recent research is to view folk and classical traditions as co-existent and available to everyone. For example, a corpus of a 1000 tales in Kannada contain no mention of *Karma*, yet the women who tell these tales use karmic notions in other forms of speech. Other dimensions of the relationship stand out if we think of folk and classical as "codes" in a culture. Not only are folk and classical traditions coexistent, they are cooperative. They complement each other as two ends of a continuum, between control and release of energy (Ramanujan, 1986).

Metaphors built up in songs are symbols, personalized expressions that later may become regularised into conventional idioms of meaning. This statement reminds one that behind or underneath any folk and classical problem, one knows very little about the role of individual experiences in the formation of Indian culture. Moreover, the theory that personal songs are vehicles for new cultural meanings is particularly interesting because it rests on the dual nature of folklore. It is traditional, yet it lives through variation. The fixity of form confers authority and familiarity, while variations allow changes in content. Folklore is thus an effective agent of cultural innovation.

Coomaraswamy (1936) has argued that in India folk and classical traditions share a common base and should be contrasted with popular or 'burgher' culture. This observation helps us to formulate the position of folk-lore in Indian civilization; its forms and features may be unique, but on some deeper levels, its conceptual structure may have classical analogues.

The psychological (and thematic) continuities between classical and folk traditions are mentioned by Ramanujan (1986), who turns one's attention toward variation in the image of women and goddesses. In the Rama story, as one knows from the classical to the folk texts, Sita becomes more dominant and powerful, so that in the folk story she actually replaces her husband on the battlefield against Ravana. The same movement — from mere static to more dynamic forms appears at other levels of the texts.

The volatile energy in folk traditions (Ramanujan, *ibid*) poses a psychic counterpoint to the maintenance of control in classical traditions. But 'classical' is not simply order and 'folk' disorder. In folk traditions, a woman may express rage, but she is also controlled through ritual, often through the process of deification. This is why the heroines of folk epics become deified virgins, why the folk 'Sita' is likened to village goddesses, why sisters must play the game in a ritual setting, and why strong women in the bow songs songs become goddesses (Ramanujan, *ibid*). Also, oral perceptions differ from classical texts in that they use a greater array of delivery styles and manipulate them more subtly.

The division of social roles along gender lines is nothing new to social sciences. But the role that gender plays in performance is still a relatively unexplored area. Linian and Young (1986) predicted accurately that gender should and would become a central focus for future folk-lore studies. The role of gender is so basic and pervasive as to defy generalization, but a division might be made between scholarly considerations of gender in the act of performance, and representations of gender roles in the "texts" as performed. Clearly, neither of these areas of interest can be addressed without addressing the other. Gender is one of the basic parameters of alacrity (Appadurai *et al.*, 1991).

Importance of Oral Traditions

In short, the point about experience to which the chapter on approaches and methodology elaborates, implies a respect for the full human qualities of those whom one is researching; this is more than just establishing warmth and rapport in the collection of field data. This is where the importance of oral traditions comes in, because these survive in a particular society only because these fulfil diverse functions. For example, these may be grouped into — recreations, amusement, education, socialization, social control, protest, propaganda, communication of new ideas, knowledge and values.

Folk-lore is both benefactor and beneficiary — it is an active agent of social change, as well as an enthusiastic and lively receptor of the changes taking place in the society. This dual existence and many faceted role of folk lore are its real strength. It is a dynamic force of culture. Society is based on individual relationship of man with man and their mutual actions and interactions. The seed of social change lies in these relationships. Society in a sense is the changing pattern of social relationship (Islam, 1985).

Oral traditions are remarkable primarily because of two reasons. Firstly, there is incredible continuity preserved through the transmission of ideas, knowledge, religion and culture over the centuries and secondly despite the absence of formal means of communication, transport and the written word, the tremendous unity of tradition across the country, which is obvious even despite regional variations and linguistic diversity.

Folk-lore, folk musical and dance traditions have been passed down through many generations, adapting to changing times, whenever necessary and yet retaining in their contemporary form, an extra ordinary vitality (Sondhi, 1985).

Folk songs among the entertainment media of rural India are prominent in performing a communication function. They impart knowledge about the weather, health care and improved agricultural technologies. They are an agency of social control or socialization encouraging the moral values of the community. It is clear that the oral tradition is the key to the whole process of communication.

The characteristics of folk music is such that it is conducive to the social change of a mass scale. We find that in folk music there is directness and simplicity in the narration. It deals with the local specific subject and the music is simple, therefore, easy to learn and easy to sing. Thus, it is easy to modify also. So, it is quite obvious that these characteristics would make folk music an ideal vehicle for mass communication, not only in a local and specific manner, but rather in a national sense.

Folk music is a medium par excellence for mass communication and should be used for education and development. Singers are also well known and much liked by the audiences as well as respected for their talented skills. If they are willing to co-operate they might also serve as excellent discussion leaders and change — promoting agents, in the rural and remote areas where modern technology and the audio-visual aids cannot reach the masses.

Folk Songs as Entry Points

It is clear from the above that our approach to the study of women's image and folk songs suggests a radical departure from many of the earlier studies which take a recourse to the one-to-one question and answer methodology. Bearing in mind that Indian civilization is well-known for its multi-dimensionality and multi-layeredness, this is why folk songs need to be examined within the framework of processes and events, and not simply as things and products. They are thus seen in terms of a continuous process of flux, with interactions at many levels. In short, there are two processes that are going on simultaneously; one of change in the context of development, and the other of interaction, dialogue and communication between one variable — unit — and other similar units; viz. songs are linked to dimensions of social issues, emotions, culture and ecology. In short, moments of time are encapsulated in the artistic expressions of the folk communities in order to recreate and repeat. This is how there is such a richness of folk forms in music and dance (Vatsyayan, 1976).

Why and What of Folk Songs

> "Once upon a time a passer-by saw an old woman searching for something, under a powerful street lamp. When asked, what she was looking for, she said, "My house keys". In fact she had lost her keys elsewhere but since it was dark where she had lost them, she was searching for them under the light!"

One is indeed tempted to apply this parable, narrated by Ramanujan (1986) to the present context and state that oral traditions can provide the best grass-roots perception of women in society. An analysis of other sources ignoring this vital source would be like the old woman's search for her keys (Ramaswamy, 1994).

Folk songs form a particular genre of folk tradition. Jan Vansina (1961) while discussing the historical methodology involved in the use of oral traditions, classifies folk songs as second traditions, since they are a narrative they go through changes and interpolations in being handed down. Folks songs can be categorised as 'soft evidence' in contrast to archaeological or inscriptional evidence which is relatively 'hard' or authentic.

Nevertheless, anthropologists, social scientists and historians are increasingly making use of this source material to build up a structure of society. The important criterion, for determining the usefulness of folk tradition, is the extent of its prevalence and therefore songs prevailing widely in popular consciousness are an important index of that society (Ramaswamy, 1994).

Ramaswamy (1994), studied Tamil folk songs with special reference to women and the 'domestic'. Although the focus was on the 'domestic', songs sung in other situations were also analysed; for example, work songs, because women often sing about their domestic situation in the domain of the 'public'.

According to one definition, "a folk song is a lyrical, short, simple, less artistic rhythmic song of a community. It often reflects the socio-cultural heritage, the environment and the life of the community living in a particular territory" (Srivastava, 1974).

Folk songs are one of the oldest means of the expression of any community. They are important because they reflect different aspects of tradition, customs, rituals, aspirations, values, attitudes, and so on. In general, songs are deeply rooted in the life of the people and therefore allow one to narrate the many faceted aspects and dimensions, interlinkages which songs tell us about the particular community. The chief characteristics of these songs, simple melodies, is a fine blending of words with the tunes, which is highlighted by the spontaneity that springs from the emotions of common people arising out of their natural surroundings.

Songs handed down, by generation, by word of mouth, are indeed created by socialised individuals, or by groups, within any given cultural-ecological region. The imprint of their style is not due to the presence of individual personalities as is the case with modern societies. The characteristic of folk songs earns a place in society because their content satisfies psychological and social needs; and, this is why they are carried forward by the people themselves. Songs are constantly innovated as well and their vitality remains because they are amenable to change; even today as people make provisions to put fresh content into them.

Functionally songs in this manner provide endless relief to not only the singers but also to the community as a whole. They give respite from everyday monotony of life. They reduce the tedium of hard work, and a very important function often is to provide an outlet for suppressed emotions and desires which cannot be expressed in prose, in ordinary language. For example, whenever there is injustice and oppression, the victims find some solace in expressing anguish the form of folk songs. In this way songs not only reflect an expressive musical form but are also indicators of changing socio-political variables. In fact, when the basic framework of any of these oral communities changes, then such oral traditions reflect change in the songs means which act as a guiding force in maintaining continuity of cultural institutions. This is because songs represent also many aspects of social behaviour, the loves and hates, ecology, and world-views. Thus, folk songs are not to be taken at their face value, and taken for granted as mere songs (Barua, 1963).

As stated above, the contents of a song not only satisfy socio-psychological needs, but also make due provision for incoming drastic changes such as in the modern age, by the people themselves. Folk songs allow members of the community to find emotional outlets, especially as they are sung, understood and learnt on many occasions, viz. birth, *mundan* (tonsure), sacred thread ceremony, marriage, festivals, in the fields, in the household and on other special occasions.

One can discern in the songs a world view and an attitude which is immensely human. This is obvious in the fine blending of words and melodies that appear to spontaneously arise from the basic emotions arising out of simple surroundings and the environment. These songs form a part of oral literature of the community which is handed down from generation to generation (Upadhyaya, 1964). Folk songs are thus crucial indicators of such communities, as established "texts" - documents - which are the most authentic and unshakable witness to ethnographic fact (Elwin & Hivale, 1944). In short, folk songs testify to a celebration of life in the midst of work, during festivals, and act as powerful indicators of the lifestyle of the people(Choondal, 1970).

Objectives of Folk Song Study

The main concern of the present book is to examine the relationship of folk songs to the life of the community, both individual and collective. The conceptual-theoretical-background emphasises the fact that folk songs are to be understood as a matter of actual experience, of participation and of keen observation. It is worth noting that it is at this experiential-participatory level that folk songs are able to provide a cohesiveness to the community, inspite of the great diversity and multiplicity of themes, forms and styles. This is because of the quality of spontaneity, involving the participation of every one, with no barriers between the creator and the actor, the performer and the audience. There is an absence of a self-conscious artist and sophisticated stylisation which gives folk songs a capacity forever renewing and rejuvenating themselves while maintaining a continuity with tradition (Vatsyayan, 1976).

The concern of the present book is restricted to a specific area, as stated above, to the study of women — their images — in terms of oral traditions as reflected in folk songs because women are the carriers, active bearers of tradition especially as they are not effected merely by the written word (Deva, 1989). This is especially true at the rural and folk level. According to Ananda Coomaraswamy (1936):

> "...even more significant than the religious and knightly culture the product of less quickly changing conditions and impressive too in its naivete, is the picture of the women of the people which we can gather from both folk song and lyric".

This work takes on newer direction in studying women's images because the content of folk songs provides us valuable insights into the images of women and their life, within the community (Katarya *et al.*, 1987).

Folk expressions of culture tell us about women's lives as they speak from their hearts, for the sheer joy of living together in the community, and the other social behaviour. It is a significant method for focusing on cultural values and other areas of their life-styles. This is unlike the interview and other related methods whose main focus is to gain information about social issues. But the latter techniques conceal many motives and attitudes of the respondents covered by the area of cultural values. And it is here that folk songs are able to reveal the deeper layers of the community (Bhargava, 1972).

Women's Images and Folk Songs

Folk songs reflect the position of a woman, as an integral part of any society, they form the "window" which allows us to glimpse into the many expressions of her significant role in that society, beyond the stereotype images of women. Folk songs not only tell us about sex discrimination, her social authority in the family and her relationships with other family members, they tell us about other cultural behavioural and ritualistic activities which are clearly etched in the songs. Therefore, the entry point into the community through songs becomes crucial, especially as this research investigation involves the methodology of participant-observation in the production of knowledge.

Bearing the above approach in mind, the process of field work involves many changes which are brought about in both the researcher and the people one is studying, i.e. the women within the cultural milieu. Perhaps, this is especially true because of the consciousness of the concept of gender equity which today has become a matter of great concern to all those who participate in the problems of women within the framework of developmental programmes. This aspect would require another study, of course.

For my purpose the area under examination for in-depth study is deliberately circumscribed to that of women, their images as reflected in the folk songs which are sung on many auspicious occassions. To illustrate, no celebration of the birth of a child, marriage, religious rituals and so on, are conceivable without the singing of songs by women; and, of course, during ritual performances, telling of tales, calendric annual festivals and so on. In this way folk songs are indicators of the social position (status) of women, their authority in the family, their relationships with other members and the constraints of occupation, physical location of space in the life patterns. As it was noted, in Garhwal every women is the creator of her own folk song through which she communicates something about her life patterns, her emotions, her feelings, her position in the family, her relationships with the community, with the environment in which she grows. In short, she creates her own socio-cultural history in the creation and expression of these songs that are a form of communication. The creator expresses herself through the medium of a song and this creation in turn gives an insight into her life, her community and tradition.

Conceptual Framework

Within the broad framework of the preamble given above, certain pertinent and relevant questions were formulated, which are given below:

A. *WHEN do women sing these songs?*
   1. Time of family life cycle,
   2. During changing seasons associated with agriculture.
   3. Leisure time.
   4. Rituals and other occasions.

B. *WHERE do women sing these songs ?*
   1. In the village,
   2. In the forest,
   3. In the fields,
   4. In the *melas*,
   5. In the country side,
   6. At home.

C. *WHO among the women sing?*
   1. Women of all ages,
   2. Is it less among younger age group ?
   3. Women who are exposed to other media of communication ?
   4. Do women of all communities sing?
   5. Do women sing all types of songs ?

D. *WHY do women sing, and WHAT is their context?*
   1. What is their own perception of their songs?
   2. Do they identify themselves with their song?
   3. How significant is the song in their lives?
   4. Do they express themselves in any other medium — painting, dance, weaving, spinning,etc.?

5. Are songs linked to their aspirations, desires, feelings, and emotions?
6. Do songs give us an insight to the ecology of the area?
7. Are songs sung to enact rituals, ceremonies related to the life cycle of a women's life?

E. *ARE folk songs changing ?*
1. Do they reflect the issues of concern to the women in their daily lives in the contemporary context?
2. Are new songs being created all the time,i.e., are voluntary organisations working with women using folk song for creating awareness about social issues ?

Significance of the Study

The concept of gender equity and its impact on national development has become a matter of great concern to all those who are participating in the problems of women and developmental programmes. It is thus in understanding women's position that this research takes on a different direction than the conventional methods of studying images of women. This is done by taking up case studies of folk songs as these give us insights into oral histories, and family histories interrelated to other folk material.

One of the objectives of the book is is to present a multifaceted image of the woman, as reflected in the folk songs of Garhwal. The significant point in this context is that songs not only reveal the various images of women etched in them, but also highlight how women create their own songs. Women use songs as a medium of expression - it is their channel of communication. They breathe life into the song, and that song in turn tells us something about them. This creative act of creating one's own songs, breathing life and meaning into them has tremendous implications and relevance for providing insights into the cultural and social significance of the lives of women and their imagery. In terms of communication the creator of the song is empowered by the act of that creation — the song belongs to her — there is greater identification with the medium; she takes responsibility for creating that song, for breathing life into it. It is her song, her life, that she sings about.

Folk songs provide valuable data about the life of women, their relationship in the society, and the cultural values, as well as her world view. In societies where cultural values are transmitted orally, songs and allied areas provide us with knowledge which would normally not be easily available. These songs are not merely created for some romantic fulfillment of the people, or for pleasure only. It is the serious expression of social and cultural situations, of the unparalleled imagination of the lives of the women of Garhwal. In this way it becomes possible to portray the cultural life of these people.

Until recently, many earlier published studies have stressed the context of woman's images in terms of oppressed, bereft of parental love, as tortured wife, and an unhappy mother. While to some extent this may appear to be true but this is not so if one views these events within the totality, say, of situations arising in the family, between husband and wife and so on. In other words, songs are not just concerned with poetic melodies and sentimental romantic events. In reality every song significantly introduces and portrays prevailing social circumstances, situations and cultural life.

In Garhwal it is difficult to think of a folk song without the woman. She is the life of the song. In fact it is this element which is highlighted by the content analysis of these songs. It may be pointed out here that other scholars have worked in this area as well. But the focus of these researchers is not the same as this thesis. The first ever research oriented investigation into folk songs of Garhwal was done by Bahulkar (1964) and Chatak (1973); and later by Nautiyal (1975). In all the above mentioned researches in folk songs, nowhere have the problems related to women's conditions been totally investigated. However, Nautyal(1992) has worked on the historical, social, cultural aspects - emphasising the psychological images - of the woman of Garhwal. Her focus has been on performance genres and literary texts which depict traditional images.

A complete study of the Garhwali woman was and is still a necessity in the context of Garhwali folk lore. Some research has been carried in the context of folk literature and songs. But there has hardly been an earnest effort to provide insights into the images of women in Garhwal with a background of her wholeness as is available in the folk songs. This is why the objective of this book is to fulfil this long lacunae in the study of a rich source material for understanding socio-cultural images of women in this Garwhal region of the Himalayas.

The present study clearly attempts to show the multifaceted image of the woman of Garhwal who has changed many hues and colours. Folk songs very beautifully reflect this change in her image. It is like an artist working on a picture — the sketch keeps changing as he adds various colours.

In my research, I have tried to study completely situations related to or projected in the context of women's lives as reflected in the folk songs. These songs indicate different extensions of Garhwali woman in old traditional ways as also in ordinary earthy lives. These are poetic expressions of a woman's state of mind, whereby her cultural elegance is integrated with traditional beliefs. These are a woman's creations which allows her to introduce her poetic strength of sentiment, word power and also give shape to her social problems. The above examples reiterate the fact that folk songs have a tremendous potential, since women are the carriers of oral tradition, and folk songs are a significant aspect of this tradition, the need to look at them as indicators of women's status and lives cannot be overlooked as a medium for mass communication.

Keeping all the above considerations in mind, this study addresses itself to the following research questions :

1. Do folk songs reflect women's lives?
2. Is there a correlation between the image and reality, i.e., do images etched in the folk songs correlate with the actual life patterns of the women in the community?
3. Are folk songs changing in content to include social messages related to the lives of women ?

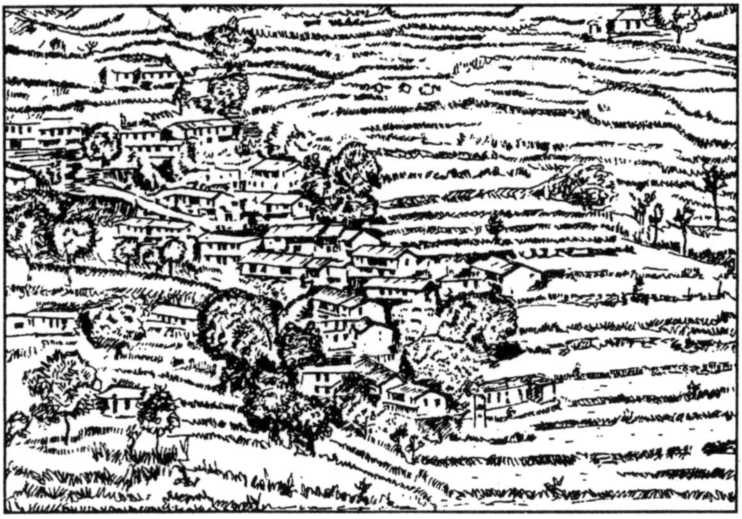

Village Settlement Pattern amidst Terraced Hill-sides — A distinct feature of Tehri Garhwal

2

GARHWAL — A PROFILE

Introduction

The northern part of Uttar Pradesh lies in the lap of the Himalayas. This hill zone includes the districts of Dehradun, Uttarkashi, Chamoli, Pauri, Tehri Garhwal, Pithoragarh, Almora and Nainital. This zone forms 17.4 per cent of the total geographical areas of the state. The altitude varies from 250 to over 3500 meters above mean sea level. On the basis of altitudinal variation it can be categorised as sub-tropical, sub-temperate and temperate, and alpine zone.

Known for centuries as Devbhumi, the abode of the Gods, the territory in the Central Himalayas referred to as Garhwal, was unified by Ajaypal of the Panwar dynasty by constructing garrison fortresses on strategic hill-tops in order to consolidate his authority. Later the British for administrative convenience divided Garhwal into Tehri and Pauri. Today, Garhwal consists of the districts of Uttarkashi, Pauri, Tehri, Chamoli, Dehradun and spreads over some 5,50,000 sq.km. (Map 3).

General Climate, Flora and Fauna

Climate

The weather is unpredictable, and a whole range of weather conditions may be experienced in the span of a few hours. It differs from place to place due to geographical differences. The average temperature in the valleys varies from 3-30C while the higher hills are covered with snow even in summers. The annual rainfall ranges from 670 to 2500 mm. About 70 to 80 per cent of the total annual precipitation is received during June to September. Winter rains are scanty, accounting for only 10 per cent of the annual rains. In the hills, the climate in general is humid temperate but variation exists which largely depends on the altitude (Negi, 1990).

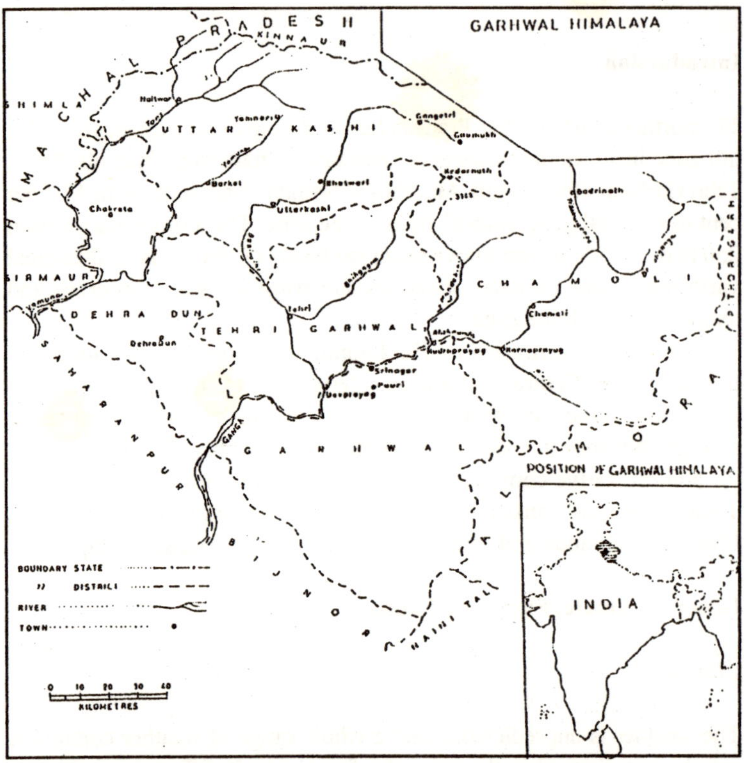

Map 3 : Garhwal Himalaya — The Five Districts

Flora

The upper reaches of Garhwal are covered by ancient and majestic forests, conifers occur in unbroken masses extending over many miles and present a scene of magnificent grandeur unknown elsewhere. Today most of the forests stand vastly depleted, and show little evidence of their past glory. The entire forest area spreads over 6,90,721 hectares. Among the flowers are primrose, gentian, poppy, buttercup, golden kingcup, yellows daffodil, blue poppy and 'Brahmkamal' or 'Lotus of Brahma'.

The reported area under forest in the zone is about 64.5 per cent. Good forests accounts for only 15.5 per cent of the forest land and 4.4 per cent of the geographical area. The great variations in altitude, rainfall and soil throughout the U.P. Himalayas support a variety of forest ecosystems, but the extent and quality of the forests is receding rapidly. Human intervention has altered the composition of the natural forests and reduced species diversity, while land clearing for agriculture and settlements has already reduced the area under forest cover (Source: Forest department, Govt. of U.P. Van Panchayat Afforestation Project).

Due to different type of climate the soil also differs from place to place. It varies from sandy loam to pebbles and *kankar*. The slopes of the hills have been converted into terraces for cultivation. The slope of the hills even in valleys is too steep. The soils on the whole are shallow and less fertile.

Fauna

Fauna is well distributed, but leads a precarious existence today. Once the large deer Sambar was quite abundant at heights above 3000m, and the smaller member of the deer family, the Kakar or the Barking deer inhabits forests around 2,500m. The *Kastura* or Musk deer is found between 2,750 and 3,700 m. The rarest and the exotic species of wild life is the snow leopard found on hill ranges from 1,500 to 5,500m (Dilwali and Pant, 1987).

Topography

The topography of Garhwal is mostly rugged and the entire region is mountainous with vast tracts of bare rocks and forests. The lower parts of mountains, where the river flows, are covered with fertile narrow terraces for cultivation. The snow line is reached at some 150 kms from the foothills.

Plate 2 : Village Settlement Pattern and terraced hill sides — A distinct feature of Tehri Garhwal

Sometimes, fairly large villages are situated on flatter ground bordering the big rivers, though they are usually 20 or meters above water level to avoid damage during floods. Most of the valleys are accessible by narrow and steep bridge paths, except a few curvilinear roads that link up the major river valleys.

People have build their houses near water resources, mainly springs and water pools, often perched precariously on spurs of mountains. Most people travel on foot and transport of goods is on the head and back. A most typical village near the road is characterised by a few tea shops and storage houses abutting near the road side, followed by terraced farming culminating into hamlets at higher levels. The agricultural area is located between 500 to 2000 km, Bhagirathi, Alaknanda and Bhilganga are important for wheat, manduwa and vegetable cultivation. The Chamba-Mussorie, Chamba-Gaja, Koshiyar-Chandrabadni and Kandeyal-Nagara belts are known for fruit cultivation. These belts are situated at higher altitudes. The five rivers, viz. Bhagirathi, Alaknanda, Mandakini, Bilangana and Balganga traverse the district flowing from north east to south.

Forests

Forests serve as the most valuable natural wealth and ecological stock not only for the areas but for the entire country. The flora is correspondingly different types in different parts as it is characterised by change in climate and other topographical features.

The area may be divided into three broad vegetational zones, mainly on the basis of climate, altitude and with some over-lapping transitional factors.

Lower or Tropical and Sub-Tropical Zone

This zone covers the Shivalik ranges and valleys of the lower zone or Sub-Himalayan tract and is the extension of sub-deciduous forest of the Bhabar areas. It ranges roughly between 300-1200 m. in height and is dominated by deciduous and sub-deciduous types of forests of *Sal, Shishum, Gular, Tun, Khair, Dhak Sernal, Haldu, Kali Papri* — these being the common species found in the area (local names).

Temperate Forest Zone

This zone is dominated by coniferous forests and approximately covers the areas from altitude of 1200-2000 m. *Kail* and *Deodar* is quite abundant along with Banj, Burans, Panger, Kharsu, Moru, Devidan, Thunner as the other common species.

The Alpine Zone

This is the zone of alpine and sub-alpine areas and ranges from 2000-4000 m. above m.s.l. It marks the limit of tree growth at about 3900m. On lower levels of this zone species of *Guggal, Dhup, Kadvi, Kathur, Ranushi*, etc. are distributed in varying conditions. There are also many medicinal herbs found in this zone. (all local names)

Garhwal is full of forests and they are part and parcel of the life of the people. People largely depend on the forests for their supply of fuel, fodder, building material, medicinal herbs, honey, gum, spices, fruits, berries and roots . Besides, forests give shelter to a variety of animals and birds which are an integral part of the ecosystem of Garhwal. For this inseparable dependence on the forests, people worship the forestsd as deities. (Singh, 1986).

Historical Background

Garhwal is a land of legends and mythology. The land is closely associated with legendary heroes of the *Ramayana* and the *Mahabharata* epic, as many place-names indicate along with evidence from many social customs and cultural activities of music and dance related to Shiva and Vishnu, Shakti and Ganpathi within the general belief system of Hinduism in general. Recorded history begins only from the ninth century and is not relevant to be given here for our purpose (Dilwali and Pant, 1987).

Myths and Legend

From time immemorial Garhwal has been a destination for the devout, the five Kedars (seats of Shiva), the five Badris (Shrines of Vishnu, and the five holy Prayags (confluences) are the cherished goals of the pilgrimage centres, *tirathsthans*; located in two adjacent areas which have been identified as the domain of Shiva Kedarnath, and the realm of Vishnu, Badrishetra. Although at times the entire Uttarakhand is referred to as Kedarkhand, specifically the tract of land lying between the valleys of the Bhagirathi and the Alaknanda.

In other words, most parts of Garhwal have a sacred landscape and setting. Their sacredness is associated with gods or mythological personages and saints. Most people of Garhwal are worshippers of local deities together with Shaivism, Shaktism and Vaishnavism. The people have awe, reverence and respect for the mountainous environment of Garhwal. Even though various forms of Vishnu and Shiva are widely worshipped, local gods and goddesses are also highly revered in this mountainous region, where exist the pilgrim routes to the shrines of Badrinath, Kedarnath, Gangotri and Yamunotri. Local gods and goddesses live in such natural settings as high mountain passes, thundering waterfalls, snow-clad peaks, rivers, streams and so on.

What is interesting to note is that in Garhwal, culture, nature and religion are intertwined in the lives of the people. For instance, in the southern region, along the *yatra* routes, the culture is intermixed with those pilgrims who come from the plains. But basically the Garhwalis are close to nature, hard working and honest. While the men wear trousers with loose shirt belted at the waist with a cord called *tigra* and a woollen cap the women wrap themselves in a black woollen blanket tied at the waist with a piece of cloth and a scarf around the head. Both are fond of jewellery, the women with more variety.

In the extreme north, the Bhotias with Mongoloid features are Hindus with Tibetan influences, and are concentrated around Malari and Mana areas. They are found even in Chamoli district where they shift south to avoid the harsh winters. Tall and handsome Gujjars who are truly nomadic, move from one pasture to another with their herd of buffaloes and sheep along with their entire household (Bond, 1990).

Various customs and traditions are founded on the Hindu religion, such as the trinity mentioned above of which Shiva is the most widely respected, along with Narayan in some areas. Parvati is worshipped in different forms as Durga, Nanda and Mahakali. Ganpathi is popular only in isolated areas. Thus most of the fairs and festivals are associated with the worship of one of the above, during the time of harvesting and cultivation; now-a-days the trade fairs are held at Gauchar in Alaknanda valley and Malari beyond Lata with emphasis on music and dance as a recreational and entertainment activity (Bond, 1990).

The science of astronomy and astrology specially in Deoprayag is used by *Brahmins* since people depend heavily for everything on these skills of forecasting, and of its auspiciousness. Whatever happens, the reigning deity of the house has to be worshipped.

At the social level, the traditional caste divisions are followed here. Marriages are arranged by the elders but interactions with the culture of the plains has changed many customs including widow marriage, for example. Most of the ceremonies of *Nath* (nose-ring), sacred fire ceremony and holy seven rounds,etc. are allowed to complete the marriage ceremony. Early marriage and dowry systems still exist in interior areas. Funeral rites and rituals are followed strictly according to the scriptures and are performed near a river or water pool. (Bond, 1990).

Fairs and Festivals

The fairs and festivals follow traditional Hindu observances, such as Diwali, Dussehra, etc. which are also good times to meet relatives and for getting new clothes clothes and jewellery for the children and women who wear colourful dresses. Most of the festivals are observed during the traditional seasons of *Chait* (March which is the new year), *Bhadon* (August and September), *Kartik* (October and November) and *Magh* (January).

On the first of *Chait*, Hurkiyas and Dholi-dancers move about from village to village singing, dancing and collecting gifts. *Bhadon* is the monsoon season while *Magh* is the lean period in cultivation and the Garhwali make full use of this leisure in various recreational activities. *Makarsankrant* is considered a holy occasion to take a dip at a prayag, at a time when rhododendrons come out in a gorgeous bloom (Bond, 1990).

People

Caste Structure

Present day Garhwal is inhabited by people coming from many ethnic backgrounds. They can be divided into the following groups or castes, briefly as follows :

1. *Kols or Koltas or Doms*: Believed to be original inhabitants of Garhwal, are dark complexioned people considered to be low castes such as carpenters, sweepers, weavers, blacksmiths and so on.
2. *Rajputs*: They appear to have come from south or the adjoining tracts of Himachal Pradesh via Hindu Kush through Kashmir. But later Rajputs came after Mughal rule to escape oppression. They are agriculturalists who took to other professions and joined the army in large numbers.
3. *Brahmins*: These are primarily considered to be the descendants of the priests who migrated from the plains, or those who came to visit religious shrines. Some of the place-names of villages indicate the original home from where they migrated from, viz. Ajmer-patti,Udaipur

patti, Telangi or Telangana,etc. Some examples of surnames also indicate this, viz. Karnatak, Telang, Rawat, Joshi, etc. (Negi, 1994).

There is a great degree of cultural variation between British Garhwal and Tehri Garhwal. Tehri Garhwal was independent and developed into a feudal order. The kingdom of Tehri was a custodian of the temple of Badrinath.

There were three predominant castes in Tehri Garhwal; Brahmins, Thakurs and Doms. The lowest of the strata (Doms) were not allowed to own any material property like land. They were the artisan class. Tailors, blacksmiths, ironsmiths, carpenters and musicians called *Oujis*, all came under this caste. The *Oujis* were the singers of the narratives from the epics like the *Mahabharata*. They travelled from village to village performing these narratives. During the marriage ceremony, it is the *Oujis* who sing the Mangal songs, welcoming the *Barat*. The women from this caste called *Mangalacharins* sing the Mangal song during the various ceremonies like the ceremonial bath given to the girl with the paste of *Haldi* and *Chandan*.

In the month of *Chait*, the*Oujis* of a village would travel to the villages where the girls from their native village were married into. They were the messengers or communicators for the emotions and feelings expressed by the daughters for their parental home in songs. They would come back and sing these songs to the mother and father, who wept on hearing the hardships encountered by their daughters in their in-laws home.

According to Shri Beharilalji, secretary Lok Jeewan Vikas Bharati, Budakedar, the *Oujis* kept alive the narrative epic tradition by performing for the village people. They were highly respected in the socio-cultural milieu of the village community, in this aspect, and any event of importance which happended in the life of the community would find expression in a song created by the *Oujis*. At a camp — *Shivir,* Sevadasji, an *Ouji* from village Gongarh, sang stanzas from the epic *Mahabharat* and the description of Shiv-Parvati's wedding.

Food Habits

Most of the people have been engaged in agrarian economy, working in agriculture, horticulture, forestry, sheep rearing and livestock farming.

In the context of food habits, diet and dietary regimes of the people are influenced by the following :

1. Food and nutritional requirement: food preparations

(Report, Joint Indo-Canadian Project on Development of Garhwal Himalayas, 1992).

Basic Information about the Tehri Garhwal District

Tehri district was formerly a princely state and was merged in the State of U.P. in 1949 and was formed into a separate district. It has now three tehsils: namely, Tehri, Pratapnagar, and Deoprayag. This district is bounded by Uttarkashi in the north, Pauri in the south, and Chamoli in the east; and, Dehradun in the west (Map 3). The geographical area of the district is 4421 km, with ten blocks in the district. According to the 1981 census the total population of Tehri is 4,97,710; out of which 95.8 per cent are ruralites and the rest are urbanites. The density of population is 113 person per km.

The physical regions of this zone are the Himalayan and sub-Himalayan tracts, which consists of the outward succession of ridges of decreasing height from more than 3000m. to 6000m. The hills contain very little leveled land. The sub-Himalayan tract is 20-25 km wide and runs almost parallel to the southern most boundary of the Himalayas with elevation ranging from 600 to 6000 m.

Socio-economic profile of Tehri district

Tehri Garhwal is, as stated above, one of five districts of the Garhwal region in west U.P. and is the gateway to the sacred shrines of Badrinath and Kedarnath. The general information about it is summarised below as given in the Census Record of 1981 - Tehri :

General Information

S. No	Particulars	Year	Information
1.	Total area	1981	4421 sq.km.
2.	Population	1981	4,97,710
	male		2,38,327
	female		2,59,387
3.	Total No. Villages	1981	1953

Occupational Status

The occupational structure of the women gives valuable information about their socio-economic profile, as follows:

Ninety per cent of the women are engaged in agriculture, as it was reported that each household possessed its own piece of agricultural land. Only 10 per cent were doing any jobs and service within the village or outside. These included small jobs as primary health care workers and Mahila Mandal Dal leaders under the voluntary organisations working in the area. (Savitribehn, Mahila Mandal Chief, Village Sabli).

The contrast in the occupational patterns of the men and the women, wherein 54 per cent of men practice agriculture and 90 per cent of the women are engaged in agriculture alongwith household work, clearly reveals the high rate of migration in the hilly areas. The NGO personnel in village Sabli supported the statement saying that there was a heavy drain of educated rural youth to menial jobs in the cities and to the army. It was also observed that while the women were involved in agricultural and household work, the men were either engaged in gambling or drinking. A woman in village Sabli said, " Except the ploughing no other agricultural work is done by men". The women also complained about the lazy attitude of men, which put extra burden on them.

Educational Status

During discussions with NGO representatives in Chamba block, it was found out that a majority of women were illiterate. A number of women were educated till primary level; and there was a lower level of literacy among the rural women. This low level of literacy among rural women was very surprising considering the data available on educational structure in the district wherein there are 998 junior basic schools, 221 senior basic schools, 108 high schools and 2 degree colleges (1989 Census Report, Tehri districts).

It was observed that the reason behind the low literacy levels was ignorance and a dismissive attitude of women towards education, "Why do we need to be educated, we only have to collect fodder and fuel from forest. There is no need for education for all this".

Non-accessibility of schools because of long distances and hazardous pathways of hills were some factors influencing the decision to not to send children to schools.

A few of the respondents who had completed high school education belonged to the younger age group and indicated that orientation programmes at school had highly influenced them for continuing their education : "We were told about a nursing training centre in the school, so we completed our education and did this training. Now we have got a job

Pathways to understanding a culture — Chir Forests near Village Budakedar

3

THE APPROACH
A New Methodology for the Understanding of Culture

Preamble

Ordinarily, it is a truism to state, that the foundation of scientific research is to be as objective as possible. The training of the mind towards 'objectivity' is perhaps clearer in disciplines like biology, chemistry, physics, and so on, than is the case with the arts and humanities. The 'objective' approach is an attempt by the researcher to be both clinically detached and dispassionate in his/her observation and analysis. However, how far this is possible when studying humanities, is far from clear. At any rate, the drawback of this form of perception is that it atomizes phenomena under investigation, and is a selective and isolated vision of reality. In the process, it relegates from one's purview a whole range of other perceptions, i.e., the world of wonder, of aesthetics and ethics. The things of great beauty are also crucial to the quality of being human, which includes the capacity for empathy, compassion and love. It may not be far wrong to state that this fragmentary approach which ignores the 'subjective' aspect of being human, especially when it comes to investigating human societies, has in many ways been the cause of modern civilization's current state of alienation, loneliness, and the increasing violence that is so widely prevalent today. (Malik, 1995).

In view of this state of affairs, a select group of researchers in many parts of the world have begun to ask such questions as; what is the way to humanize the method of understanding human societies without demolishing the merits of science, rationality and objectivity ? Attempts are being made to find ways and means that may allow us to inter-relate many of these layers, in order to seek wholeness. Wholeness means that all parts belong together, that they partake in each other. It is within this overall interconnectedness that the idea of participation arises — each part, each one of us participating in the totality. In other words, participation is an implicit aspect of the wholeness of the 'participatory universe'. Nothing would exist if this was not so (Skolimowski, 1994).

The Notion of Participation

Thus, without elaborating on the philosophy behind the 'participatory universe', it is clear that participation is at the core of social life, it is the song of joy of individual experience. It is these experiential moments of oneness which bring about the richness and meaningfulness to our lives. On the contrary, the more the inability to participate, the more the feeling of separation, and the more is the feeling of estrangement and alienation. It is this song of life, this song of participation, which is amply illustrated by the women of Garhwal in terms of both individual and collective experience. It was possible for the researcher to learn and appreciate the significance of this approach through her own participation in the lives of the women she studied; and, conversely their participation in her life. This is the approach — core-methodology — of this thesis, and one of its major contributions for setting up clear guidelines for the approach to field research, whereby new methodologies may be evolved.

To elaborate, deep participation means empathy, an almost complete identification with the subject of one's attention. Empathy or identification is a crucial aspect of the meaning of participation, since this is what gives meaning to wholeness, i.e., empathy necessarily implies the idea of responsibility, which can only come about because there is participation in the whole. (Skolimowski, 1994). To illustrate, the women of Garhwal spontaneously show a high level of participatory-ecological responsibility not only to their environment but also to their family, household, and areas of social interaction, and so on. It is this multi-layeredness that maybe deciphered in the songs, provided one has the ability to move behind the explicit to the implicit experiential knowledge embedded in the songs.

It is in this sense that songs of women become a crucial and important source material for understanding the images and life-style of the women of Garhwal. It is this approach in looking at the material evidence that is central and not peripheral to their life. Thus, central to this study is the notion of empathy, participation, and responsibility; all these form a circularity of wholeness, in terms of flowing into each other, one partaking in the meaning of the other. This perspective is radically

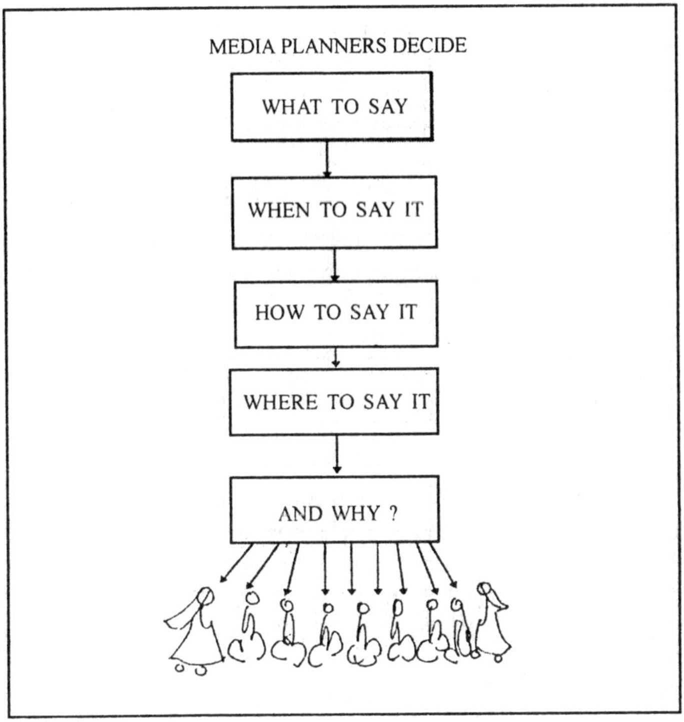

Fig. 3.1 : Linear model of communication

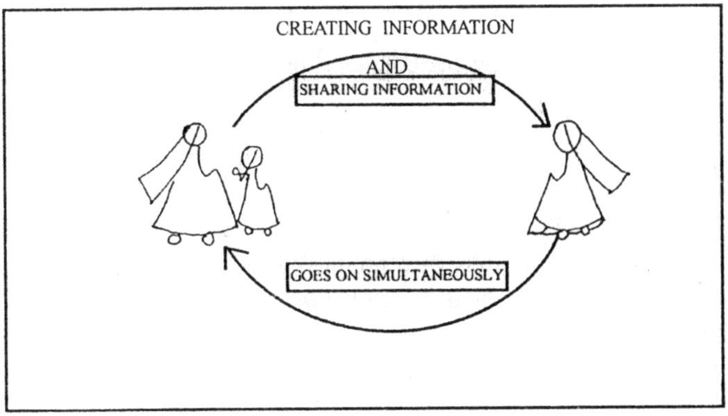

Fig. 3.2 : Participatory model

different from the 'normal' linear 'objective' approach of the social sciences. The latter, from this researcher's viewpoint, is only a kind of 'cold' act, since it tends to treat human beings as objects, within the context of a linear methodology. However, the connectedness of isolated entities may also be observed within the context of the partcipatory model. (Fig. 3.1 and 3.2). (Seth and Capila, 1988).

Thus, participation is that process which allows for creative intervention. Now, the question which may be asked is: How does one translate these general insights into specific methodologies? How do we create a new rationality woven around the central concept of participation, in order to learn the new methodology? The way the songs, the 'material' has been looked at in this thesis, it provides very significant answers in terms of the new directions that is the goal of 'participatory' research programmes, wherever human communities are involved. The validity of this approach for India is very appropriate because here cultural traditions are largely transmitted by oral means, as mentioned in the introduction.

In short, the time has come when we need to adopt appropriate participatory methodologies for social science research programmes. All this effort requires a new form of perception, a new way of acknowledging the totality of the human phenomenon, a different spiral of understanding other than that of 'objectivity'.

Briefly, some of the main prerequisites required for an enquiry into participatory research may be outlined as follows:

(i) Empathy;

(ii) Communion with the object of enquiry;

(iii) Learning to use the 'other's' language, literally and metaphorically;

(iv) Communicating with the 'other';

(v) The ability to penetrate from within, in-dwelling in the 'other'; and

(vi) Learning the ability to transform one's consciousness so that it becomes part of the consciousness of the 'other'.

Someone may be sceptical about the above guidelines, especially from the view point of minds trained in the rigours of 'linear objectivity'. It needs to be pointed out that this approach is not so difficult as it sounds, since most of us in our personal lives know, feel the sense of participation with the other. For instance, all of us know the experience of loving and being loved; of the experience of personal pain which enables us to understand the pain and anguish of others; of the deep experience - communion — with works of art, songs and dances, music, etc. which allows one to in-dwell in that oral — audio-visual — world which is beyond texts and words. This is the dimension of a participatory process which naturally implies empathy, belonging, sharing, giving/taking, and so on. This commonsense everyday knowledge — experiential and conceptual — really has deep metaphysical meanings. To illustrate, emphathetic participation implies a positive identification. it is to empathise and become one with the other, it is to beat the same rhythm with another, it is to understand through compassion and from within (Skolimowski, 1994).

Again, someone may point out that these vague emotional responses will only lead to a fuzzy methodology where nothing specific could be validated. The need therefore is to clearly show how not only to evolve new strategies and perceptions for field work but also how to formulate a different methodology for extracting information other than what hitherto was possible in 'normal' research programmes. In this research, the notion of the terms such as in-dwelling, empathy, looking at things from within; all these thrusts are crucial because these allow one to show how a new kind of dialogue becomes possible between the 'subject' and 'object'. The wider implications being that in a general sense human kind today also needs to carry on a compassionate dialogue between cultures, between communities, and also with plants, animals and the environment.

Bearing the above in mind, the questions which this researcher asked herself and evolved, in the context of intellectual strategies — meaningful, rational questions — and new sources of imagination, are as follows;

(i) What ought to be revealed, and in what language?

(ii) How am I to evolve an ongoing dialogue?

(iii) At what level, in what forms and terms is this dialogue to be maintained?

(iv) How do I come close to the kind of sensitivities which the other embodies, and operates through?

(v) What is the range and limits of my own sensitivities which I need to evolve in order to establish a true rapport?

(vi) How do I translate all this into my own academic and non-academic terms, and then into inter-subjective terms?

In short, how does one make a transition from 'objective' consciousness to compassionate consciousness? In some ways, the integral approach of this research is an initial attempt to provide inroads into these new areas. This perspective, it needs to be pointed out, has very wide human implications for understanding the predicament of the crisis within which humankind is caught up in. It is time that social sciences moved into alternate modes of inquiry. However, the rational and the intuitive, the rational and the compassionate are not antithetical to each other; at a deeper level of analysis, both are aspects of each other.

Participation implies the development of manifold sensitivities, so that wholeness is revealed in the multi-fariousness of its participation — part in the whole, and whole in the part. In some ways one may call this holistic thinking, ecological thinking, i.e., it means transcending the boundaries of objective thinking; its purpose is not only to acquire objective pieces of information, but to heal, to maintain well-being, and to enhance life; to make life more vibrant and radiant. All this area in some ways defies giving precise definitions of this approach. However, as other ways have to be devised, this book is one such attempt to show that reverence for life, and all that it entails about creativity and process, is an indispensable part of the value of being human, of his or her modality of existence in the joy of daily living. Participatory thinking is co-creative, which does not impose any strait-jackets on any one (Skolimowski, 1994).

Field Work and Experience

While it is true that knowledge is embodied in words, yet most social experience — such as field work — lies beyond language. For example, processes — experience of both the 'self' and the 'other' — are difficult to render in words (language categories). The latter by their very nature fragment and breakup the reality they are supposed to represent. There is the inherent unidimensionality and linearity of language because in emerging from its so-called domain of objectivity and rationality it blocks out another kind of experience,i.e. subjectivity and intuition. However, the contention, as stated above, is that this need not be so in any exclusivistic terms as both the domains are crucial for any kind of understanding and in fact go hand in hand. The spoken or written word — prose — involves one of the senses, the other senses (say, smell, touch, feelings, sight, rhythm and so on) are very important in the expressions of traditional cultures and societies.

In fact, as stated in the introduction, this is especially so in cultures dominated by oral means of transmission of heritage where songs, music, dance, poetry — are important. While this point may not be disputed, the moot point remains to show what means and methods may be evolved which will allow us to put across such creative understanding of field work in the context of experience. A crucial first step is to be aware of the issues and seeing that such fusion is possible between the two poles. This itself is an important step in contributing to methodological frameworks which are now emerging from this and many other studies (Hervik and Kastrup, 1994).

There are thus serious methodological problems to be faced not only in the context of what constitutes any theory of knowledge, but those which face any field worker in order to arrive at any understanding of 'other' cultures and societies. The route which is to be traced from field experience to the formulation of analytical results is not an easy one. After all the value of field work cannot be underestimated because it is a crucial process whereby knowledge is produced. It is clear today that there is no sharp distinction between objective and subjective knowledge; between theory and practice or empirical studies which were taken to be self evident at one time. But these distinctions which arose out of scientific knowledge of the external world are themselves no longer valid in the sciences.

Until recently, the experience of the researcher in the field was reluctantly dealt with since what mattered most was 'objective' analytical results, a kind of straight narrative-description of 'those' people by 'us'. These distinctions (valid only as categories of deconstructed objective entities) are no longer as absolute as before since the observer and the observed are closely linked, i.e., one's biography merges in the process of knowledge production. This initial statement does not in anyway minimise the focus of field research since its impact is in the nature of transformation at many levels both for the individual researcher and the cultures and societies he or she is studying. (Hervik and Kastrup, 1994).

However, one must be clear that subjectivity as such and experience thereby is nothing secret and hidden. It is not anything mystifying that cannot be shared, understood and communicated. In understanding creatively women's images in such an area as folk songs these remarks are indeed very pertinent. This methodological shift from structure and function to process and events is exemplified throughout this study. In short, the holistic view of multi-layeredness, multi-levelness in horizontal and vertical terms is important to be borne in mind. This is especially the case in understanding creatively women's images in their songs and associated activities which is the particular focus of the many faceted society of the Garhwal region. Thus the contextual shift from the static (pattern) approach to a dynamic (process) one is very significant.

Participant — Observation : Lived Experience

'Lived experience' is a prerequisite for obtaining any relevant information during field work since the non-verbal cannot be simply 'called-up', it has to be experienced, participated and performed so to speak.

The issue of participant-observation involves a high level of sensitive awareness, allowing little room for preconceived notions and concepts about the 'other'. It involves a reflectivity in which there is also a shared reasoning i.e., there is an attempt to see logical connections within integral terms since just saying 'I saw it myself' will hold little water. It is what one may call a shift from implicit knowing to explicit understanding. This is important because otherwise even if one were able to fully record all that was going on audio-visually of the 'native', it would tell us nothing in terms of contribution to knowledge. For example, most people speaking their language are not necessarily aware of the rules of grammar — this would be the job of the specialist, and in our case the researcher's goal of seeking some form of coherent understanding, of some causal connections between the different strands within the culture (Hervik and Kastrup, 1994).

Thus, the linguistic model and the cultural model are interlinked in actual behaviour — 'lived experience' as stated earlier — of both concerned parties. What one is methodologically doing in this context of emphasising experience is to start from the idea of a dialogue between this contact of the two — the 'self' and the 'other', enroute to the production of knowledge process which is the goal of the researcher. Cultural models and categories, one discovers, have to be experienced comprehensively, if only to understand the practices (images in our case) and motivations of one's self and of the other. The internalisation of the holistic social and cultural experience is important in this interpersonal realm since it allows one to move beyond conceptual worlds of people to a totality that comprises thoughts, feelings and emotions. The researcher believes that understanding cultures is not merely about information categories (although these may be later on useful for some other purposes), it is a learning process that can only come by participatory-experiencing. Every field worker has of course been acutely aware of this discrepancy between what is observed (participatively or otherwise) and what is recorded. Reiterating the significance and the emphasis of this approach is an integral aspect of this study of women's images as reflected in the songs.

Functional Importance of Participant-Experiencing

It is clear that experiencing allows one to understand different notions of events and processes; the latter are to be seen as a flow, like life. This is what is to be seen in the various categories of songs that reflect inner experiences which form the very core of lived and the shared culture of Garhwal. Some one may doubt this statement, to question the idea of how much of experience can truly be called shared experience. But some insight and creative understanding is possible through empathy since being in the shoes of the 'other' is well-nigh an impossibility. The centrality of the methodological issue is on how to deal with this flow of inter-subjective human experience without dehumanising it as has been the case in presenting cultural models in terms of 'objectivity'.

Once this proposition is accepted other avenues do open up. In this way it becomes possible to come closer to discover many ways of representation of 'other' cultures. For example, in Garhwal, as has been elaborated later on, songs reflect group identity and the notion of female bonding. 'Her' song is 'our' song — such is the tremendous sense of identification by women of all ages and groups, especially when it comes to songs reflecting longing for the parental home. This feeling links all women, since it is a felt experience of 'longing'. This lived experience is not taken to be something restricted to the personal self as in modern societies. There is both empathy and sympathy for this common feeling of longing which is shareable since there are no hierarchies involved at this level, no boundaries to transgress. The experience itself unifies the women into a universal whole.

What is significant to note here is that the study of folk songs is not one of seeing these as objective entities for mere analytical purposes. The latter is crucial too at one level for contributing to a body of knowledge. But the emphasis here is that all this knowledge has to be integrated within the experiential dimension both for the researcher and in understanding the 'other' culture. Folk songs are thus events and processes that are part of a larger whole of the total culture, interwoven with various manifestations into the very fabric of the life of the women. To illustrate, folks songs reflect a world view, and the women-centredness of that society. Folks songs help us to understand a community and its life, and act as powerful indicators for looking at women's lives particularly and the culture in general. This is thus another way of contributing to the general production of knowledge in a humble way, throughout this book.

Thus, in the community under study, songs are a part of a living - lived - experience, a tradition which is created anew in the now, everyday. It is an expression of one's being, of one's experience in day-to-day life. While it is transmitted through generations by word of mouth, the creator or experiencer breathes new meaning into it. Singing by memory or recall through rote is more than just rendering of the song.

What one experiences personally is the 'lived experience', an aliveness of the song and its words which alone tells one of the lives of the women. How this is to be translated into knowledge is another crucial question since the written word is to be supplemented with audio-video means even if that will only slightly approximate to the experience felt in the field. It does not tell one about the sense of identification which the women feel with the song. The women are not mere passive receivers of another form of entertainment as in modern times. They are active participants and the researcher herself becomes a participant-observer in this sense because the lived experience invokes, evokes and provokes something inwardly. It is in this sense that the study of folk songs for understanding women's lives takes on a significant dimension.

Social Experience and Knowledge

As stated above, the knowledge we formulate about the 'other' is filtered or refracted through the knowledge we have built for ourselves,i.e., we are interpreters of cultures and can observe 'others' only through our own cultural and experiential biases. But this is not all so subjective, for at any given time there are accepted norms of what knowledge is conceived to mean, i.e., the knowledge of the 'self' and of the 'others' comes together in terms of some subjective and creative understanding; say, about new sights, sounds, rhythms, silences, feelings and tastes amidst many other cultural paraphernalia. This does not mean that language is not important in that culture and that they are not linguistically sophisticated. It is just that in the naturai flow of interaction, especially in music and dance and so on, there is something behind the words — a hum of another kind — which takes into account a large sensory inventory which cannot be frozen into the written word that becomes the so-called field record (Kohn, 1994).

The human approach to a cultural model must encompass all 'experience' even if in terms of categories - taste, smell, sound, shape, colour and so on. Moreover, while linguistic categories may be gradually learnt, cultural learning may just have to be picked through sheer participation — doing the right thing at the right time, by feeling something beyond language that gives some meaningfulness and vibrance before these are classified and explained away. One can of course only attempt to approximate to the verbal and non-verbal experiences in terms of the shared experience as a participant — observer and as far as possible it is to share emotions. May be there can be a lived understanding of the situation, event and process. Primarily, "I must feel and learn to express my own experiences". The point that is being made is that in most field work reports the early experiences and feelings of the worker tend to be forgotten, at best confined to reflexive introductions. The methodological question remains, how can the field worker make her experiences of the 'other' accessible if words do not do justice to them? Different media are necessary, and the relevant tools and techniques for it, since lived experience is the stuff of art, poetry, music, songs, and so on.

The content of culture, which we learn about through our experiences with others, is much more than what we can confine to texts — our learning is much more than a textual interpretation. "We cannot live other people's lives and it is bad piece of faith to try....we can but listen to what in words, in images, in actions, they say about their lives .... it is with expressions — representation, objectifications, discourse, performances, whatever that we traffic", says Clifford Geertz (Kohn, 1994).

Summing Up : Creative Understanding

Participant-observation methodology is founded on an idea that we can understand another culture through sharing the experience of the practitioners themselves as far as possible. It is important to get at what people do because there is so much cultural practice that is never verbalized. Therefore there are many other representations of culture beneath writing and speech. Thus contextualisation of context is also determined by the experiential luggage of the participants, i.e., such events which form a pattern within the culture, and experience as a process whereby experience is transformed into knowledge which is shareable. It is thus both information-processing and knowledge-processing which makes sense to the informant and the participant-observer. One assumption is that the informant and the researcher make sense in essentially similar ways; both experience along parallel lines without explicit discussion. The interpretations of the informant and the researcher get intertwined in this way. This procedure is of crucial methodological importance : it is at this point that we become maximally able to compare the researcher and the informant.

Understanding in this way through empathy is a creative process operating at the practical and interpretative levels; understanding through action by responding to particular situations. These are supplementary features that are not observable to the senses. Interpretations thus lie between two markers, on the borderline between analogic and digital communication. Later on it can take on a scientific aspect, but the idea of making sense is essential for both the scientific and normal discourse, the difference is probably one of degree rather than of kind.

Of course, there will always be the question whether experience can really be shared and if so, what kind of sharing is feasible. The coming together of the informant's and the researcher's experience become part of the sharing processes in order to compare and contrast, and to develop ways of creative communication.

At this level the participant-observer is another node, present in the field at two points in time, and bent on understanding social and cultural processes which unfold in the study of women's images as seen in folk songs, for example each time one shared with a woman some space, there was more shared space between us; creating meaning in the making of the research process. The researcher, in her attempt to acquire the analytic gaze, tries to subsume the metaphors of the informants and make them into objects of analysis, at the same time as she creates metaphors at her own angles for the organization of the final text. It is an attempt at information-processing that has taken place in a complex web of social interaction in the field of action (Rudie, 1994).

It should be clear by now that the emphasis is less on a criticism of the textual material and more on the dialogue which takes place in terms of a one-to-one dialogue with a woman or a group of them. This is different to those of field-workers who rely on interview method in which speech is important for empirical research even for oral historians.

Thus, here knowledge is derived from areas which are beyond language — prose — and this is not some extra-sensory perception but that which is derived from all the senses — through sight, taste, sound, touch and smell; and bodily movements — their stillness, vigour or dynamism. It is in this context of the songs and the images derived thereby that they begin to make sense in a profounder way — rather than some mere banal brief interludes — towards the contribution to the learned areas of knowledge.

However, despite this inability to replicate others' experience, given the subjectivity, one could get something through creative understanding especially in case of music — song and dance — because there is some commonalty of rhythmic vibrations. The stress is on 'lived-experience' rather than confining it to only some distilled external representations, separated from every day life practices which are taken for granted and not treated as significant (Okely, 1994).

This is why the field worker has to comprehend the 'other' through the full range of sensory knowledge and arrive at a new intuition learned in field work. The total experience is also used in unarticulated and unconscious ways to make sense of field notes long after the events. The point to note is that in the dialogues of various orders, there are adjustments, exchanges which affect both the parties concerned — the informant and the fieldworker undergoes significant changes in their sensory perceptions and knowledge. The nature of this encounter is seldom mentioned in most literature of methodological issues in academic circles (Mahajan, 1991).

The important issue here to understand is that the so-called subjective experience cannot merely be dismissed, it can be understood with an approximation to empathy as a creative understanding which will of course always be partial — needless to say. The shared experience and knowledge cannot remain in the background and taken for granted as 'given' in this area of participant-observer interaction. The songs of women go beyond any linear chronology, or life-history and are akin to some representation of descriptive reality of that culture. The images represent some perennial dimensions within and those that are common to other cultures, and this is why there is great affinity developed between the subjects and the field worker. There would naturally be differences, since the internal memories and associations of each would be different. The verbal and the non-verbal encounters merge into a continuum since often minimum words were needed in this form of communication in specific situations that require many hours of work in the field.

The emphasis is on the fact that the total representations of the senses in understanding other cultures or representing them is crucial. We may call this as knowing the taste or essence of the culture through the focus on songs by women. For example, the spatial sense in terms of where the women are comfortable to sing or be with each other — in the forests cutting grass,etc. — is important to understand because the total ambience needs attention in terms of when and where the songs are sung rather than seeking the mere why. Removal from that spatial ambience does not replicate the same essence of this aspect of culture — it is out of context.

In short, over and above the intellect, linguistic utterances, the full range of bodily senses — experiencing — is an important means for approaching others' experience — beyond the linear, pre-ordained format. It is not implied here at all that the linguistic means is therefore redundant or subordinate to this form of knowing. I wish to draw attention to the context within which not only songs but other areas take place and to bear this in mind; the often contradictory and hidden meanings behind utterances and silences. One may call this grounded knowledge, a most appropriate medium available which most field workers have unconsciously relied upon in their field reports yet disembodied it in the name of objectivity (Okely, 1994).

Of course at the end of it all one has to transform this total experience into words where too one has a choice, to write descriptive prose or poetry or audio-visual cassettes — multimedia representations. It is important to convey a sense of what it is like to participate in other societies and cultures; that is why this stress on changing a course in the methodological approaches. In short, finding ways and means to capture that which goes without saying — so to speak — the non-linguistic aspects of tacit knowledge that is transmitted through songs and allied aspects. The extent to which the meaning of these symbols and practices is shared, is empirically examined by analysing everyday recurrent experiences of women, by a woman participant-observer and not from a man's viewpoint. The methodology aims at situating us on the same plane as the subjects we study and observe, while to understand and explain we go beyond. For example, in seeing experience as a process, the knowledge of images emerges through memories that evoke emotions and frame judgments and understandings, and are externalised through language and symbols (Ask, 1994).

Thus the actor's place in social reality makes her perceive and comprehend as subjective those relations — material, economic and interpersonal — which are in fact social and, in larger perspective, 'historical'. The boundaries within which the woman has to move, the terrain — physical and mental — has to be taken into account to probe the embodied cultural understanding and the process of socialisation. This is where a field worker has to start if she wants to comprehend the images of women from folk songs.

Interacting with Village Women outside the Ancient Temple at Budakedar

4

CONTEXTUALISING THE SONGS
The Natural and Socio-Cultural Framework

This chapter discusses the analysis and classification of folk songs which are presented within the following six contextual sections (frameworks) :

Section I. Natural Environment : The Ecological Perspective

Section II. Songs of Celebration : Life-cycle Events

Section III. Social Relations

Section IV. Work Roles/Activities Performed

Section V. Aesthetic Depiction

Section VI. Dissent, Protest and Social Change : New Songs on Contemporary Issues.

The first section deals with songs relating to nature and ecology in the context of women's lives. The second section describes songs in the context of life-cycle events, viz. birth of a child, *mundan* ceremony and all aspects of the wedding ceremony are analysed with special reference to the images of women as reflected in them. The third section focuses on various dimensions of the social relations of the women of Garhwal as reflected in the songs. The fourth section highlights the work roles of the women of Garhwal: Her daily routine and her position in the family in the context of her contribution to the community life are also emphasised. In the fifth section songs describing the beauty of the woman of Garhwal have been analysed. The sixth section highlights the aspects of dissent/ protest and social change as reflected in the songs on issues related to women's lives.

NATURAL ENVIRONMENT
The Ecological Perspective

Deodar Forests — Village Budakedar

The Himalayan mountains laden with dense Deodar forests
The peaks of Badri and Kedar
The rivers Ganga and Jamuna,
And Gaumukh the source of river Ganga
Adorn our beautiful land

SECTION-I

NATURAL ENVIRONMENT
The Ecological Perspective

The songs of the women of Garhwal Himalayas clearly reflect a deep bond with Nature and the Ecology of the region. In the context of the Natural Environment four distinct categories emerged, which are divided into the following sub-sections :

(i) Songs in praise of the land.
(ii) Songs about the seasons.
  (a) *Barahmasa.*
  (b) *Ritugeet.*
(iii) Songs about trees/forests.
(iv) Songs about water scarcity.

In Garhwal, the phrase 'mother nature' is no mere cliche. Every individual sees nature as his or her mother, friend and inspiration and loves it as such. The trees, the rivers, the mountains are all inextricably bonded to the life of the people; every Garhwali participates in the changes of seasons — celebrating and laughing with the blooming of flowers in the spring, and crying with their withering in autumn. It is for this reason that in Garhwali folk songs one finds abundant references to the forests, rivers, mountains, birds and animals. (Information from Ganga Prasad Bahuguna.)

Songs in Praise of the Land

Women sing in praise of the natural beauty of Garhwal. In fact a number of songs collected from the villages around Chamba and from the interior valley of Budakedar, reflect an innate sense of pride in their land.

Song 1

In our heavenly land of Uttarakhand !
Himalayan peaks are like the Brahmi Kamal
A symbol of spiritual and religious sanctity.

The Himalayan mountains laden with dense Deodar forests
The peaks of Badri and Kedar
The rivers Ganga and Jamuna,
And Gaumukh the source of river Ganga
Adorn our beautiful land

Simple people,
The abode of Sadhu's
This land has been purified thus.
Pilgrims from various lands
Throng to the Himalayan shrines

The multi coloured flowers in the meadows
The snow on the high peaks
Shimmering like gold
With the sun's rays
Make this land heavenly!

The fog creeps up the hill side
Playing hide and seek with the Deodar trees
The monsoon rain covers the hillside with wild flowers

This Himalayan land is beautiful!
As beautiful as the Brahmi Kamal
The Lotus amongst lotuses.

(See App.I, p.270)

Note : The Brahmi Kamal or 'lotus of Brahma'is a yellow sweetly scented flower growing on steep rocky slopes. It is the most celebrated blossom in the valley of flowers in Garhwal. (Dilwali and Pant, 1987).

The visual images created by this song get reaffirmed when one is sitting amongst the deodar trees, looking at the Himalayan peaks covered with snow. How true each word in the song is; how completely representative of the natural environment of Garhwal.

Ecology <------------------> Continuum <------------------> Culture

• High Himalayan peaks	• Notion of the sacred
• Rivers Ganga and Yamuna	• Religious Shrines
• Dense Deodar forests	• Simple People
• Wild flowers	• Land of Saints

All the aspects referred to in the above song, and represented (graphically on the ecology-cultural continuum) are closely linked to the life of the women of Garhwal. Dharam Devi of village Budakedar said in Hindi, " Our difficult and hard life is spent in this beautiful environment. The Himalayas, the trees in the forest, the birds, the rivers are all our friends. Our lives are deeply linked with all of them".

Song 2

We are Garhwali, this is our Garhwal
These mountains are ours
This is our land of birth
Our home, our family
Our lush green fields have abundant grain
The sounds of our bangles
The sound of the sickle cutting grain creates music, resounding
in the hill side.
This is Gandhiji's beloved land
He spun yarn on a *Charkha*,
And gave us a
Message for our lives.

(See App.I,p.270-271)

The above song reflects a deep sense of pride in their land Garhwal. The experience of the researcher while hearing women singing these songs was that the song, its text and the women singing it were all one, coalesced into one inseparable unit. One could sense a strong feeling of belonging, pride and relatedness to this sacred land.

In another song the woman lucidly describes the environment in which she grows and lives, and uses the strength of the natural beauty of her land to implore her husband to stay with her.

Song 3

The water is cool in the mountains,
Do not go away to a strange land my lord!
The Gods abide in this land
Do not go away to a strange land!
The fields are lush and green
The Himalayan peaks high and covered with snow

The forest is dense with tall Deodar trees
The water is cool and clean
My Lord do not go away to a strange land.

(App.I,p.271)

The portrayal in each song is comprehensive; for example the above song not only describes the natural environment, but it also makes a reference to the presence of the sacred. The notion of the sacred is significant and is reflected in their songs. Garhwal is known as the *Dev Bhumi*, the abode of the gods. The presence of the four *Dhams*, Gangotri, Yamnotri, Badri and Kedarnath has both religious and cultural sanctity.

The intense longing of the woman for her husband, who is away for occupational reasons is also reflected in the above songs.

In Garhwal the woman and her song are not separate. The one exists because of the other, in a symbiotic relationship. Her image as reflected in the song is an indicator of her socio-cultural environment. Thus, the song, its text or context is not an end in itself. It is in fact, the starting point of looking 'in', to a culture. This looking 'in' reveals the multi-layeredness, and interrelatedness of the song, her life and culture.

In the following song the woman links the description of the natural environment of Garhwal, with the socio-cultural practices prevalent in the society as they influence her life.

Song 4

My Garhwal has beautiful forests
Groves of banana plantations
And tall Deodar trees
'Santelu' Pradhan makes money
In exchange for his daughters
And gives *'daan'*
To attain salvation!

(App.I,p.271)

The contrast between the beauty that surrounds the woman and the legitimate sanctions that the father has to get money in exchange for his daughter and attain salvation by calling it *daan* is brought out in the above song.

Devakibehn of village Pipli who sang this song explained that about 30 years ago there was a practice called *Rada-Bada*, in Garhwal, whereby the girl's father got money from the boy's family in exchange for the daughter. This money was used by the mother to make some ornaments of gold, or to acquire some object of prestige and status by the father. Many songs collected by the researcher make a reference to this custom which in a way reflects the status of the woman in the society in Garhwal at that point. These songs will be presented later in another category. The elderly women in the group discussion, at village Pipli, however, clearly stated that this practice was no longer prevalent in Garhwal, except may be in some remote areas of Jaunpur, where the families are very poor.

The researcher met Satu, a Harijan woman in village Sabli who had been given away twice by her father. Satu, belongs to the Jaunpur area in Tehri Garhwal. She was married to an old man for Rs.800. As she did not produce a child she was abandoned by the family, and after great hardships went back to her father's home. Her present husband from village Sabli, gave her father for Rs. 1400 for Satu when he had gone to her parental village for a visit. She said he used to beat her a lot initially, but now that he had grown old and was dependent on her he was quite kind. She looks after his mentally retarded son from his first marriage. When the researcher asked her if she remembered any song, Satu could not sing. While other women could sing to express themselves, Satu could not even sing, she just wailed in anguish as though the very harshness of her life had torn the words and melody from her song!

Highlight

This section demonstrates the interrelatedness of songs to women's lives. We clearly see in these songs that ecology, emotion and culture are linked. The beauty of the land, the mountains, the rivers, are the canvas against which the image of the woman of Garhwal is painted. Nature is a close friend and comforting mother with whom troubles can be shared and the burden and hardships of everyday life alieviated.

Her longing for her gets husband intensified in this beautiful environment which she describes so lucidly in her songs. Her reference to the sacred, links ecology to tradition. Thus Garhwali folk songs highlight the link between two significant aspects of the woman's life; relating her socio-cultural environment to the description of the land.

Songs of the Seasons

The songs of the seasons are an integral part of Garhwali folk songs.

The varying patterns and characteristics of each season inspire the women to create songs reflecting their beauty. During spring, the beauty of the hillside covered with flowers, the humming of the bees intensifies the woman's longing for her husband and she creates a song to express these emotions. At other moments, the harshness of her life situations, work patterns and social relationships is interwoven into the beauty of the changing seasons.

Barahmasa Songs

The songs of the seasons are locally referred to as the *Barahamasa* and *ritu geet* which give a total picture of not only the natural environment and its changing moods, but also glimpses of the socio-cultural aspects of the lives of the women of Garhwal. In fact in the *Barahamasa* songs one finds a 'holistic' depiction of the images of the women of Garhwal.

The following *Barahamasa* song beautifully reflects the emotions and feelings of the women during the 12 months of the year.

Song 5

The month of Chet is here
flowers are blooming
Everyone is busy in their work

In Baisakhi the crops of wheat and Jowar are cut
My back is scarred with lashes
Carrying heavy bundles of wheat

In the month of Jeth
The weather has become hot
My beloved husband is still away

In Ashaad the monsoon clouds
Hides the blue sky
I have become weak like a skeleton
with only bones and no flesh
In the absence of my husband

The month of Sawan is even more painful
I am waiting for a letter

And there is none

During Bhadon
the fog envelopes the hillside
This fog has enveloped my heart too!

Asuj brings the clear sky
And the moon shining on the snow covered mountains
looks delightful
All the beauty I see around me makes me feel sad

In Kartik every one celebrates the festival of lights
Without my husband nothing is left of me -
not bones nor flesh

In the month of Poos it is bitterly cold -
My whole body shrinks with cold -
How lucky those women are, who have their husbands
with them

Magh is the season for weddings
and the union of brides and bridegrooms

In Phagun everything becomes green again -
new leaves on trees
But I sit alone like a monkey
looking emptily into the sky.

(See App.I,p.272)

The *Barahamasa* songs reflect the woman's emotional condition during the twelve months of the year, and the impact of her emotional state on her physical well being. She links the special features of each month to her emotions. For example, the *kohra* or fog of the month of *Sawan* not only envelopes the hillside, but her heart as well. The falling leaves of autumn and the barrenness of the environment in the extreme winter are linked to her body — 'no bones — no flesh'. 'Without you I am like the skeleton, just as the tree is without its leaves and flowers.' In spring, or the month of Chet, the hillsides are covered with flowers, she immerses herself in her work and this season reflects a sense of hope in her. (Fig. 4.1)

Fig. 4.1 : Visual Representation of *Barahamasa* Song

Ritu Geet

While the *Barahamasa* songs describe the 12 months of the year, and the emotions of the woman in the various seasons, the *ritu-geet* describe special features of one particular season. Songs about *Sawan* — monsoon - season feature predominantly in this category, followed by songs of spring.

Songs of Spring

Song 6

Basant *ritu* is here !
The hillsides are covered with flowers
The *koel* sings from mountain tops
Its sound reverberates in the valley!

The Manbabura flies from tree to tree singing
His voice reminds me of my husband
Away to a strange land!

In Garhwal people sit on the banks of river Ganga
And enjoy this season!

(See App.I,p.273)

Song 7

The dove chirps in the trees
Her sweet sound brings me a message
The month of April is here
Time to go to my parents' home
The snows have begun to melt
The forests and fields are lush again!
When, O! when will my brother come to take me
And bring me good news of my family
My father sits on the terrace looking sad
My mother wonders when I will come home!

(See App.I,p.273)

While the above two songs give us an insight into the special features and aspects of spring, they also describe the emotions of the woman at that point. In the first song she longs for the husband, in the second song she sees the dove as a symbol, as a messenger from her parental home. She imagines the dove brings her tidings from her mother's home asking her to go there soon! In a number of folk songs sung by women there is a reference to the dove. In traditional societies the dove was used to send messages from one place to another.

Songs of Sawan

In the month of *Sawan* there is torrential rain. After the rain subsides, the fog envelopes the hill side and the village. During this season the woman feels like the fog (*Kohra*) has enveloped her heart also, she imagines herself as Radha longing for her Lord Krishna (her husband is away) and puts the following words to her emotions.

Song 8

Listen, to me my Lord -
Sawan is here
With it, it has brought the rain and dark clouds!
The fog is moving quickly through the trees
This fog, my Lord has brought darkness
When I look at this fog, I long for you
And my *papi* eyes are filled with tears.

(App.I,p.273)

The term *papi* eyes is used quite frequently as a metaphor for desiring and longing eyes; it describes the anguish experienced by a *nayika* for her beloved. Eyes that create an illusion. She feels she sees him and yet he is not there! The special features of this season transforms the woman into the *nayika* longing for her Lord.

The harshness meted to her by her in-laws, hunger and lack of affection, hard life, all this and then the absence of her beloved husband for long periods of time, make the longing for the parental home even more intense. Not only her parents' home, she longs for the rivers , trees, mountains, birds and animals in that area. These memories, or her repeated reference to them in the folk songs give her strength and courage to bear her pain and anguish. Whenever, she finds herself alone in the forest, in the mountains, she bursts forth into a song to express herself. The natural environment provides movement, speed and spiritual salvation to her through her songs.

Song 9

Where are the beautiful mountains
Near my mother's home
where the monsoon fog has enveloped
the hillside
playing hide and seek
where is the grove of trees
where the buffalo gave birth to the calf?

Everyone must be drinking hot milk
and eating *kheer* at home
Where are the beautiful mountains covered
with the fog of *Sawan* ?

I do not have kohl for my eyes -
nor sequins to make my dress beautiful
But I love my beautiful Garhwal
The sound of rain drops, in *Sawan*
Beckons me to my parents' home
How beautiful to be home
In the month of *Sawan.*

(See App.I,p.274)

It is interesting that even though the manifestations of the month of *Sawan* are the same in the mountains of her in-laws home, she refers to how beautiful the month of *Sawan* is in her mother's home and longs to go there.

When one sees beauty, one longs to share it with a beloved or loved ones, since her husband is away, she longs for her parents, her childhood friends, her brothers and sisters in this season.

The folk songs of *Sawan* also make a reference to the prosperity and joy which this month brings to the farmer.

Song 10

In the month of *Sawan,*
The rain brings joy to the farmer
All the fields and farm lands have turned green,

'mother earth' is joyous on seeing this
wonderful sight.
Come dear sister, come dear brother
Come and sing the song of joy and prosperity
Let us grow saplings of 'oak' and 'rhododendron'
And sing in celebration of 'mother earth'
and prosperity.

(See App.I,p.274)

The month of *Sawan* is indeed special for the woman. Its distinct characteristics — heavy rain, dense fog, the singing of the *koel*, the ripening of the maize crop, the song of the peacock:

Dear peacock please do not sing
The sound of rain reminds meof my mother's home!

All stir different emotions in the women of Garhwal and they burst forth expressing themselves in songs. The songs of *Sawan* thus become a vehicle for their feelings and emotions. She refers to the month of *Sawan* as *rasila* (something filled with essence and that endears itself to one).

It is also the season when she longs for her friends and peer group. The following song is sung by a young girl to her friend before she is married. The song has a carefree sentiment about it. The girl is happy in her parents' home. She is enjoying the season of *Sawan*. Even though she talks about work to be done it is with a sense of joy. The song reflects a close bond with her peer group.

Song 11

Dear friend, come let us cut grass
High up in the mountains
There after we will go to the '*mela*'
For the Goddess.
Our sisters will also be there
The mountain breeze
Makes my *saree* fly
Let us tie the *saree* around the waist
And go to the '*mela*', dear friend!
The month of *Sawan* is here!

(App.I,p.275)

In Garhwal there is a custom to send all the married girls to their parental home before the rains. One reason for this is that the rivers and streams get flooded and the roads get blocked due to landslides, thereby inhibiting movement from one place to another. For those girls who are left behind in their in-laws home, this season becomes difficult to bear and hence songs are created to express this emotion.

Song 12

The fields and grass are filled with dew drops !
It is raining heavily
The roads are blocked with landslides
The rivers and streams are in spate
All the daughters and daughters-in-laws are at home
While I go to the forest to get fodder
How will I go to my mother's home?
All the roads are blocked.

(See App.I,p.275)

The *Barahamasa* songs and the *ritu-geet* clearly reflect the symbiotic relationships of nature, its changing moods and aspects, and the emotions and feelings of the women of Garhwal. "In poet Kalidasa's Ritu-Sambhav we find abundant references to the changing seasons and the emotions of the individual," said Ganga Prasad Bahuguna.

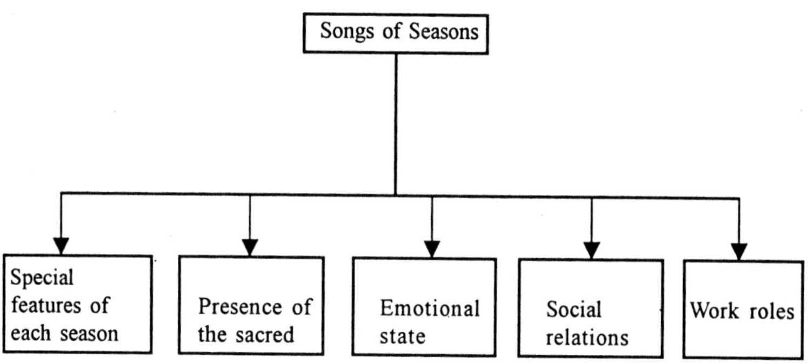

Fig. 4.2 : Representation of songs of season

about 30 years old and is widely sung by women in the interior villages of Tehri Garhwal."

Song 14

Dense forests look beautiful!
Grow more trees in the front yard and
backyard of your house and your fields
The yield from crops will increase
Grow garlic, onion, and cumin seeds

Our land Garhwal, is the land
Of Gods and Goddesses,
Keep your land beautiful
Grow more trees!

Trees give you fruit
The sound of swaying branches
Will fill you with joy!
Keep vigil around your trees

Garhwal, our land is Parvati's birthplace
From Lord Shiva's hair roots
Emerges the mighty Ganga!
Keep this sacred land beautiful
Grow more trees.

(See App.I,p.276-277)

The last four lines reinforce the notion of the linkages between the mythological dimension and phenomenal existence. It is this significant correlation which permeates the very fabric of the life of the people of Garhwal. The message of grow more trees is beautifully linked to the sacred and to the natural environment. Since women go to the forest for fuel and fodder twice a day, these songs are created by them, for them.

Song 15

Dear sisters, do not cut trees
If you cut trees, the soil, mud, earth
will disappear

No fields, nor houses will remain on the hillside

Trees give us fodder for animals
Keep our environment clean; the air pure
Nurture and care for the trees
Like your own children
Look after them, raise them with care.

(See App.I,p.277)

"There is a great sense of ecological preservation in the women. They understand the value of the forest and its relationship to their lives. These songs are sung by women when they are in the forest, or when they get together in groups at their Mahila Mandal meetings. Ecological awareness and preservation of the forest is not only a concern of the power elite who give a voice to these issues at seminars and conferences. It is very much a day to day concern of the women of Garhwal. They create songs to express these issues, and this simple form of communication, which is their channel of communication has tremendous impact in the community", said Ganga Prasad Bahuguna.

Song 16

Do not cut trees
Protect them!
Trees keep the mud intact on the hillside
The mountains look beautiful with dense forests
Even the seasons are dependent on trees
The rivers Ganga Yamuna are dependent,
On the trees of the Himalayas.
The life of animals is linked to trees
Do not cut trees
Protect them!

(See App.I,p.277-278)

At an environment camp at Budakedar organised by the NGO — Lok Jeevan Vikas Bharati, 300 men and women representing 11 NGOs from Tehri Garhwal and belonging to various villages had gathered to express their ideas and concern about environmental issues. Surja Devi, head of the Mahila Mandal of village Thati (Budakedar) said,(in hindi), "We are made of earth, with mother earth we have a deep relationship. We have knowledge about every tree, fruit and leaf in our environment. Our lives and our songs are deeply linked to them".

A number of the songs cited above were recorded by the researcher at this venue. The group sessions with women did not end at mere recording of songs, the meaning of each and every song recorded was explained by them. They talked about the relationship of the song to their lives. There was total participation of the women at every stage of the research. In fact on one day during the camp they asked the researcher to accompany them to the forests of Budakedar. It was here that one experienced the silence, the hum behind the words, the total communion of the woman with nature. The forests, its trees, birds, flowers and animals are very much an integral part of her life.

Vishweshwar Dutt Saklani was awarded the 'Indira Gandhi Vriksh Mitra Puraskar' for his work related to growing trees in Saklana district in Tehri Garhwal in 1993. The researcher met him at a meeting of NGOs in Chamba and he sang the following song which he had composed himself on the deep and intense relationship of the people of Garhwal with the trees and the forest.

Song 17

Trees are my parents, trees are my God,
Trees are my friends, trees are my children
Trees are my body, Trees are my soul,
Trees are the wealth of Garhwal!

Grow more trees and make this earth beautiful!
From the dust of my being/body, may trees grow
Let humanity learn a lesson from trees
They give food to the hungry
Water to the thirsty
Shelter to the tired and homeless
Let us learn to be selfless, grow more trees
And make the world a beautiful place.

(See App.I,p.278-279)

The brief encounter with Vishweshwar Dutt Saklani was special for the researcher. When I shared with him that I was documenting the folks songs sung by women he remarked, " The folk songs are the voice of the women of Garhwal. Women are the back-bone of Garhwal. Every women is the Rani of Jhansi in Garhwal. The songs of the trees in a way reflect the knowledge, concern and relationships of the women of Garhwal to the entire eco-system". This song describes the beauty of the wild berries growing in the forest. When women go to collect fodder and fuel-wood, they eat these berries and quench their thirst.

Song 18

Your black skirt
And your beautiful golden yellow blouse
makes you look so beautiful Dear Hissar
I cannot find words to describe your beauty.
You quench the thirst of people
By the juice of your fruit
Other fruits and berries in the forest
cannot match your beauty!

You beckon people to come near you,
From far and near
Dear Hissar you are indeed special
I cannot find words to describe your beauty.

(See App.I,279)

The relationships of the women of Garhwal with each and every bush in the forest is special. Four to five hours in a day are spent in the forest with friends. These songs are composed and sung by the women to express this relationship and a sense of oneness.

Songs about Water Scarcity

Civilizations are based on a combination of water, land and people. When this combination ceases to be infused with a normal relationship between man and man, and man and nature, civilizations decline and give place to new combinations of these elementary values. Not only is water the basic need of our life, but it used in innumerable ways by man. As population grows and society develops, we need more water for domestic, agricultural, and industrial uses. Science has made the use of water greater in every field of human activity. The basic use of water is in the home where it is used for drinking, cooking, and cleaning. There are great many areas in the Himalaya where there is a great shortage of water even for the basic needs of drinking and cooking. Human beings and animals use one single source, the former with cans in their hands and latter with their mouths. Dearth of water is responsible for utterly unhygenic conditions in quite a few villages. It is reported by medical men that as many as 85 per cent of man's diseases are caused by contaminated water since water is the best carrier of germs, bacteria, and viruses. Water is, therefore, of vital importance to a society, and all problems associated with it are social in nature (Naithani, 1963).

Water scarcity in the mountains is related to the seasons and poses a great constraint on the life pattern of the women who have to go twice a day to get water from water sources which are located at great distances from the village.

Song 19

In the month of Jeth
The sun beats strongly
My lips are dry
Dear sky, create rain and quench my thirst
It is evening
And the water vessel lies empty
All the daughters and daughters-in-law of the
    village
Are waiting for water to come
The path to the spring
Is steep and arduous

The water comes drop by drop
There are so many vessels to fill
Oh Sky fill my vessel
Without water there is no life
No food, no rest.

(See App.I,p.280)

This song was composed by the young girls of a village where there had been acute shortage of water due to a long hot summer, deforestations and other environmental factors related to the presence of water in natural springs.

Fig. 4.3 : Water Scarcity in the Mountains

Song 20

Even though its raining, the water sources have
gone further away
Dear Mother!
Because of water, I cannot complete my other tasks
The mountain path is steep
And the water in the springs comes only drop by drop
In the summer afternoons
Water becomes even more scarce
It is easy to get food dear mother
But difficult to get water!
I prayed to the Gods for water

But alas there is none -
The sources have dried up
Where do we go now
Day and night we think of water -
Our life source.

(See App.I,p.280)

Deforestation in the mountains has created changes in the bio-diversity. The water sources have dried up and drinking water is now available at a greater distance from the village. This phenomenon poses a direct constraint on the woman's life pattern. She has to walk a greater distance to get water, and the time spent on this activity has increased.

Highlights — Woman and Forests

Woman in these hill-areas are often heard to say, "When we were young we used to go to the forest early morning without eating anything. There we would eat plenty of berries and wild fruit...drink the cold sweet water of the *Banj* (Oak) tree roots. In a short while we would gather all the fodder and fuelwood needed, rest under the shade of some huge tree and then go home. Now with the trees going , everything has gone too.."

Many examples from India show that women, despite their long and arduous working schedules, have a great interest in defending and restoring the ecosystem. The *Chipko Andolan* in Garhwal is a well-known example of women protesting against the destruction of the forest.

In the Reni forests of Chamoli district of U.P. in 1974 women were confronted with the prospect of 2,500 trees being destroyed by commercial enterprise. The women were alone, for their men had left home. When the contractors arrived, they went into the forest, joined hands and encircled the trees (hence *Chipko,* to hug); and, louder than ever before, the Himalayan hill reverberated with six words which shattered the calm and quiet secluded forest since the morning :

Aaj Himalaya Jagega
Krur Kulhara Bhagega

The Himalayas will awake today
The cruel axe will be chased away.

The women told the cutters that before cutting the trees, they would first have to cut off their heads. The officials consulted each other and finally, the contractors had to withdraw and the forest were saved.

Due to an increase in the destruction of forests the ecological stability in this Himalayas region has been damaged. The resistance to this fact has been strong both by state and private agencies; women have fasted, guarded the forests. As a result of these actions by women to preserve their environment, Mrs. Indira Gandhi issued a fifteen year ban on commercial felling of trees in the forest of U.P.

Dasholi Gram Swaraj Mandal (DGSM), the Gopeshwar based organisation at the forefront of the Chipko movement was by women who made leading attempts to reverse the destruction by planting trees:

> Come, arise, my brothers and sisters
> Save this mountain.....
> Come plant new trees, new forest,
> Decorate the earth. (A Chipko Andolan song).

For women — it is obvious — trees and forests are multi-functional whereas men tend to concentrate on commercial potential for timber and other goods. Trees offer 'fuel, food and fodder' — the three F's as women say and are thus associated with the very livelihood of hilly women.

The majority of women felt that there has been a decrease in the forest cover, as a direct influence of government policies and of the forest department. A woman from Budakedar reported, "All the forests have been given on contracts so there will be tree-cutting, also the forest department themselves are responsible for tree-felling".

When questioned about the reasons behind an increased rate of tree felling, the NGO personnel reported that trees were being cut to supply timber for commercial purpose in the urban areas. The women from Sabli again held the government responsible for the tree felling. They reported that a large area of forest cover in the village vicinity was cleared to construct the Ranichauri hill campus of Pantnagar university, which they had tried to save through the *Chipko Andolan.*

A majority of the women (60%) reported that the consumption of wild fruits and leaves had decreased, owing to an increased rate of cutting trees, forests are no longer near the vicinity of the village. As a result, household nutritional habits have changed especially because of the penetration of rural markets supplying new food items with changing tastes.

The women said they had started consuming biscuits, namkeens, mithai and other bakery products, along with their staple food. It was also felt that in some areas forest foods were no longer being consumed and knowledge about them was equally vanishing.

During discussions with village women at the environment camp at Budakedar, it was reported that fuel wood requirement (app. 70 per cent) was met from government forest, 20 per cent met from panchayat forests and only 6 per cent depended on their own sources like fields and farming lands. A forest guard reported that the right of free collection of fuelwood from the forest areas was a big privilege for the hill women. He also pointed out that some trees were sanctioned to meet fuelwood demand of the right holders from nearby forest areas. But the women expressed their dissatisfaction over these rights and concessions, as women from Gonful village said, "In many areas, the forest guard does not allow us to pick dead and dry sticks. Inspite of leaving them for us, he gives them to the contractors, who in turn sell them in the market".

Many women reported that only waste and dead wood was being taken from the forests, and by no means could women be held responsible for the destruction of trees. Of course this was contradicted by forest officials, and the women said that the concessions admissible by the former to them were not always conveniently available - the difficulties in obtaining fuelwood from the forests continued.

When asked whether fuelwood was being sold, the women said that it was collected for domestic use and the question of firewood being taken and sold in the market did not arise. The job of collection and purchase of fuel totally depended on women. In some cases children were also assisting their mothers in collecting fuelwood and getting kerosene from the local market, which supported the reason given by women for having more children who could share their work load. Incidentally it is interesting to note that through discussions with women one came to know that a decade ago they could collect fuelwood from a distance of 1/2 km, but now they had to walk for about 8-10 kms every day. Today only one trip was possible and that too meant a full time job considering the distances, in addition to their awesome duties at home and in the fields. Children await expectantly for their mothers long out for fuel collection.

An old woman from Sabli gave the true picture of the hill women. She said that seven women from a nearby village had set out of their homes to collect fuel and fodder from a distant forest, but instead had climbed the nearest peak and jumped into the river. She also reported several cases of the hill-women committing suicide to get rid of the back-breaking labour imposed on them, making their life miserable.

Almost all the women realized the dependency on forests for fodder and grass and few felt that the grass available from the private land was not sufficient; "Fodder from fields is not sufficient, we depend on the jungles". It is only well-to-do families which reported that they supplemented the cattle feed with feed from the market.

The common fodder trees in this area, as reported by the women were — Bihul (*Greewia opposifolia*), Kachnar(*Bahunia spp.*), Trinbla(*Ficus spp.*), Simbal(*Salmalia malabaricum*). When asked whether any restrictions were imposed on the collection of fodder, the women said that the forest department sealed certain areas from grazing in some seasons, "If the forest guard catches us, he charges a penalty".

At a discussion on the effect of deforestation on women's work, at the camp at Budakedar, 90 per cent of the women felt that the time spent in collection of fuelwood and fodder had increased with the depletion of forest cover and forest moving far away from the village premises. A woman from Aagor reported, " Initially, we could take two trips, but now only one is possible; and it takes morning to evening". It was also observed that an increased number of nuclear families had created problems for the women than those living in joint-family system where the household and outside activities were shared by all the women members of the family and children (90%). 90 per cent of the women felt that their work load had increased. A women said " I have to get up early in the morning to collect fuelwood, after finishing my household work, cook meals for my children and then I go to the forest." All the women felt that with the depletion of forest cover, fuelwood shortage had increased, forcing them to rely on alternative energy sources like stoves and electric heaters which though convenient were expensive luxuries.

With changing times in the villages the women feel that as deforestation proceeds their struggle to find headloads of fuelwood grows bitter and arduous. Blanket commercial felling of broad leaved species such as oak and bhimal and the growth of coniferous pines has directly deprived them of the feed for their draught animals, fuel for their ovens and water in their spring which has deteriorated agricultural output further.

A participatory meeting with Bihari babu — the founder of Lok Jivan

Vikas Bharati was held at the same camp. The meeting had women and men representatives from villages around Budakedar. The issues highlighted were related to :

1. Banning the use of the plastic bags for nursery transplantations, since they are not biodegradable.
2. The forest is made by itself, it is self generating, what is our participation in it ?
3. If the forest department would give the care of the jungle to the people of the village they would care for it much better.
4. There are in many folk songs indications of what is related to the exploitation of woman by the forest department.
5. According to Bhawanibhai we have to raise the consciousness of the people. "A few people cannot decide about our future". It is not God's verdict. The wisdom of ordinary human beings has more value. It is not counterproductive to the resource in the environment.

Thus, as said by Bhawanibhai we have to seek the wisdom of the people who are living in the forests and whose lives are linked to it. Their inherent knowledge has preserved the jungles for centuries; without the use of the plastic bag. The knowledge of the traditional systems has been affected only after man became consumeristic.

Therefore, it is imperative that atleast to return the forests which are around the village back from the forest department, and give the care of these to the village women.

SECTION-II
SONGS OF CELEBRATION
Life-Cycle Events

Garhwali Bridegroom and Bride — Village Kotigad, Chamba Block

They have arrived !
They have arrived, from Dev Lok
Lord Shiva, has arrived to Wed Parvati
Lord Vishnu to Wed Lakshmi
And Lord Brahma to Wed Savitri

SECTION-II

SONGS OF CELEBRATION
Life-Cycle Events

Introduction

Songs of celebration of life-cycle events are referred to as *Mangal geet* in Garhwal. It is difficult to establish when the tradition of singing *Mangal geet* started in Garhwal. However, it can be stated that the tradition of singing songs celebrating life-cycle events is indeed ancient — perhaps from Vedic times. These have been associated with the birth of a son, the naming ceremony, thread ceremony, during *mundan*, and all aspects of the wedding ceremony.

In Garhwal the singers of this category of folk songs are the daughters-in-law and daughters of the family; or the daughters of the *Ouji* community who are Doms (Harijans). The latter were the traditional singers of this category of folk songs. It was a tradition that the *Oujis* came and sang *Mangal* songs in the homes of the upper caste Thakurs and Brahmans. This practice is no longer so widely prevalent. In the village where this study was conducted it was observed during a Garhwali wedding that the young girls of the family had learnt the *Mangal geet* sung on various occasions related to wedding ceremonies.

Songs of Celebration Related to Marriage Ceremonies

Ganesh Puja

During any auspicious ceremony, an invitation is sent to the respected family members and elders of the community.

For this purpose there is a reference to the crow or *kauva* who is called upon to send the message in all the four directions.

Song 1

Dear crow, go and give the invitation
For this auspicious occasion in all four directions;

Lord Mahadev, comes to wed you today
Dear girl, on this auspicious day
We are anointing Parvati
with *haldi* and *chandan*
Brahma, Vishnu, and Mahesh
accompany the *barat* with
learned pandits
Your *tai* is blessing you
Dear girl, on this auspicious day.

(App.I,p.283)

The reference to a *suhagin* or married woman whose husband is alive is significant here, because no widows are invited to this ceremony. Only married women are considered auspicious as the presence of the male counterpart in their lives gives them a special status. Only their presence at a ceremony like this is considered efficacious for the bride to be.

In India men and women are referred to within the context of archetypal images, prevalent in that culture. Marraige is sacred and therefore images are drawn from mythology. The bridegroom is referred to as 'Mahadev', Lord Shiva, and the bride 'Parvati'. According to Shri Ganga Prasad Bahuguna, a respected leader of an NGO in village Ranichauri, " The socio-cultural environment of the family in Garhwal is deeply influenced by the presence of the sacred, and songs which are the voice of that culture are replete with images of gods and goddesses". For instance, 'Parvati' is the daughter of the Himalayas; every girl is the 'roop' of Parvati for us. The presence of the sacred influences the values and culture. Even though women have to work very hard, and participate in all activities related to life in the mountains... the aggression one sees towards women in the plains is missing in Garhwal". The connection between culture — worldview — songs — actual life patterns is clearly etched in these songs. There is a constant reference to the sacred in the mangal songs. After the ceremonial bath, the girl is asked to wear the bridal clothes.

Song 4

"Come dear girl, wear these clothes
Your father has got these specially stitched for you."

(App.I,p.284)

Thereafter she is taken to the room where *ganesh puja* was performed and is then asked to wear the ornaments made by the jewellers at the request of her father :

Song 5

"Come dear girl, adorn yourself with these jewels
Your father lovingly got them carved for you
At the sonar's shop."

(App.I,p.284)

The *Vedi* where the actual marriage ceremony takes place is made by a *mistry* who belong to the same clan. The song sung by the bride to be, on this event urges the father to get the *Vedi* made like the one in *Dev-lok*. However, instead of gold, silver and other gems she asks her father to use banana leaves, sandalwood, mud, stone and til seed, to decorate the *Vedi*.

Arrival of the Barat

The arrival of the *barat* marks the next significant event of the marriage rituals. Mangal songs are sung during this occasions by the *Oujis*.

Song 6

They have arrived!
They have arrived, from Dev lok
Lord Shiva, has arrived to wed Parvati.
Lord Vishnu to wed Lakshmi
And Lord Brahma to wed Savitri.

(App.I,p.284)

The father of the bride welcomes the *barat* by carrying the bridegroom's *palki* to the front door of the house. In Garhwal even the bridegroom arrives in a beautifully decorated yellow *palki*.

Song 7

Come, come! welcome dear *baratis*
Come and be seated on these durees
The *hookahs* are filled with tobacco

Plate 10 : The Bridegroom arriving in a yellow *'Palki'*

for the elderly amongst you,
The girl's father welcomes you
with the ceremonial tilak
Come dear honoured guests
We will serve you food and sweets, wherever you are!

(App.I,p.284)

All the children and elders in the village gather to see the face of the bridegroom who is welcomed at the entrance with the chanting of *mantras* and *aarti*. An oil lamp is placed in a brass thali and moved clockwise in front of the bridegroom. This ceremonial welcome gives him the status of Lord Mahadev who has entered the house of the bride.

The uncle of the bride's *Mama* (mother's brother), takes the bride to where the groom is seated, and a curtain is drawn between the two. This in a way makes the groom even more anxious to see his bride to be. The friends of the bride and family members tease the groom by singing the following Mangal song:

Song 8

Open up, open up! this curtain
And see the beauty of our bride
Our daughter is beautiful like *gauri* (parvati),
And you Krishna like are black like a *chamar*!

(App.I,p.285)

The Gotroucchar

This kind of joking repartee goes on in the next ceremony called *Gotroucchar* and is beautifully reflected in the following song:

Song 9

Dear bridegroom, covered with cowdung
Tell us your '*gotre*'
Your father is a son of a weaver
Your mother a daughter of *chamars*
Our daughter is as pure as *chandan*
Her mother is the goddess Lakshmi
Her father the Lord Vishnu incarnate

Tell us your gotre dear daughter.

(App.I,p.285)

Kanyadaan

After the *Gotroucchar Kanyadaan* is performed by the father. The *kanyadaan* ceremony is a very significant aspect of the wedding rituals. *Kanyadaan* is considered even more superior than *Bhoomidaan, Heeradaan* and *Motidaan* (Nautyal, 1992). The daughter urges the father to attain salvation by performing the highest *daan* when you give away a part of yourself to another.

Song 10

Dear father give *kanyadaan*
Land and jewels, everyone gives
But your dear father
Give *kanyadaan*,
And attain salvation.

(App.I,p.285)

Various versions of the above song were collected by the researcher from different villages in the area. However, while most of the songs are simply an appeal by the daughter to the father urging him to give *Kanyadaan* to attain salvation, the following song makes a distinction, in that the girl asserts herself and categorically asks for an equal share in her father's property. She refers to 'choicest gifts' of gold and silver from her paternal uncles, but goes on to ask for an equal share in her brother's property. This aspect does not exist in the traditional song cited above.

Song 11

Daughter — Dear Father, give me *Kanyadaan*,
And attain salvation.
Dear Father, give me a share in your property.
My uncle and aunt will give gold and silver as *daan*.
My brothers will give an equal share in
their property.
Father — You are the only such girl born in our family.
Will our ancestors go to heaven,
Hearing your demand?
Daughter — Jagdish Panwar a great *daani*,

Cut off his head in *daan* for his daughter.
Father — Raja Harishchandra was also a great *daani.*
He said, "The most efficacious *daan,*
for a daughter is *Gowdaan*".

(App.I,p.286)

On probing further, Kamla from village Bergani Chamba block who sang the above song said, "Songs keep changing. In songs we can express what is in one's mind. It is not customary for a girl to ask for a share in her father's property. No girl in Garhwal would do so. These lines were added by an educated girl in our village".

This amount of sharing, initiated a very interesting debate in the group comprising about fifty women of Bergani village. The elders among them said, "...such a girl should have died at birth only. The brother's home is always open for a sister. What is the need to ask for a share?".

The younger daughters-in-law and daughters of the village expressed different sentiments. Leela, who was left alone, because her husband took another wife, said, "I feel very unhappy in my brother's house; my *bhabhi* taunts me all the time. If my father had left me something, my status would have been different". She had even attempted suicide, but was saved by Shashi didi of Mahila Nav Jagran Samiti who had started the Mahila Mandal in Bergani village and had involved Leela in its activities.

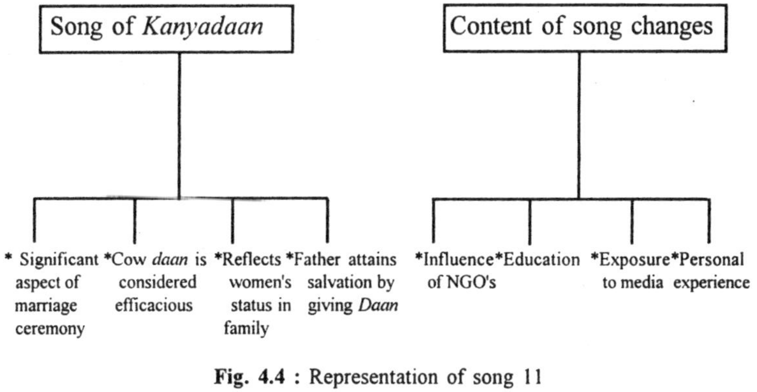

Fig. 4.4 : Representation of song 11

The above illustration shows the significance of the song in depicting so many aspects of a culture. What is important is that it reflects both continuity and change; it illustrates the linkages of culture, mythology and women's lives and yet includes a dimension of change related to social issues concerned with women's lives.

According to Raheja (1994), "In northern India, marriage is spoken of as *Kanyadaan* ('gift of a virgin'), the unreciprocated gifting away of a daughter along with lavish gifts for herself and for the people of her *sasural*, her husband's house. She is given away in the course of a complex set of ritual actions designed to effect her transformation from 'one's own'(*apni*) to her natal kin to 'other'(*dusri*) and 'alien'(*parayi*) to them. The woman is often said to undergo a transformation at the wedding, in which she becomes the 'half-body' of her husband, of one substance with him. His kinsmen become her kinsmen, and her ties with her own natal kin are transformed as well; people in Pahansu say that unmarried girls share a 'bodily connection'(*sarir ka sambandh*) with their natal kind, but that after the marriage, there is only a 'relationship' (*rista*)." (Raheja, 1994: 56).

Saptapadi

After the *Kanyadaan* ceremony 'Saptapadi' and the seven *pheras* are performed which complete the wedding ceremony. The following *Mangal geet* is sung when the bride and bridegroom take the seven *pheras* around the sacred fire solemnising their marriage.

Song 12

As you take the first round of the sacred fire
You are a *kunwari*
As you take the second round of the sacred fire
You are a *kunwari*
When you take the third round of the sacred fire
You are mother's loved one
When you take the fourth round of the sacred fire
You are your father's beloved little girl
When you take the fifth round of the sacred fire
You are your brother's beloved sister
As you take the sixth round of the sacred fire
You are about to become somebody else's
As you complete the seventh round of the sacred fire
You have become your mother-in-law's
Beloved daughter-in-law.

(App.I,p.286)

It is significant to note how on completion of the seventh *phera*, the girl ceases to belong to her parents. Her status changes by taking those few steps around the fire; which transforms her image drastically from a *kunwari* (virgin) to a *buwari* (daughter-in-law in Garhwali language). With the completion of this ceremony the parents relinquish their rights on the girl. According to Leela behn of village Ranichauri; " After the seven *pheras* are complete, we have no *adhikar* (a significant word here) on the daughter, her in-laws have all the rights now".

As can be seen in the above song the *'Mangal geet'* or songs of celebration are deeply linked to the life of the women. They are not mere descriptive entities of a cultural phenomenon in the life of a woman. They mirror deeper layers of linkages. Her emotional state, her social standing in the family and society, her relationship with her parents, brothers, sisters and friends are all clearly etched in this category of songs, celebrating life-cycle events.

Bidai

The *Bidai* ceremony or bidding farewell to the bride is indeed a very very touching ceremony. In Punjab this is referred to as *doli.* The folk songs of Punjab are also replete with touching images of the parting between the parents and the daughter. The famous song from the legend of Heer-Ranja which is sung at the time of the *doli*, brings tears to the eyes of one and all even when sung today :

> "Doli chadeya Heer Mariyan Cheekan
> Manu Le chale Babul Le Chale".

The song sung in Garhwal at the time of *Bidai* is sung by the *Oujis.* The drums are resounding, beckoning the girl to come quickly.

Song 13

Oujis: Come soon, it is time for you to leave
The drums are beating, announcing the *Bidai*
Why are you taking so long......?
Bride: Wait! Don't be in a hurry
Let me at least meet all my beloved friends.
Oujis: Come soon! Don't take so long
Your bridegroom is waiting for you.
Bride: Wait! I am coming

Let me at least meet my dear mother
Don't be in a hurry please!
Let me at least meet my dear brother.
Oujis: Come dear girl, come soon
You are keeping the whole *barat* waiting.
Bride: Wait! Don't be in a hurry
Let me meet my dear father, before I leave.

(App.I,p.286-287)

The song is tinged with sadness, the girl is delaying her departure. She wants to meet her friends, her mother, her father, her brother and sister...all her loved ones whom she is going to leave behind. This moment of separation is indeed a traumatic experience for her. The imagery of leaving her parental home for an unknown destination, the path to which she imagines is covered by thick black clouds(metaphor for the unknown), creates fear in her mind.

Song 14

Behind the dark mountains
Are the thick black clouds
Alone, I fear to go to my in-laws home
dear father
Your *barat*, dear daughter will precede you
And elephants and horses will follow you.

(App. I,p.287)

Her fear at this moment is understandable, the father's assurance in a way does not appease her and she carries this anxiety within her, as also the curiosity to know what her in-laws home would be like.

Most of the mangal songs are sung at the home of the bride. The bride's arrival at her in-laws home, however, is also marked by the singing of mangal songs. "The coming of the bride to her in-laws house is considered as a symbol of pride and good fortune for the Garhwali families", says Ganga Prasad Bahuguna, an NGO representative from village Ranichauri.

Song 15

On this auspicious day, this auspicious moment

Plate 11 : The *Ouji's* beating the drums, and singing the mangal for the *Bidai* ceremony

Comes this *suhagin*
To our home, our home comes this *suhagin*
She brings with her the fragrance of nectar
And spreads, jewels wherever she goes!

(App.I,p.287-88)

With this mangal song all the ceremonies related to marriage are completed.

Highlights of Mangal Songs

The wedding songs of Garhwal clearly express the mental and social condition of the women of Garhwal. These songs cannot be treated as mere descriptive accounts of socio-cultural events taking place in society but are deeply rooted and connected with the life of the women, and are an expression of her emotional and psychological state.

In the wedding songs the girl's anxiety, inquisitiveness about the rituals connected with the various ceremonies is reflected as also her love for adorning herself with beautiful clothes and jewellery. The pain of separation from her parental home, the uncertainty of the future and the fear of entering a new house are all etched in the wedding songs.

In the case of the building of the *Vedi*, the daughter asks the father about what materials he would use and lovingly he says, "Gold, silver, and all the jewels as they do in Brahma Lok". Keeping in mind her father's poor status and economic condition she urges him to use mud, stone, and banana leaves instead to prepare the *Vedi*.

This depicts her concern for the welfare of the society, as well as her deep and mature thinking. It is this attitude of the woman which strengthens the very foundation of a culture and society. It also in a way points to the status of the woman during the vedic times when the mangal songs probably originated, and when the woman was considered to be an integral part of the family and society.

In the songs sung during the *Bidai* ceremony the daughter's pain at leaving her parental home, the unknown fear about her new life and all kinds of doubts are expressed. She does not know what lies ahead for her in her new home which may be situated across four or five mountains. Her father tries to assure her that the cow given in *daan* to her will keep the rivers of milk flowing in her house (indicating prosperity) and that her brother's would keep coming to see her. The daughter is going to leave her home, the forests and fields, her friends and kith and kin behind. To fulfill this emptiness by material things provided by the father does not bring solace to the girl at this moment. To over shadow the emotional aspect by the materialistic is an indicator of *abhav* (lack of the essential feeling).

Images of beauty of the bride to be, are reflected in the auspicious songs sung during the various marriage ceremonies. While anointing her with haldi and chandan, reference is always made to the beauty of Parvati and other goddesses. She is not described as an ordinary girl but is compared to the sacred, the Devi, the daughter of Lakshmi, Parvati in front of whom the rays of the sun are weak, the whiteness of the river Ganga mild. Her face is as beautiful as the full moon in the sky.

Most of the mangal songs make a reference to Parvati. Her image in the folklore of Garhwal is so lofty that no auspicious occasion related to a women's life is complete without a reference to her. The marriage of every girl in Garhwali society is referred to as the marriage of "Lord Shiva and Parvati". The image of gods and goddesses pervading the whole marriage ceremony reinforce the concept of religion (*dharm*), duty (*kartavya*) and ideals (*adarsh*) as essential elements of the socio-cultural environment of this society.

Parvati is the ideal for every girl in Garhwal. Her devotion to her husband Lord Shiva is given as an example for every girl to emulate. By comparing every girl with goddess Parvati, she is made to realise the purity and sanctity of her being. Parvati is not only projected as a bride, but also as the embodiment of the universal mother. Even during the *Godharna* ceremony in the seventh month of pregnancy the goddess Lakshmi, Parvati, and Savitri are asked to bestow happiness and prosperity and fill her lap with sons.

Every family has their own ancestral gods, who are asked to participate on the auspicious occasions of the marriage ceremony,particularly during the *kanyadaan* ceremony. In the context of the religious aspect of the mangal songs the image of the mother figure is reflected. Woman is the symbol of motherhood like mother earth. She has three attributes; she is loving, she is full of material wealth and she has the ability to bring progeny into the world.

Songs of Celebration: Birth of a child

Apart from the wedding songs, other *Mangal songs* are sung at the birth of the child, naming ceremony and *mundan* ceremony. In these songs there is reflection on the mother image of the woman. When a son is born to a woman, he is referred to as the redeemer of her austerities. When she gives birth to a son her importance and status in the family increases tenfold. She communicates the height of her joy on this occasion, by beckoning the *bhaunra* to take this message to her mother:

Song 16

Dear mother your daughter has won the battle
By giving birth to a son.

(App. I,p.288)

Her bliss on this occasion knows no bounds and she shares this joy with her mother, with whom she identifies completely. Mangal songs are the embodiment and symbol of mother hood. Through these songs the woman expresses her unlimited motherly love, and makes a reference to the hardships, she undergoes to give birth to a son.

The birth of a child is no longer celebrated by the singing of songs in Garhwal. Even the songs which were sung at the birth of a son earlier, have in a way disappeared because nobody sings them any longer. During group discussions and individual interviews with the women in villages near Chamba and in the interior villages near Budakedar, the women opined that this practice was no longer prevalent "Till twenty years ago songs celebrating the birth of the male child were sung in homes. But now Garhwal has changed", says Savitri Devi, Mahila Mandal chief of village Sabli. Only one song sung at the birth of a son was collected by the researcher. This was sung by an eighty year old woman in village Gonful, 1 km from Budakedar.

Song 17

Dear son! You are the fruit of my sacrifice!
To attain you, I underwent severe austerities
And observed all rites and rituals
For you, I bathed in the Holy Kund
Of all the shrines in Garhwal
I worshipped all the stones,in the name of the Gods
Dear son, may you become that ray
Of light that illuminates the mountain peaks at dawn!
My dear son,may you become the'light'of my *kul* (family).

(App.I,p.288-89)

Just as in the mangal songs related to marriage the bride and bridegroom are referred to as 'Shiva and Parvati' or 'Sita-Ram'; in the same way the new born son is referred to as Lord Krishna or Mahadev. For every mother her son is 'Narayan'. He is the greatest salvation of her motherhood. With his birth are linked her dreams and aspirations which find expression in the form of folk songs.

In other parts of India also, the birth of a son is celebrated with great pomp. Songs sung at the birth of a son, are referred to as 'sohar songs' in the Hindi speaking belt of the country. Research studies on women and folk songs of Haryana (Katarya, *et al.* 1987)(Kakkar, 1988), revealed that the birth of a son was indeed a very significant event in the life of the woman. No songs were sung celebrating the birth of the girl child.

In group discussions with women in village Ranichauri, Sabli and Dargi (Chamba block), it was expressed by the women that attitudes towards the girl child had changed considerably in Garhwal. "All girls in Garhwal are sent to study till class 12. There is tremendous sense of pride in educating the girls. In fact the mothers do not expect the school going and college going girls to help much in the domestic chores. They are happy to do the work themselves, rather than burden the daughter", said Vimla behn, Mahila Mandal chief of village Dargi.

A number of girls were under going training to be nurses, working as *balsevikas* in the Balwadi programmes or assisting NGOs in their activities. However, they were not able to see the relevance of education to their lives after marriage. Most of the newly married girls in the villages near Chamba were educated till class 12.

After marriage their work roles were the same — the only difference was that they were no longer intimidated by their mothers-in-law, and asserted themselves in the family. Surprisingly, it was the mother-in-laws who were complaining about the daughter-in-laws.

In the village Pipli, where a Mahila Mandal has been established by Mahila Nav Jagran Samiti, older women enacted a play about their daughter-in-laws. Some of the issues they highlighted were :

— emphasis on dressing up, using lipstick, make-up,etc.
— answering back their in-laws.
— watching television, most of the time.
— sitting and chatting with their husbands.
— singing less folk songs.

Songs of Celebration : Naming Ceremony

Songs sung to mark this life-cycle event were entirely difficult to find. In fact the researcher could not collect even one song for this occasion.

Songs of Celebration: 'Mundan' Ceremony

The next significant ceremony is the *Mundan* ceremony, referred to as '*Churakram*' in Garhwal. The mother expresses her deep love and concern for the child, by requesting the barber, *nai*, who shaves the head to be gentle and not to hurt her child:

Song 18

Dear *nai*, my brother
Do not give any pain to my little one
To you I will give a pair of sandals
A shawl to keep you warm
To you, I will give clothes and a *pagari*
Please do not hurt my child
Dear *nai*, my brother be gentle
Do not hurt my child.

(App.I,p.289)

The maternal instinct, motherly feeling, of the woman gets heightened and finds expression in the above song. She honours the *nai* who performs the ceremony by referring to him as her *dharm-bhai* (foster-brother). Through these songs the woman expresses her unbounded love for her child, for whom she undergoes severe austerities, bathes in the Holy *Kund* and worships all stones as images of Gods and Goddesses.

The mangal songs envelope beautifully the life-cycle events related to a woman's life. The transition in society and the changing position of the woman in society are reflected in these songs. In reality these songs portray the mental state of the woman. From times immemorial the image of the woman has been changing in the context of the depiction of her beauty and her status in society, but the image of the woman in relation to motherhood and the honour bestowed on her therein has remained the same. This journey from girlhood to marriage to motherhood is beautifully etched in the mangal songs.

SECTION-III
SOCIAL RELATIONS

Moments of Social Interaction — Walking to the forest, Village Ranichauri

My Beloved Dove,
Go ask my mother, when she will send for me
All my friends have gone home
But no one has come to fetch me.

SECTION-III

SOCIAL RELATIONS

In this section the patterns of familial interaction are explored with the woman as the pivot. This section is presented with focus on the following aspects :

Social Relations - *Khuder geet.*

(i) Parental Home.
  (a) Mother/Daughter.
  (b) Father/Daughter.
  (c) Brother/Sister.
(ii) In-laws Home.
  (a) Husband/Wife.
  (b) Mother-in-law/daughter-in-law.
(iii) Dialogue Across the Hills - *Baju Band geet.*

(a) Social Interaction with peers and kin

Patterns of familial interaction as reflected in the folk songs give us an insight into the position of the woman in the family, her social roles and her emotional state. In Garhwal the category of folk songs which reflect familial interactions and the emotional and psychological state of the woman are referred to as *Khuder geet*. The word *Khuder's* etymology is from the word *khud*, that which touches the self, which is dear to one's self; and, the absence of which creates a void, a longing which gets expressed in a song. The term *Khuder* is given to a category of songs which reflect anguish, pain, and sorrow of some kind.

Khuder geet reflect the heart-rendering account of the life of the newly married girl in her in-laws home; and her intense longing for her parental home. The mountainous terrain, absence of the man, harsh treatment of the in-laws economic deprivation, the status of the woman in Garhwali society, and the authoritative nature of the mother-in-law. All these factors contribute to her longing and misery, which she gives voice to as a *Khuder geet*. Garhwali folk songs are filled with images of the hard life of the woman in her in-laws home. In the context of the above it becomes imperative for her to look for support, comfort and love from her parental home.

These songs are generally sung in the forest when she is with friends or alone. None of the songs reflecting parental longing are sung in the precincts of the home. Vimlabehn of village Dargi, near Ranichauri said:

> "At home, in front of the mother-in-law and other elders we cannot sing these songs. Songs remembering the mother or longing for the husband are sung in the forest."

The locale of singing is a very significant aspect in the study of folk songs of Garhwal. Songs of celebration of life-cycle events, and songs sung in memory of famous people, or an event; religious songs propitiating the goddess, or songs describing the beauty of the woman are sung in the domestic environment. Songs reflecting longing for the parental home and the husband, songs mirroring relationships with members of the family are sung in a supportive environment, which is the forest near the village. Women from village Sabli participating in a group discussion on, why this category of songs, was sung in the forest, stated :

> "The trees, plants, birds, fruits and flowers in the forest listen to us. They do not answer back or belittle us in any way. They just listen and absorb it. In a way our song frees us from our emotions."

Parental Home

Mother/daughter relationship

From many other accounts and sources it is evident that there is deep affection and compassionate attention bestowed by mothers on their infant daughters. Folk songs all over India bear witness to this close mother-daughter relationship. " I turn the stone flour-mill with the swiftness of a running deer; that is because my arms are strong with the mother's milk I drank. A mother's unconscious identification with her daughter is normally stronger than her son. In her daughter the mother re-experiences herself as a cared-for girl"(Kakkar, S., 1986).

Most profound perhaps of all relationships is the bond between mother and daughter — a bond which is felt to be part of all growth, of all continuance and creation. The bringing to birth of one like oneself, who in turn will bear another, is an image engraved everywhere in Indian culture. Hence a singer need not seek far to find metaphors for mother-daughter continuity, and often a single word will go a long way in this regard.

In the song mirroring mother/daughter relationships, the woman wants to negate the pain and torment experienced by her in her in-laws home by the 'cool shadow' of love and affection she gets from her parents. In all the songs she addresses the mother — with whom she identifies totally and completely.

> " Who understands pain and longing more than the mother who has herself undergone and experienced all this in her own life." says Dharam Devi of village Budakedar.

In short, the common experience of pain intensifies the bond between the mother and daughter.

Much of the significance of a crying song lies, not in its open declarations, but in its allusions. A single word opens, for those who share the singer's world, on to complex realities with multiform meanings; but for those who do not share the singer's world, the meanings are closed and opaque. Words have meaning according to the cultural context. This density of word-pictures greatly deepens the song - deepens it, first because much of the song's meaning is not immediately accessible, but takes intimacy with the singer's sub-culture, and time to "sink in". To the extent that the meanings expressed by the song are encoded in the culture, they may be unconscious or partly conscious, perhaps even for the singer herself. The song is deepened, secondly, because this dense imagery touches upon dimensions of human relations that no words express directly (Egnor, 1986).

Song 1

Girls with mothers go to their parental home
But I have no mother or father
who will call me ?
Dear mother, I remember you so much,
Those with brothers will be called home,
But alas! I have no brother
Dear mother, I long for you.
My husband is away to a strange land

For years he has not written to me.
I am the only child born in a poor family
Dear mother, I miss you so much!
My eyes are filled with tears.

(App.I,p.290-91)

In this song a girl who has no parents, whose husband is away in the army, cries out to her mother, to be called home.

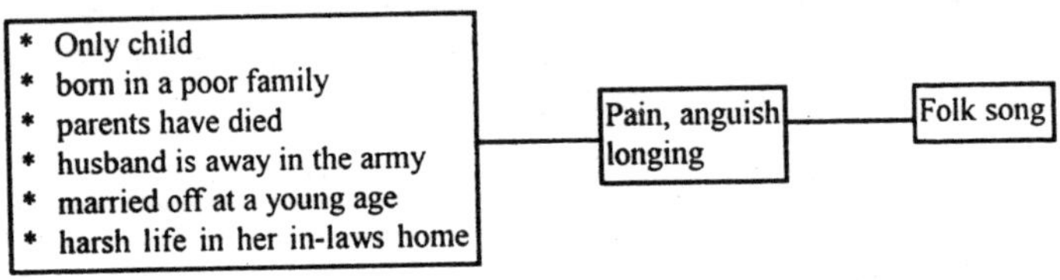

Fig. 4.5 : Representation of song 1

Song 2

Dear high mountain peaks
Lower yourselves
Let me see my mother's home.
Dear, tall deodar trees
Lower your branches
So that I can see my mother's home.

(App.I,p.291)

The above song was the most widely sung folk song in Garhwal. The song reflects anguish and longing for the parental home and is a dialogue of the woman with the deodar forest.

The woman addresses the high mountain peaks asking them to bend, so that she can see her mother's home which is situated across various mountain ranges Similarly, she requests the tall deodar trees to bend a little to enable her to see her mother's home. Mountains do not bend, neither do trees, asking for the impossible is only an indicator of the intense longing she has for her parents home. The lines are tinged with poignancy. The woman talks to the forest, because the forest is the embodiment of mother-earth. It listens but does not talk back to her like a

Fig. 4.6 : Graphic Representation of Song 2

mother-in-law or husband.

The intense longing for the parental home which she cannot express in her home environment she expresses in dialogue with the forest. There is a feeling of liberation, a freedom of space and she feels in complete harmony with nature. To speak to the mountains, to the trees, to the birds—to make them participate in her emotions, is an integral feature of the folk songs of Garhwal.

Song 3

My Beloved Dove,
Go ask my mother, when she will send for me
All my friends have gone home
But no one has come to fetch me.

(App.I,p.292)

Song 4

Dear 'kafu', go and sing near my mother's home
My mother will hear your voice
And send my brother to fetch me.

(App.I,p.292)

Song 5

The month of January-February is here
The high mountain peaks will be ablaze
with Rhododendron flowers.
All the girls have gone to their mother's home
Alas! I am the unfortunate one.

(App.I,p.292-93)

The songs of mother/daughter relationship referred to as *Khuder geet* also make reference to the deep relationship of the woman to the natural environment. "Nature is a great friend, the forest is warm nurturing, the birds listen, all this is our world. They share our joys and sorrows", says Leelabehn of village Ranichauri.

The songs of the seasons highlight the special features of the changing seasons as also the emotional state of the woman. The canvas of the *Khuder geet* which predominantly focus on the emotional and psychological state of the woman is the natural environment of Garhwal. Thus emotion, ecology, culture are inter-linked and interconnected. So many aspects of a woman's life get highlighted as we look at each category of folk songs.

Some folk songs addressed to the mother make a reference to the life and work roles of the woman in her in-laws home.

Song 6.

The night is dark, dear mother!
The night is dark
Do not send me to my *sasural*
At Deep Danda (a place-name)
Do not get new clothes stitched for me
Nor make sweets for my in-laws home!
Do not buy me a pair of sandals
Or comb my hair into braids.
Dear mother, I will not go to my *sasural*
It is too painful for me there.

(App.I,p.293)

The dark night is a metaphor for the life of the woman in her in-laws home. She implores her mother not to perform all the rituals associated with sending a daughter back to her *sasural*, namely:

1. buying new clothes

2. preparing sweets
3. purchasing new sandals and
4. combing her hair into braids.

The following song illustrates her life in her in-laws home and the work roles she performs.

Song 7

Dear mother, I feel scared in the forest
Near my *sasural*
Without you, my 'life-source' is dead
The unkind daughters and daughter-in-law
Of this village
Leave me alone, and walk away.
In the courtyard at home,
The buffalo and cow keep calling out!
But nobody gets up to give them fodder
Their pride and status is all false
Dear mother!
The heavy load of grass I carry on my head
Falls in fear of encountering wild animals!
My sisters-in-laws
Keep sitting at home.
When I bring grass from the jungle,
Then I go to fetch water
From a great distance.

(App.I,293-94)

The images etched in the above song give a clear picture of the life of the woman of Garhwal.

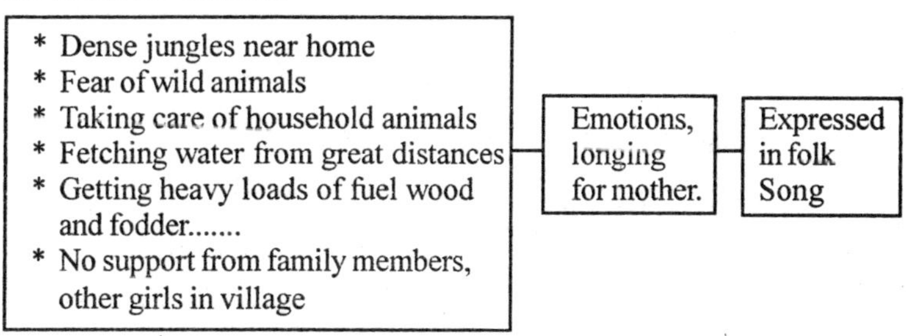

Fig. 4.7 : Representation of Song 7

Fig. 4.8 : Graphic Representation of Song 7.

This is an extremely popular folk song in Garhwal with both men and women. Interestingly in Garhwal even men sing songs about women's lives. According to the women of Ranichauri, Sabli, Dargi (near Chamba) and from the interior valley of Budakedar, Aagor, and Gonful- this song truly represented their life. There is a great degree of identification with this song which has come down by word of mouth from generations, with new phrases being added to it, as experienced by the women.

In the above song the daughter tells her mother that when she goes to collect fuelwood to the forests near her in-laws home in the mountain, she feels very scared and longs for her mother. She goes on to say, "The daughter and daughter-in-law of the village, where she has got married, are not kind and gentle. They do not accompany her to the forest, and they also do not care for the animals in their backyard. Their pride is all false". This reflects strained relations with other family members in her in-laws home. In the dense forests there are lots of bears who frighten her and the heavy load of grass that she is carrying on her head fall to the ground. Women walk great distances (10km) in dense forests to collect fuelwood for the family and have to encounter these animals.

The trees on the peaks of the mountains are laden with red Rhododendron flowers, but she does not hear the sound of the beautiful birds which sing in the trees - a sound she was so familiar with during her childhood.

The above lines reflect a close link with nature and the daily work pattern of the women of Garhwal. A number of songs show a deep link between the ecologyof the area and life of the women.

New content is added to songs all the time, reflecting a kind of continuity. Interestingly the husband understands the pain his wife goes through to collect fuelwood and grass — so he tells his mother:

> Have coal instead of wood
> and cut the leaves of
> trees if there is no grass
> but do not trouble my wife
> anymore as she is too overworked.

The last few lines were added to the song about ten years ago, showing that there is a loving relationship between the husband and wife. It was observed that the older women, above 40 years, sang more of these (*khuder*) songs and even cried during the singing session. In a group discussion session at village Sabli, where 20 women had gathered in the house of Shakuntala, grand-mothers who had their grand children in their laps, had tears streaming down their cheeks when they sang any song remembering their mothers.

The following song is based on a true story of a Garhwali girl who was killed by her husband in anger by a *darati* (agricultural implement) because she had cooked *chapattis* and he had asked to eat rice instead. His extreme anger under the influence of alcohol reflects in a way the position of the woman in the household and the authority of the male. According to the older women in the village, this song was composed and created by the women of Garhwal, soon after the incident took place. The song is addressed to the mother and Sushila tells her whole story in it.

Song 8

Dear mother what kind of a husband
did you find for me,
he is always drunk
You got me married at the young age of sixteen
to a far away destination
Oh! mother you have killed me in a way

One night he came home at midnight,
I was cooking *chapattis*
He asked to eat rice instead
He took off his watch,
and put it in the almirah
and went into the next room.
He brought a *darati*
I thought he was joking and smiled at him
He cut me twice with the *darati,*
I fell sideways - bleeding profusely
My younger brother-in-law cried in vain
when he saw me fall and my head cut off

My husband put me in a sack and
And buried me in a deep pit in the forest.

Six months from now, at the festival of Diwali
Dear mother, call my younger sister Vimla
And give her warm milk to drink,

which you would have given me.

My friends must have come to their mother's home
They will all go dressed beautifully to the *mela*
Alas! if I was alive I would
have been there.

I lie here alone, in the shadow
of this tall deodar tree

Dear mother, I pray that there is no
unfortunate girl like Sushila born to any mother.
(App.I,p.294-95)

Many questions arise in one's mind after listening to the above song which was interestingly sung by a young man, an activist working with the Mahila Samakhya Project in Tehri. Songs get created on events which move people in a society. Vimla behn of village Dargi said that this event had not taken place in her life time(she was 70 years old), but her mother talked about Sushila's story which shook the entire community across the length and breadth of Tehri Garhwal. This song is illustrative of:

(1) intense anger and authority of the man,
(2) alcoholism and its effect on family dynamics,
(3) helplessness of other members of the family, and
(4) what is most significant is that it is addressed to the mother, with whom Sushila shares a deep bond.

Her story/song in a way frees her from the actual event which confines her to a space.

> "Sushila's song frees her. By talking to her mother she feels lighter. In the cool shadow of maternal love she finds peace", says Savitri behn of village Sabli near Ranichauri(Chamba block).

Ramanujan (1986) defines "Women's tales" as tales told by and centered around women, which does not preclude male exposure to and interest in them. Whether Tamil, Kannada, or Paxto, women's personal narratives maybe seen to share the general function of recapitulation in functional narratives; the construction of a self. Ramanujan points out that " the whole tale is the tale of her acquiring her story, making a person of her, making a silent person a speaking women. Fictional tales and narratives grounded in concrete personal experiences suggest that fantasy and reality often address similar concerns. Finding a personal voice in male-dominated galaxies of possibilities seems to be at the center of female-related gender issues as well as in the description and analysis of the emergent production of games"(Korom, F., *et al.*, 1991).

Trawick (1991) in her research, also bridges the gap between emotionally laden accounts of individual experiences and genre production. She detects a tangible transformation between life and song; songs clarify and strengthen certain life events, in this case fragmentation and suffering in human relationships. Margaret Trawick addresses two rather abstract issues; one the relation between art and life; and two, the relation between people and place. The assumption in the case of the former is that an artistic performance is not an object that can be grasped in isolation from the life of the performer. Rather the artistic act is continuous with the performers or singers ordinary life; it is a rendition into greater meaning of this life, and is as much dependent on it as a rosebush is dependent on its rose. A related assumption is that every human being is in some way an artist, a being driven to produce something of surprising beauty, even under the most adverse conditions. We must recognise that person to be a creator not just a survivor - someone for whom creation may be even more important than survival

This act of creating one's own songs, breathing life and meaning into them has tremendous implications and relevance to the significance of the study of folk songs.

In terms of communication the creator of the song is empowered by the act of that creation — the song belongs to her — there is greater identification with the medium; she takes responsibility for creating that song, for breathing life into it. It is her song, her life, that she sings about.

According to Grima (1986) who worked with Paxto women in Afghanistan, 'Gham' is a key cultural word-term in the women's everyday performance of Paxto. In a woman's life, 'Gham' begins with her marriage, when she is cast from security of her mother's home into an environment of hostile relationships with a mother-in-law, sister-in-law, living day after day in the same house with no release from them. Just as marriage marks the introduction of 'Gham' into a woman's life — so does it mark the opening of the story of her life. The opening line of their story was always "My life has been nothing but misery" or there has been no joy in my life. A women's life is perceived almost entirely within a framework of hardship and suffering, beginning with her being severed from her mother. Many women agreed that the time before marriage had been one of happiness.

A number of folk songs collected in various sessions with village women from Ranichauri, Sabli,—and Dargi reflect this intense longing for the parental home. In fact the woman (Vimlabehn) who was singing this song would burst into tears.

I wondered how she could feel like this at her age - she had her grand children in her lap and was 60 years old. On probing further she shared that she was married at the age of 12 in village Dargi which was located across four mountains from her parental home. The physical inaccessibility in those days added to this anguish, as there were not so many roads and buses and it was not easy for her to go to her mother's home. The hardships encountered in the in-laws home, getting up at four in the morning, grinding *manduwa* a coarse grain, making tea for the household, going to the jungle 10kms away barefoot, coming home at one, cooking food, bathing the animals, feeding them fodder, going to collect water from the spring (4-5 kms) away, coming back at three and then going again to the forest for the fuelwood and fodder, all added to her extremely hard life at a young age.

Father/daughter relationship

A Garhwali girl addresses a passer-by whom she meets on the way to the forest:

Song 9

Girl— Which village do you come from - dear brother,
Help me to forget the longing I have for my
parent's home

Boy — Do not cry dear sister, wipe your tears
Be courageous like a man in your in-laws home

Girl— What did my father get by educating me till class 2,
What did my father get by getting me married in the
mountains

Boy — Your parent cannot remain yours forever,
And your brother and his wife are also not
yours forever — they have their own life

Do not cry
my dear sister, wipe your tears
Become courageous like a man in your
in-laws home
And everything will be fine!

(App.I,p.295)

This song is sung by an educated girl who lives in the lower Himalayas (Rishikesh, Haridwar). She has been married into the mountains near Chamba and sees no value of her educated status in her married life, since her work roles require different skills. When she sees a young boy playing the flute near the forest path, she addresses him and implores him to alleviate her anguish for her parental home.

The advice the passer-by gives her is to become courageous like a man. It is interesting to note how courage is associated with a man, when all the hard work is done by the woman alone, braving the forests and wild animals in the cold winter and rainy season, walking long distances to fetch fuel, fodder and water; and, participating in all agricultural tasks. According to Dr. M.L. Dewan, Director, Trees For Life, Ranichauri, Chamba block, 93 per cent of the agricultural tasks are performed by the women in Garhwal.

At the emotional and personal level she gives vent to her feelings in the form of questions, the answers to which she seeks from her father. The passer-by's reference to 'become courageous like a man' is perhaps asking her to gather herself. His advice is philosophical in a way, addressing a fundamental dilemma faced by women across cultures. He asks her to become conscious of the fact that 'no one remains your forever', and urges her to get on with her life with courage. Men are known to be courageous at the emotional level and perhaps the reference to the man is only symbolic of that attribute.

This song is significant from many aspects with reference to a woman's life. The following points were noted after recording the song in Budakedar. About 20 women who were attending the *'shivir'* on environment at Budakedar, participated in the discussion :

(1) It is easier for her to talk to a stranger about her personal anguish or longing than address the same questions to any member in the in-laws family. The stranger is unknown, the family members 'known' in one sense.
(2) The locale of singing is also significant here. Personal songs of

this nature would not be sung in the precincts of the home, as stated earlier. The passer-by in this case becomes a part of the forest which is viewed as warm, and a space where she can express herself.

(3) Finding no value for her educated status (10+2) in her new role is a question that was reflected not only in the songs but came up again and again for discussion at various meetings with women in Garhwal.

Did they feel that education would change their role in family and society? Does one see education as freedom from drudgery — is it in opposition to working and performing one's day to day activities?

According to Dharamdevi, Mahila Mandal chief of village Budakedar, "Today's daughter-in-law has so many facilities, and education is her greatest advantage. Even though she does all the household work, and goes to the jungle, she is able to plan her work better. She is not scared to express herself". Dharamdevi's profound explanation had all the younger women in the group looking up to her with surprise, as though she had created a shift in their way of thinking about themselves.

Some folk songs reflect the position of the father in the family and his role in decision-making regarding the daughter's life. Whereas, for emotional and psychological sustenance she addresses the mother, in the following songs the daughter addresses the father because it is he who decides where she is to be married and to whom.

Song 10

Father — Dear Kamla, you are a young woman now
I will get you married in the mountains.

Daughter — I beg you, dear father
Do not marry me into the mountains
life in the mountain is extremely hard
People walk barefoot
The men drink alcohol
And come home late at night
I pray to you dear father
I touch your feet dear mother
Do not get me married into the mountains.

(App.I,296)

The young girl Kamla is apprehensive about getting married into the mountains. She lives in the foothills (Rishikesh) with her parents, and fears that her life in the mountains will be very hard.

Song 11

Daughter — Dear father, what are the social customs
Where you seek a life partner for me?
What clothes do they wear there?
What food do they eat there?

Father — They wear woollen *sarees* there
And eat *jhangora* and *manduwa*
(barley and coarse grain millets)

Daughter — Dear father, I will never go there
Dear father, I will go nowhere!

Father — Come daughter, I will take you to
Nagni (a small village off Chamba) *Bazaar*
And give you a thousand rupees

Daughter — I will not go to any *bazaar*
Nor do I want rupees hazaar (one thousand)
(App.I,p.296-97)

The life-styles and socio-cultural customs vary to a large extent from the lower, middle and higher mountain ranges. The work-roles performed by the women also change according to the altitude and the terrain. In the above song the girl who lives near Nagni village (at a height of about 3000 feet above sea level) asks her father about the customs prevalent in the upper Himalayas near Harsil (Uttarkashi district) at a height of about 8000 feet above sea level. Since it is cold in that region, women wear wollen clothes and eat coarse grains which they have to grind in the stone *chakki*. The girl refuses to go there even though her father tries to bribe her with a thousand rupees. Significant features of the song are as follows :

1. The father takes decisions regarding marriage of the daughter.
2. Social customs, life-styles vary with altitude within the same districts.

3. The girl is always apprehensive about her life and hence the questions addressed to her father (fear of the unknown).

Songs reflecting patterns of familial interaction are also indicators of the socio-cultural environment of a particular family and the community.

Song 12

Dear father,
Why did you give me away
Across four mountains!
Dear brother, why did you accept
money for my hand in marriage?
My mother-in-law abuses me
My step-brother does calls me names
I cry looking at the path that leads
to my home, Dear father!
Why, Oh why!
Did you get me married
Four mountains away!

(App.I,297)

This song makes a reference to the social customs prevalent in Garhwal, wherein the girl's father/brother(representing the male authority in the family) accepted money from the boy's family in exchange for the girl.

When the girl finds herself in a strange environment, and has strained relations with her in-law's family, she feels isolated and alone. She gives voice to her anguish through a song addressed to the father. It is interesting to note that most of the songs reflecting father/daughter interactions are in the form of questions.

— Does the father answer the girl's questions?
— Are there any simplistic answers?
— Is the song only a psychological release of pent-up emotions?

When the researcher asked the women of village Sabli to comment on the above questions, Vijaya Bahuguna, a primary school teacher, said:

> "Who has ever got answers to such questions. Songs are the voice of our lives. By singing, by giving voice to our pain, we

feel better".

Song 13

When I was a little girl
Then I was your beloved, Dear father
Now I come to your house Dear father
Only when I wish to.
Why did you marry me off to an old man
To such a far off place
My friends tease me and
make fun of me!
Their remarks jibe me like a sharp knife,
My mother-in-law ill treats me
And gives me only one *roti* to eat
When will I do my work
And when will I breast feed my baby
Dear father, I am very unhappy
My husband's away to a strange land
I want to jump in the river and die
Or strangle myself to death!

(App.I,p.297-298)

Highlights of Song 13

1. Married at a young age
2. To a man much older than her
3. To a far off destination
4. Harsh mother-in-law/not enough food to eat
5. Heavy workload at home
6. Teased by peer group
7. Husband away for long periods of time, no support
8. Wants to end life.

Fig. 4.9 : Song mirrors so many aspects of a culture

The above song illustrates how rich each folk song is in reflecting so many aspects of a culture with special reference to women's lives. The categories are not mutually exclusive, but infact the linkages present a continuum, a movement which connects each layer with the other. Each song is a holistic representation of the women's life in Garhwal.

Brother/sister

This song is sung by a Garhwali woman both to her mother and her brother, describing the hardships she faces in her in-laws house.

Song 14

Daughter — Below the *pipal* tree
there is a small stream of water
that flows 'drop' by 'drop'
In my *sasural* dear mother
my life is very hard
The mountain paths are steep
And I have to use a stick to climb up and down

Brother — Dear sister your *kismet*
destiny is like this
What can we do about it
I did not know the people in your in-laws home
would be like this
you have been cheated

Sister — When the 'dove' sings in the tall deodar trees
I am reminded of the life in my mother's home And
my heart writhes with pain

Brother — When I go for my work dear sister
I think about you and cry dear sister
This is what is written for you
What can we do.
Do not cry and complain
People laugh at your fortune
And malign our family.

(App.I,p.298-99)

The sister seeks comfort by sharing her pain with her brother and mother, while the mother listens, the brother tries to give her a 'fatalistic' explanation about destiny!

The women's movement in our country has challenged the notion of destiny which is so deeply engraved in the psyche of all woman. Since there is no other rational explanation for pain, suffering, hardship it is all put under the umbrella of destiny.

In the rural areas the brother represents to the woman, a figure of authority and dependability. He may be able to do something about my life, the woman feels. But again he has nothing to offer but -- "that you are destined to suffer, do not cry, people will laugh and malign our family." In a way representing a different kind of male stereotype.

In-Laws Home

Husband/Wife relationship

It is interesting to note, in terms of socio-cultural aspects, that in Tehri Garhwal after the British Raj, the men were recruited in large numbers into the army, and the women stayed back alone in the village for long periods of time. At that time the age of marriage was 12-16 years, and when this young girl found herself in a strange environment, without the support and affection of her husband, her intensity and longing for her husband was heightened. Most of the folks songs in the category of *Khuder geet* reflect this anguish and longing.

Song 15

As the monsoon mist
creeps up the hillside
flitting amongst the deodars
I long for you - my swami (lord)
I want to throw myself into the deep gorge
All my friends have received letters -
so many of them!!
But your letter eludes me
My parents are not alive

My brother and *'bhabhi'* are away to a
strange land
And you are also away!!!
As the monsoon mist
creeps up the hillside
I long for you
Without you, I want to kill myself
by falling into the deep gorge of the mountains.

(App.I,p.299)

Estranged from her husband who is away for occupational reasons for long periods of time — the woman in Garhwal sings expressing her anguish and intense longing for her husband.

The absence of the husband for long periods of time is a significant aspect of the life of the woman of Garhwal. She performs a dual role in the family bearing the responsibility of a wide range of activities alone. In adverse circumstances (both economic and climatic) her undaunted courage, ability and skills to perform various work roles related to the household and outside, and her undying love/longing for her husband are all indicators of her special 'beingness'. Ganga Prasad Bahuguna, an NGO worker from village Ranichauri, very aptly said : "Women are the backbone of the society".

Not only does the woman sing songs in the absence of her husband, the husband also expresses his feelings through songs.

Song 16

You my beloved *'chanda'*

Are as pure as the water of the river ganga
Your heart is as pure
And you are compassionate and kind
I feel you crying *'chanda'*
But Alas! I am so far away from you
What can I do.
The *'kafal'* fruit must be ripe
All the girls and you must be going
to the jungle to eat it
The trees would be laden with
fresh fruits and leaves
And you must be eating fresh vegetables
from the fields
Dear *'chanda'* I am sending you
two thousand rupees
Remember we got married on the 20th
of this month
You are my lovely 'chanda'
I miss you a lot.

(App.I,p.299)

There is a sense of rhythm and rhyme in the above song, for example the words 'Chanda' and 'Ganga'. The river Ganga has special meaning to the people of Garhwal. The river permeates their culture and life-styles. For the husband his wife 'Chanda' is not only a woman but an embodiment of goddess Parvati and he likenes her to the pure river Ganga. The notion of the sacred is also inherent in the folk songs of Garhwal. The song clearly reflects the loving relationship between the husband and wife. The husband also longs for and misses the wife. It is equally unnatural for him to live without his wife, and family for long periods of time. The reference to the " I '11 send you two thousand rupees" is significant here, because Garhwal is referred to as the 'money-order' economy.

Song 17

Why does the sound of the flute
reverberate in the hillside.
Today I experience a sense of fear and sadness
Dear gods and goddesses of this universe
protect me -

I am all alone today
I will sacrifice a goat at your altar
dear god -
please protect me
Devi Bhagwati, I beseech you
to keep my honour intact
I will offer a beautiful *'chunni'*
at your shrine
The sound of the flute fills the hillside
I long for my husband
Yet, I experience a sense of fear
Why does the sound of the flute
Fill the environment thus.

(App.I,p.300)

The beauty of the natural environment of Garhwal, the fog coming up the hillside, the sound of the flute reverberating in the mountains all heighten the longing of the woman for the husband. Here her image is that of a *Virahini*, one who longs for her beloved. The protection that she seeks from the gods and goddesses is not from the fear of being attacked, but the fear that she may be drawn to the man playing the flute. Women of Gonful village (near Budakedar) who sang this song said, "We feel very safe walking in the forest, the fear is only from outsiders, the forest rangers, etc. However, the long absence of our husbands, makes us long for them even more and it is possible to feel unnerved at the sound of the haunting flute".

In this song there is a reference to the money-lender who troubles the wife to recover his money as the husband is away. She sings this song in the form of a dialogue.

Song 18

Wife — When the money-lender arrives
I tremble with fear

Husband —Why do you cry
Why do you carry pain in your heart
People laugh at your state

Wife — My father, promised me a 'gold-*nath*'

But alas! he did not give me anything.

Husband —There is sin in the mind's of the people
All this forebodes the fall of *Hindu-dharam.*
Don't worry, my dear
The house and land are in you care
While I go to earn some money in a strange land.
Wife — Dear husband! Do not utter such words
My eyes fill with tears
When you speak thus!

(App.Ip.300)

The money-lender is a significant feature of the village economy. Since the husband is away for occupational reasons, as no employment facilities are available in Garhwal; the money-lender extorts money with interest and suppresses the women, at times terrorising them. The women wishes her father had kept his promise of giving her more gold, so that she had more security, and would not have to face the demands of the money-lender. The husband is sympathetic and in a way understands the plight of the wife. His reference to the fall of the *Hindu-dharam* refers to the unecessary demands of the money-lender on his wife. The women look after the house and land in the absence of the man.

Song 19

Husband — Dear Radha wash my clothes!
And give me food
I have to go to war
And may never return

Wife— Wash your hands and eat food
but tell me where the war is

Husband —The war is near the border, dear Radha

Wife — You stay at home and cook
I will go to the border and fight

Husband — You stay home Radha and make rope of the fabric
If you go to the border -

People will make fun of you

Wife — Dear lord! If you will go away to the border How will I survive your absence.

(App.I,p.301)

During the time of the British Rule, the enrollment of Garhwali men into the army was done in large numbers. Even if the man was posted to a family station the wife was left behind to give a helping hand in all the household tasks. The alien atmosphere of the in-laws house, the hard tasks to be performed; all have added to her anguish — she wants to accompany her husband to the border, she wants to fight in the war — but ultimately this is not accepted. The woman has to stay behind, to look after the home and hearth. What is significant in the above song is her undaunted courage.

You stay at home and cook
and I will go to the border and fight.

Song 20

You my dear *Swami* (lord) are in the city of Delhi
You travel the whole day by car!
While I walk on stones
To the forest, to cut grass,
My hands and feet have become torn with deep marks
I have become weak
Doing such continuous hard work
Please get transferred to Kotdwar
I will meet you at Haridwar.

(App.I,p.301)

In the above song, the woman shares her hard life with her husband:

— walking long distance to get fuel fodder
— walking bare feet on sharp stones
— clothes/hand/feet are torn.

She contrasts this with his life in Delhi, where she thinks he is travelling by car (symbolic of a comfortable life). Her request to get transferred to

Kotdwar in Pauri Garhwal represents the cry of the women of Garhwal, who stay for long periods of time away from their husbands.

At a *Shivir* in Budakedar on environment from the 17-20 May, 1993, 300 men and women had gathered from neighbouring villages. *Sevadas,* an *Ouji* (traditional folk singer) from village Gonagarh sang a very old folk song which he called " Rami-Burana ka geet". Surjadevi, Mahila Mandal head of village Budakedar said that this song truly reflected the socio-psychological state of a woman who had not set eyes on her husband for several years. When he comes home 12 years later disguised as a *sadhu,* and starts a conversation with his wife while she is working in the field, she retorts back that she does not talk to strangers. On reaching home she finds that her mother-in-law is warmly feeding the same *Sadhu.* The daughter-in-law urges the mother-in-law not to be so kind to this stranger, because he had said some offensive things to her. On finding out that the sadhu is none other than her husband, she is shocked and sorry about her behaviour.

Song 21 *(Rami-Burana ka geet)*

Sadhu — You who are working in the fields
Tell me what is your name ?

Woman — Oh wandering *Yogi (sadhu),* why do you ask my name
What do you want from me
My name is Rami, my father's name is Rontu
I come from village Pali and
I am the wife of Sethu

Sadhu — Why are you working alone
Where are your father-in-law and mother-in-law?

Woman — My mother-in-law is at home
My father-in-law has passed away

Sadhu — Come dear woman!
Come and sit near me
Will you not do that for me?

Woman — Oh *Yogi* do no speak thus to me
Your sisters will come and sit near you !

The man goes to the village and straight to his parents home. He asks his old mother for some food, as he is hungry.

Sadhu — Dear Mother give me some food !
I have come a long way.

Mother-in-law —
Rami come cook for this *sadhu*
He is our guest today

Rami — No, I will not, he said some bad things
to me in the fields.

Sadhu — Cook and serve me in your
husband's *thali*
I will only eat in that
And stay hungry otherwise
I have come home today after 12 years.

(App.I,p.301-302)

The above song is an indicator of the long periods of absence of the husband, and the dilemmas associated with this predicament.

Is the loving relationship reflected in the folk songs only a result of the absence, the long period of separation? Discussions with women on this issue revealed that their lives were indeed different from other women, who got married and had the support of their husbands in various ways. "Just his presence in the house, would make a lot of difference. But he is not there leaving us alone to cope with so many things, house, children fields, jungle, family relationships", said Khushadevi of village Kotigad (Chamba block). It is the observation of the researcher that during various discussions, informal meetings and so on, the women hardly ever talked about their husbands. They talked about their lives, their hard work, their children and their relationship with their mother-in-laws. But the uppermost aspect of their conversation was the longing for the parental home. They seldom complained about their husbands, and the non-participation in their lives. "It was as if something is given, and how often does one question the given".

Mother-in-law/daughter-in-law

Woman is the pivot, the centre of family life in Garhwal. There is a proverb in Garhwal, "That just as a 12 year boy is trained to fight in battle, similarly a 12 year old girl is trained to look after the household and related activities". This training is given to the girl right from the 12th day after her birth.

Subsequently, her whole life is spent in caring for her family, the fields, the domestic animals etc. As stated earlier, the geographical terrain is not conducive to employment opportunities for the men of the family, and they have to migrate outside Garhwal, leaving the woman alone to cope with so much.

To add to all this the mother-in-law's harsh treatment of her daughter-in-law makes her life even more miserable. The following few lines beautifully depict this:

Song 22

Just as vegetables cook
in a pot of hot steaming oil
Such is my plight (my destiny)
In my mother-in-law's home!

(App.I,p.302)

A number of Garhwali songs reflect images of harsh treatment meted out to the daughter-in-law. These songs are mainly addressed to the mother, and they make a reference to not wanting to go to *sasural*, getting very little food to eat, the hard work that has to be performed in the in-laws home and that even though the girl is beloved of her parents, in the eyes of her mother-in-law she is always 'bad'.

Song 23

My hands and feet are torn
With hard work
My mother-in-law sends me to collect grass
In a forest
Unknown to me.
The slopes are bare and devoid of grass
Yet I bring green grass for the animals
When I come home and drink some milk

My mother-in-law retorts
"Did your father provide for this milk?"
She complains about me to my husband,
And gets him to beat me.

(App.I,p.303)

The above song reflects the treatment of the mother-in-law of her daughter-in-law and the hard work that she performs daily. The taunting words hurt her like daggers; she wants to cry and escape her destiny. The forest is her only friend where she talks to the birds and trees through the medium of a song and feels somewhat relieved.

In a study on portrayal of women in the folk songs of Haryana (Katarya, *et.al.* 1987), it was also seen that to counteract the harshness of the mother-in-law, or the home environment, the woman turns to nature to relieve her suffering.

"Fetch water from the well
Without a rope or a bucket", says the mother-in-law.
"Do not cry loved one of thy parents
We will fill your pitcher", say the birds
in the fields.

The song in a way takes away a lot of the pain and anguish experienced by the woman.

In fact a majority of the *Khuder geet* present a very harsh picture of the mother-in-law. However, it would be unrealistic to hold the mother-in-law solely responsible for the unhappy experience of the daughter-in-law in her in-laws home. The socialization pattern of the girl child in the parental family, economic deprivation, lack of job opportunities for the husband, the daughter-in-law's educated status and unhappiness at participating in all agricultural tasks are some of the factors that contribute to this pattern of familial interaction between mother-in-law and daughter-in-law.

Song 24

When will I grind the grain
and when will I breast feed my child
My mother-in-law is very bad
She wants to hit me all the time.

She gives me coarse *roti* to eat (rye bread)
And stale food to eat.

(App.I,p.303)

Song 25

My heart is enveloped with fog
My mother-in-law abuses me about
my father and mother
she gives me stale food to eat
with only salt.

(App.I,p.303)

The above two songs reflect the treatment of the mother-in-law with reference to the food she gives her daughter-in-law to eat. The type of grain grown in a village and the food eating habits of a community are a significant feature while deciding a daughter's marriage. Wherever there is abundance of rice and wheat in the fields, the people from that village consider themselves superior. Since a woman's life is so inherently linked to the agricultural tasks she performs in her in-law's home, there is a reference in the songs of Garhwal to her wanting to know "what kind of food they eat there and what kind of clothes they wear there" (Song 11).

After marriage she has to grind the grain eaten by her in-law's family, that is why she talks about being given *Manduwa* and *Koda-ki-roti* to eat (both coarse grains) as harsh treatment on her mother-in-law's part.

The songs sung by the women not only reflect the patterns and dimensions of familial interaction but also give us insight into so many aspects of life in the community.

During group interviews with village women on various occasions, the discussions would invariably centre around their relationship between the mother-in-law and daughter-in-law. In the context of the women of Garhwal this relationship assumes greater significance, because of the absence of the husband and the nature of the work performed by the women. The older women in the age group 60-75 years had very unhappy experiences to share. The age of marriage also contributed in a way to this problem. Most of the women in this age group had been married between the age of 12-16 years. Gomtidevi of village Sabli (75 years) said;

" My life was so hard, I was 14 years old when I got married. My mother-in-law used to wake me up at 4 in the morning to grind grain, then reluctantly she would give me half-a-glass of tea and send me off with other girls to collect fuel-wood from a forest 15 kms away. When I came home at 3 p.m. tired and hungry she would weigh the load on my head, if it was less than 30 kgs she would taunt me, and then give me very dry *roti* with salt to eat. I would swallow it with some water, and then go to the forest again at 4 p.m. to collect grass for the animals. When my husband came home on holiday (he was 10 years older than me) I did not know what married life means, so I would hide in my mother-in-law's bed and refuse to go to him. She would beat me with a stick and force me to go to her son. But he was kind, if it wasn't for him I would not be here talking to you ."

Plate 12 : Interacting with Gomti Devi, Village Sabli, Chamba Block

The lines on Gomtidevi's face, her expression in a way reflected her whole socio-cultural history, her biography. "Our songs emerge from our lives. They are linked to our emotions and experiences", she said. The content of the songs discussed above and her brief life sketch are illustrative of a process. A song is thus not merely an objective entity but a process.

The women in the age group 45-60 years, had a different story to tell. Some of them had just become mothers-in-law and they shared with the researcher that they were infact frightened of their educated daughter-in-laws. At a Mahila Mandal meeting in village Pipli, which the researcher attended with Shashi Raturi of Mahila Navjagran Samiti Chamba, Devkibehn the head of the Mahila Mandal Dal and Khushadevi, another village woman, enacted a play about the new daughters-in-law. Some of the issues highlighted in the play were —

1. Emphasis on dressing up, and using make-up,
2. Less respectful, answering back their mothers-in-law,
3. Watching TV most of the time,
4. Sitting and chatting with their husbands very openly without covering their heads,
5. Shirking hard work,
6. Singing less folk-songs but more film songs.

Both Devkibehn and Kushadevi are such wonderful actors, they had all the women in the meeting including the young daughters-in-law in splits of laughter. It is interesting how emotions which cannot be expressed easily in conversation can be expressed so lucidly through songs and drama.

The folk songs of Haryana are also replete with images of daughters-in-law cursing their mothers-in-law, and giving voice to their suppressed emotions. The following song also reflects similar themes.

Song 26

Dear "sasuji'
Do not fight with me day and night
I will run away to my husband.
My husband will come in a rail
I will burn you alive with *tel* (oil)

(App.I,p.303-4)

The daughter-in-law tries to assume a position of authority threatening her mother-in-law with dire consequences if she continues to fight with her day and night.

Song 27

Wake up dear daughter-in-law
It is 10 o'clock in the morning
Eat your breakfast.
When it is time to grind corn,
You hide in your room,
And laugh wearing dark glasses.
When you go to cut grass
You walk so slowly,
And do not do any work
Except helping other women carry their load
What should I do,

My misfortune that I got someone like you!

In English you say, "where is my watch?"
My son is a simpleton,
But you are growing fat and healthy
Eating *kaju* and *badam*.

(App.I,p.304)

The changing roles enacted in the play at village Pipli are reflected very vividly in the above song. Songs are not static, they are dynamic and created all the time mirroring the changes in the images of women. The image of the daughter-in-law is so different in the above song than in the earlier songs.

Dialogue across the hills — *Baju Band Geet*

Social Interaction with peers and kin

A significant feature of the song sung by the women of Garhwal is a dialogue across the hills in the form of questions and answers. According to the classification of Garhwali songs by Chatak (1973), Nautyal, S.(1971), Babulkar (1964), these songs are referred to as *Baju-Band Geet.* According to Kusum Nautyal, *Baju-Band Geet* are an aspect of the love songs of Garhwal. This is a dialogue between women cutting grass and wood in the jungle, and men who could be grazing sheep or cattle nearby. The dialogue could also be between the forest ranger and the woman cutting grass.

Q— You, who is cutting the branches of the oak tree which village do you come from.
A— Whichever village - it is of no concern to you.
Q— Why are you cutting the trees in the reserved forest.
A— Fie to the king, who handed this jungle to the sarkar (govt.) (Nautyal, K. 1992).

This dialogue with the forest-ranger throws light on the fact that since women's lives are so inextricably linked to the forest, they have

Fig. 4.10 : Dialogue across the Hills — *Baju-Band Geet*

to deal with this kind of verbal repartee and at times exploitative comments by the outside agency present in their environment. Some *Baju-Band Geet* also reflect the relationships between the *'Devar'* and the *'Bhabhi'*.

> Dear Bhabhi
> You have not recognised my immense love for you
> The fog is enveloping the hillside
> Show me your beautiful face

These songs are also referred to as *Jhangu*. This word emanates from the location where these songs are sung, which is the jungle. These songs are created on the spur of the moment, depending upon the situation, relationship and need for expression between two people engaged in this dialogue. Just like a conversation has no pre-determined format, in the same way *Baju-Band* songs are not bound by any traditional format. They are created anew everyday and not handed down by word of mouth from one generation to another as are the other songs.

At a group discussion with village women in Ranichauri, when the researcher asked the women to sing some *Baju-Band geet,* there were ripples of laughter in the group and infact some women looked embarrassed, and the others were surprised that I had heard of this category of songs. Khushadevi of village Dargi said, "*Baju-Band* geet are associated with man-woman interaction or dialogue across hills; this could be between *jija-sali, devar-bhabhi, patrol-ghasiyari* or between any man and woman wanting to get to know each other. But now-a-days this kind of dialogue is rare and these songs are sung between friends who go to get fuel wood and grass from the jungles".

Khushadevi's intervention initiated a lively discussion and the women shared with the researcher many significant aspects of this dialogue across hills. When they go to the jungle with their friends they move to different slopes to gather grass/fuelwood. Since the forests are now located at greater distances from the village, there is danger of wild animals and strangers. The voices of the women singing helps to keep wild animals away. It also helps to combat loneliness and more significantly it enables them to share their innermost feelings with their friends.

The verse is created spontaneously to depict what the woman is feeling at that particular moment. The content can vary from talking about the husband/beloved's absence, cruelties of the mother-in-law, longing for the parental home or anything that may come up for her at that moment.

The following song illustrates some of the aspects referred to above. It was sung by Devakibehn and Kamlabehn in village Pipli (Chamba block). Since recording these songs in their natural context, i.e. from one hill to another was difficult, the two women were asked to recreate their spontaneous dialogue for the purposes of recording. However, the recording was done in the forest, under an oak tree.

The pitch and intonation of the *Baju-Band* songs is entirely different from the other songs recorded by the researcher. The sound waves carry the words across the hill in a kind of a floating, wafting sound which leaves one spellbound. Again, one experienced the oneness of the song, its words, the woman, the forest, the sky, the earth and the sun, as if the whole universe was participating in this dialogue. The experience of listening to the song in its natural context, experiencing this total participation was of great significance to the researcher, as one of the objectives is to include the experiential dimension as a construct of knowledge.

Song 28

Friend A — It is time to go home now.
We have not collected enough grass today
What will we take home.

Friend B — So what if we have not got enough grass
On our way home, we will cut
the branches of the 'brinal' tree.

A — Basant Ritu is here
If we do not collect grass
What will the animals at home eat.

B — You are worried all the time we'll find
something.

A — We do not have nice clothes
Even the ones we have are laden with mud
Those who have nice clothes have gone to the
town for a visit

B — Why should we go to town
Let us go to our own 'New Tehri Bazaar'
There is a line of taxis there
It is nice to see the taxis on the streets of New Tehri

A — How will we go to New Tehri
We have to go to the Jungle - collect grass
The Jungle is everything for us
Our life is spent mostly there

B — Come on *Bhabhi,* that's enough
Let us go home now.

(App.I,p.304-5)

The images created in the above songs are varied and yet the central theme of each stanza is the same. The focus is the women herself, and all her utterances reflect some aspect of her life. While friend A takes the position of articulating her anxiety and apathy about various aspects of her life, friend B takes the position to show her friend another dimension to living than just complaining.

The content of this dialogue reflect the following:

(1) Collecting sufficient quantity of grass for consumption of domestic animals is an important daily task and a priority for women.
(2) Because of the hard work performed by women, their clothes are laden with mud; this stanza is symbolic of the fact that they do not get enough time to wash clothes, nor do they have enough time for leisure where they can dress nicely and go for an outing to the town.
(3) The importance of the forest/jungle in the lives of the women is referred to here. Six hours of a day are spent(spread over two visits) in collecting grass and fuel wood for domestic consumption.

Friend B seems to have a different attitude to life, or she takes this position to counteract the anxiety expressed by her friend.

(1) "So what if we have not enough grass We will cut the branches of the 'bhimal' tree", she says, providing a solution to her friends query.
(2) The reference to the taxis in the New Tehri Bazaar points to an element of modernisation in their environment. In fact she say she likes the

sound of taxis. Friend B puts an end to this dialogue by saying, "that's enough now, lets go home now".

Sometimes if they feel like continuing their interaction, they move to another part of the slope or hill and start singing again. The length of the dialogue can vary, and the content could be entirely different.

There is a pattern to the songs sung in the form of a dialogue between friends across the hills. The first line has sometimes nothing to do in content and thought with the second line, but is there only for rhyming.

Song 29

A — The cow gives milk
In every season of the year
I long for my parental home

B— When the cow is chewing the cud
I remember my mother's home

A — The wheat has been roasted
who else can we share our sorrow with

B— There is an insect in the butter milk
my hands and feet ache with the hard work I do.

A — When the hillside gets covered with fog
I long for my mother's home

B— When I think of you dear friend
My heart wants to weep

A — The leaves of the Thimli tree
Without you, I do not feel happy doing any work my friend

B— Without you, I feel like committing suicide
The roles are changing

A — If we keep meeting, we will always be near each other

B— I will grind *'Kodu'* in the *'Okhli'*

You silly, if we remain alive of course we
will keep meeting.

(App.I,p.305)

The interaction between A and B in the above song is centred on the relationship between the mother and daughter, and reflects the intense longing of the daughter for the mother. The pattern here is entirely different from Song 1. There is no question and answers, but just rhmying statements expressing the same sentiments. Some of the images created in the above song are as follows:

(1) In every season of the year, they long for the mother.
(2) When the hillside gets covered with fog, they remember the mother.
(3) The friend B has got married into another village, but is visiting her parental home, which is the in-laws house of friend A; so they talk about missing each other.
(4) The dialogue reflects the close bond between the two friends to the extent that one says "without you I feel like committing suicide", " If we keep meeting, we will always be near each other", " who else can we share our pain with, but each other".

All three significant statements, reflecting that this dialogue between the two friends provides them not only a forum of creative expression, but also psychological relief from stress.

" When the words leave my mouth or reverberate in the air, I already feel free, free of so much I contained within me", said one of the singers of the above song. When one listens to the women singing in the forest one actually experience this liberation, this sense of freedom.

The following song also reflects some aspects of the mother-daughter relationship, and in fact through this central theme links other features of kin relationship which affect the woman's life.

Song 30

A — There is a pile of books
My brothers are close to my mother
I am my mother's enemy
That is why she has sent me away
B — Just like butter cannot be formed from
residual butter milk

In the same way leave alone meeting even
seeing my brother's wife is impossible for me.

(App.I,p.306)

Friend A, sees herself as her mother's enemy because she has been sent away, while her brothers stay with the mother. The bond between the mother and daughter is a vital point of reference here, so also is the idea of separation, of division, of being cut off.

Friend B, uses the metaphor that just like it is impossible to get butter from residual buttermilk, in the same way leave alone meet, it is impossible for her to see her brother's wife: implying that she is longing to go to her mother's home and meet her family. The stanza reflects a loving relationship between her and her *Bhabhi.*

The two line stanzas throw light on so many aspects of the woman's life, her work roles, her kin relations, her emotional and psychological state and her integral relationship with the environment.

The pattern and structure of these stanzas is unique. The first line has nothing to do in meaning and content with the second, but is crucial for its rhyming quality. A great deal of skill is required by the singer to create this pattern, spontaneously and express what she wants to say. The key word is the last word of the first and second line.

Concluding Remarks

During field work a word which was extremely significant to the women was the word *Khud* - pain, suffering, anguish, longing; quite similar to the word Gham used by the Paxto women (Grima, 1986). When the women would gather in one home to sing and talk to me, the singing would invariably begin with a *Khuder geet*, which is a song reflecting intense longing for the parental home. Grand-mothers, mothers, daughters would all have tears streaming down their cheeks, as if their suffering was common- reflecting a kind of bonding which is a very significant aspect of the lives of the women of Garhwal. This coming together, sharing a common concern, brought a kind of intensity to the singing sessions. When one woman spoke the others would listen, as though she was narrating their story itself.

According to the women of Garhwal, songs were an expression of the hardships encountered by them in their daily lives. Even though they participated in all household and agricultural activities in their

Plate 13 : "When the pitcher is full to the Brim — it overflows. This overflowing is our song. It can be out of joy, or out of sorrow." — Vimlabehn, Village Dargi - Chamba Block

SECTION-IV
WORK ROLES AND ACTIVITIES PERFORMED

Fetching water from long distances. The Women of Village Aagor, Bilangana Block

I bring water in a heavy vessel
With no support on my head ...

[illegible]

मंगल सबद का गीत

[illegible]

SECTION III

SONGS DESCRIBING SOCIAL RELATIONS

खुदेड़ गीत

[illegible]

SECTION-IV

WORK ROLES AND ACTIVITIES PERFORMED

In the context of the women of Garhwal, songs describing their work patterns, their daily routine, and the joys and hardships associated with their work roles are of great significance, especially keeping in mind the objective of drawing up a holistic image of them as reflected in their songs.

An understanding of the natural and socio-cultural environment is necessary in order to get the correct perspective about their work pattern. The mountainous terrain, absence of the male for occupational purposes, lack of health care and other related facilities, economic deprivation, type of agriculture in the hill communities, physical inaccessibility from one place to another, natural disasters; all these contribute to the extremely hard life of the woman in the mountains.

Songs Describing Daily Activities and Work Roles

A number of folk songs make a reference to the daily routine of the women of Garhwal.

Song 1

I wake up early in the morning
And gather cow-dung
Not a drop of tea, do they give me
I grind Basmati rice, in the *Chakki,* for them
While they give me coarse Manduwa to eat!
During Sawan-Bhadon(when it rains)
I walk barefoot to the forest
My *dhoti* is torn,
I do not have a scarf to cover my head
I bring water in a heavy vessel
With no support on my head

I bring heavy loads of grass
On my bare head
Can you see my plight dear father !

(App.I, p. 313-14)

Fig. 4.11 : Some work roles of the women of Garhwal

Song 1 — Highlights

1. Wake up early.
2. Gather Cow-dung
3. Grind grain in *Chakki*
4. Walk long distances to Jungle barefoot
5. Fetch water
6. Fetch fuelwood/fodder/grass

Songs are life-centred. They emerge from the day-to-day activities that are performed by women. The above song so lucidly describes the work roles. A number of songs cited in the section on social relations particularly those focusing on mother-daughter, father/daughter relationships make a reference to the work pattern of the women of Garhwal. In fact the songs of the seasons especially the *Barahamasa* songs describe the various activities related to agriculture which the women perform during the year. The above salient points reiterate the fact that songs throw light on various aspects of life of women in a community.

Song 2

I am illiterate
Dear God, please be my saviour
And take care of my family
Carry my boat across the river of life!
In the bitter cold months
I bring grass from a far-away forest
(Dhamilidhar 10kms away)
In the month of Ashad
I have to wake up early
And transplant rice in the fields
Then I clean the cow-dung from the animal shed
And throw the manure in the fields
I have no time to get a letter written
Or to post it
My husband is away for so long
I will send him a telegram.

(App.I,p.314)

Fig. 4.12 : Visual representation of Song 3

In every song the multi-functional role performed by the women of Garhwal is etched so beautifully. In the above song she turns to "God the saviour, to carry her boat across the river of life". In the alien atmosphere of the in-laws home with no support, and the absence of the husband, it is but natural for her to turn to God to give her strength and courage to perform her difficult tasks.

"The presence of the sacred counteracts the harshness of our lives", said Laxmi Devi who sang this song at Budakedar. Laxmi, is the daughter of Seva Dasji, an *Ouji* (traditional musicians from lower caste) who sang beautiful songs from the epics.

Song 3

In the hot sun
I feel thirsty
I am perspiring, threshing wheat grain
In the fields
The months of April and May are here
All my friends have gone to the *mela*
In the hot sun...........

(App.I,p.314-15)

Women perform all the activities related to agriculture in the mountains, except perhaps preparing the land traditionally called *hul chalana.* The wheat crop is harvested in May and threshing is done soon after in the hot season.

Song 4

The hot sun is beating on me
As I go to collect grass from the jungle.
But alas! I find no grass
I walk for miles and miles,
In search for grass
Not a handful do I find !
My complexion was golden like *haldi*
Now I have become dark like a *tawa*
Roaming in these jungles,
Oh! what a hard life I have !

(App.I,p.315)

The above two songs refer to the work roles performed by the women and the constraints imposed on her due to seasonal variations. " Whether it is raining, snowing, extremely hot, or even if one feels unwell, we have to go and fetch fodder and grass from the jungle", Says Roshani, a 35 year old woman from Gonful village. Bhawani Bhai, head of the remand home

Who will spread the 'asan' for their comfort?
Who will look after the household!
And who will give fodder and water to the buffalo?
Who will clean the grain?
And take it to the flour-mill to grind.
Oh! how much I have to do,
With no help from my sister-in-law.
One is lost in the memory of her parent's home
The other is breast-feeding her child.
I feel so troubled in this house-hold!

(App.I,p.315)

The position of the woman in the family structure also influences her work roles as is evident from the content of the above song. The woman singing this song is obviously the third daughter-in-law. The burden of the major activities falls on her because of the authoritative nature of her mother-in-law, and the older sisters-in-law.

Work Roles <--------------------> Position of woman in family structure

---

In this context the song of *Jiri Jhamki* is significant, which is based on a real life story. This song was collected by Dr. Kusum Nautyal during her research in Garhwal. It is believed that the water needed to irrigate the fields belonging to a family in Garhwal disappeared for some reason. To get the water, the family Goddess had to be appeased, and for this purpose the youngest daughter-in-law of the family concerned is chosen for human sacrifice. The selection of the girl is based on the hierarchy of the family. If the father is chosen, the power and glory of the family is destroyed; by sacrificing the mother the home and hearth is finished. The elder brother cannot be sacrificed because he will carry the power and glory of the family forward; and the elder daughter-in-law cannot be sacrificed because of the perpetuation of the family. Hence the innocent younger daughter-in-law is chosen for human sacrifice!(Nautyal,K. 1992).

The song clarifies or throws light on the following situations :

1. The custom of human sacrifice may have been prevalent in Garhwal.
2. The status of the woman in the family is governed by her ranking in the family/kinship structure.

While the first situation is no longer present in Garhwal today, the second point still influences the quality of life of the woman in her in-law's home. " This is more true of families which have still maintained the joint family structure, than of families which are nuclear", said Shashi Raturi of Mahila Nav Jagran Samiti, Chamba.

Song No.5, "Who will bring grass from the jungles", was sung by a woman from Budakedar which is situated in an interior valley. The family structure in those villages is still joint, and women in the family do feel the kind of constraints expressed in the song. However, in the villages near Chamba (an important town of Tehri Garhwal) it was observed that a majority of families were nuclear in structure. Even though four sons would be living in the traditional home, their hearth was separate and they had separate rooms. Of course in these situations while the work roles of the woman were not influenced by her position in the family, her being alone gives rise to so many other problems related to her work roles.

The following song reflects the hard work that has to be done in relation to bringing fodder and grass from the jungles. Silu is a *ghasiyari* — a woman who cuts grass, she belongs to a poor family and has come to her parental home for a visit. Her mother implores her not to go to cut grass :

Song 6

Mother — Dear Silu!
Do not go to cut grass today
Your little baby has to be breast-fed
I know it is time to go to the jungle
But, stay home
Come, eat some hot rotis

Silu — I do not feel too well today
Let me go to the jungle

Mother — Dear Silu!
Breast-feed your baby before you go
She will be longing and cry for you !

(It gets dark in the evening and Silu has still not returned from the forest.)

Mother — Dear girls !

Have you seen my Silu!
She went to cut grass, with all of you.
Friends — We saw her tie her bundle of grass
When we walked back to the village.
Mother — Silu, Oh Silu!
All your friends have come back
Your little baby, is hungry
and crying for you
Come home quickly!

(App.I,p.316)

Silu had slipped from the mountain and fallen into a deep gorge. The harijan women from village Gonful near Budakedar, who sang this song said, "Silu's song brings tears to our eyes even today. Women have to undergo severe hardships to get grass from the jungle for the family. This activity is performed on a daily basis, sometimes even twice a day, depending on the requirement".

Several variations of the same song were collected by the researcher. One significant aspect emerging from the location where the song was sung and its content is that the work patterns and daily routine of the women from the interior valley of Budakedar were indeed different from those in the villages in the vicinity of Chamba.

There are some songs which reflect the status of the women in the family linked to her work roles. Her emotional state also gets highlighted, creating a holistic depiction linking work roles to status in the family, and to emotions.

The following song was sung by a group of women whom the researcher met on the way to the forest beyond the village of Budakedar. A passer-by asks a woman: who is walking from the forest to her village? Why is she crying ? What is her pain?

Song 7

Man — Dear girl, why do you cry?
Why is your heart sad today?
Woman — I am Pratima, from whom
Fortune has shied away
Even death eludes me!
Man — The tears flowing from your eyes
Are like pearls

Like dew drops that moisten the green grass
And glisten in the sunshine!
Woman — Dear wandering brother,
Do not ask me anything,
What will you get by hearing my song!
My life is like a dark night,
even during the day.
My life has been spent in sorrow and pain
Even *Yamraj* has no need for me.

My parents were my enemies
To marry me off in this family
I work so hard day and night like a beast.
The colour of my *mehendi* has turned to
the colour of blood
My husband was killed in the army
Now I have nobody
My life has been spent crying and weeping
The rivers of Ganga and Gomti
Are my only salvation,
I will go and become, one with them !

(App.I,p.316-17)

The song is tinged with a great deal of sadness, the dialogue with the passer-by becomes significant for the expression of this emotional state by the woman. Her reference to "my life is like a dark night even during the day", creates visual images about the quality of her life within the family. 'Dark night' is a metaphor to describe her extremely hard life, as Beni devi of village Hadamb near Chamba said, "It is dark at night, but in our lives it was dark even during the day".

The work roles performed by the women which have been highlighted in songs 1-7, the harsh treatment of the mother-in-law, and the absence of a loving supporting husband, all contribute to this "Darkness during the day".

This song was sung by Surja devi who was 65 years old. Women in this age group had greater identification with this song than the younger women in the group, because the song was more reflective of their lives when they were young. The older women had tears in their eyes, while Surjadevi sang this song.

Another significant line in the song is " I work so hard day and night/ like a beast".

Relationship of Work Roles to Geographical Terrain

Relationship of work roles <--------------------> geographical terrain

In Garhwal because of the nature of the geographical terrain, the question of where the house of the girl to be married, is located, assumes great significance. This has been pointed out by Kusum Nautyal (1992) in the relationship of work roles to the geographical terrain. For instance, girls from the plains (Rishikesh, Haridwar,etc.) denigrate the life patterns of the women from the middle and upper Himalayas. Girls from villages located near rivers (where irrigation is primarily done by river water sources) do not want to get married into villages located in high mountain ranges because there instead of rice coarse grains like *'Koda* and *Thargona'* are grown in abundance. Songs clearly reflect this conclusion about the location of the village as expressed by the daughter to her parents. These have been discussed in detail in the section on social relations, namely,father/daughter relations.

The woman is well acquainted with the hardships associated with her life patterns in the mountains. The geographical terrain greatly influences her work roles. In a song addressed to her beloved she says :

Song 8

Come take me to that place
Where the land is plain
Where agriculture is done on even land
Where there is water near at hand!

(App.I,p.317-18)

The song is tinged with emotions related to her hard life in the mountains. She wants to escape from this life, and her imagination creates another world where all this is not taking place. She begs her lover to take her to a land where the fields are located on even land, and water for irrigating the fields as well as for domestic consumption is close at hand.

Women walk long distance not only to get fuel, fodder and grass, but also to fetch water. The springs that were located near the village have dried up, and the water sources have become more remote. While piped water supply is available in villages located near roads, in the interior villages this facility is also not available and women have to walk long distances to fetch water.

According to William Sax(1994) : "Women provide agricultural as well as domestic labour throughout India; on them depends the reproduction of children and lineages as well as crops, and their fertility is often the subject of myths. Female labour is particularly important in Garhwal, where women are responsible for the lion's share of agricultural as well as household production. In addition to cooking, raising children and caring for livestock, they are also responsible for planting, weeding, and harvesting crops, processing grain, gathering firewood, and cutting grass for fodder. Men generally do the marketing, tend the livestock if no children are available for the task and perform needed repairs of the house, terraces, or irrigation canals. They are also very fond of cards. Ploughing is the only specifically 'male' task. The life of a Garhwali woman is often one of unrelieved hardships, and the men are surprisingly easy about this. As my neighbour once said,

> Here is the hills, a man without a woman will die of starvation or become a *yogi.* Why? Because women do all the work. From feeding the children to milking the buffalo to cutting the wood to weeding to harvesting to raising a family. What do we men have to do? Plough. It's not like that in the plains—there the men work and the women don't. But it's like that here, and on Kumaon side, and in Pauri.

Whenever I interviewed Garhwali women, I always asked them what the most important aspect of a woman's life was. Almost without exception, they replied 'work' or 'the fields', and when I would ask what a young bride could do if she was mistreated and in her husband's home, the answer too was nearly always the same: "She can flee to her parent's home. She can become a female ascetic (*mai/jogin*). Or she can kill herself".

Some Interviews

In order to understand further the relationship of songs to the daily life pattern of the women of Garhwal, interviews with three women of different age groups are presented to illustrate their work roles and daily routine.

Benidevi, Hadamb village, Chamba block, age 65, caste brahmin

Hadamb is situated at a distance of 3 kms from Chamba. The Mahila Navjagran Samiti has adopted this village for its activities. The predominant caste in the village is Brahmin. There are only two *Harijan* families. The pandits who perform all the celebration rituals related to the life-cycle events no longer enjoy the patronage of the monarchy of Tehri-Garhwal. The remuneration given to them by the people of the village is not enough to sustain their livelihood. A large number have left this profession and are in the field of education.

According to Benidevi, the head of the Mahila Mangal Dal of the village, " When I was young....it was dark even during the day time.....my life was like a dark night.... I would get up at four in the morning and grind Manduwa' — then walk barefoot to a distance of 10-15 kms to bring grass(weighing 30-40 kgs). We would return at lunch time and the mother-in-law would give me a *basi*-cold *roti* with only salt to eat. Household work in those days was considered no work. Work meant getting fodder/ grass, water and fuelwood. The rest, washing utensils, clothes, sweeping the house, cooking, bathing the children,etc. were considered leisure time activities....Added to this was the enforced silence we had to keep while in the house...... There was a lid kept on our mouths then; it is only now ever since the Mahila Mandal has been formed that we are able to speak freely".

The above statement by Benidevi reflects change, and the impact of the NGO's which have strengthened the concept of women's empowerment through group discussions — giving them an opportunity to speak, to express themselves. "Today, the daughter-in-law has so many facilities,viz. electric grinder for *atta,* water in the taps, electricity, and of course her education is her greatest advantage. Even though she does all the household work and goes to the jungle, she is able to plan her work better. She is no longer afraid to express herself", says Benidevi, summing up the transition from her life to the present day woman of Garhwal.

Vimla, Hadamb village; age 26 years; Harijan

Vimla was married to a man who was married earlier. She is the second wife. The first died after the birth of her youngest child. She has three children, two boys and a girl. Vimla sings beautifully, the tone, clarity, pitch of her voice is indeed special. When I asked her if she had learnt music in school, she laughed and said in Hindi: "Does one learn how to sing?! One sings because of the grace of God; I listen to songs and then create my own songs. Even now my father cries when he listens to my songs on the cassette". Vimla has a positive attitude to life, such as when she says, "My husband is very nice, he cares about me a lot, even though he lives in Delhi I feel very close to him. He is 15 years older than me. He is crazy about my singing. When I go to stay with him in Laxminagar in Delhi, he asks me to sing for him".

The work roles that Vimla performs are the same as any other Garhwali woman; perhaps, more tedious because she is poor and as a *Harijan* has to work on other people's land. There is no income except the Rs. 1000 her husband sends her. Regarding the daily work she says, "This work is not difficult at all. I have done all this from childhood. I can run up the hillside blindfolded. God has given me some skills. I cut grass, quicker and better than a lot of my friends. I enjoy cutting grass on the hillsides. My friends and I sing everyday. In fact, in Delhi I hate mopping and swooping the floors, there are no open spaces there, the sound and noise of vehicles and the lights disturb me, and I often have a headache."

> "My sons aged 7 and 9, participate in all the household activities with me. My older son also sings well and composes his own songs. My mother-in-law looks after the children, when I go to get fuelwood, fodder, grass from the mountains."

Vimla has a very special presence, she is very poised and self-contained in her world, saying " Music is my life..I sing while I work... The songs of Garhwal are specially significant in the lives of women. We sing in the forest, in the fields, and in the household during festivals and celebration of life-cycle events. It is rarely that a woman will burst forth into a song within the house. But when we are in the forest, the environment, the trees, the wild flowers, the sky, the sound of running water all inspire us to sing."

"Nature takes away a lot of the harshness of our lives. The sight of the four pilgrimage points — Gangotri, Badri, Kedar, Yamnotri — fills us with a sense of joy." Vimla's statement reflect the fact that the sacred is intrinsic to the women's lives, it is not separate, and Garhwal to them is the Land of the Gods.

Shakuntaladevi, village Sabli, age 45, caste Thakur

Shakuntala was married at the age of seven in the Unyal village near Surkanda devi, her husband died two years after marriage. She came back to her mother's home there after. She gets up at 5 a.m.in the morning, and does *lipai* of the kitchen, goes to the toilet, washes her hands and feet, lights the *chullah* with fuel-wood and makes tea for the whole family.

Then she takes out the *Gobar* from the room where the domestic animals are kept, and milks the cow. She then makes *Bajra ki roti* with *chutney* for the whole family and then goes to the forest to get grass (30-40 kgs of weight) from a distance of 14 kms. The children are left in the care of the elderly members of the family. Come home from the jungle, cook lunch, feed the family, and only then eat food herself. She would then have a bath (every 3-4 days), then after lunch she would go to work in the field.

"We are born from the earth, and we know everything about our land", she says, "After working in the field she would go to fetch water for the family(3 kms away) each water vessel weighing 20 kg... Our life was extremely hard, now things have changed comparatively. Because I was a widow my brothers and their wives treated me very harshly in the house, and this would pain my mother....The men do not do any work, at all, why should they, when women are there to do the work?...Since the last 30 years men have stopped participating in the work patterns of the family. Ever since the men started getting jobs/service they men stopped working at home, and the whole burden fell on the women. My elder borther used to grind the corn with her mother....Women sing songs for their own entertainment. When a woman is suffering she expresses her pain in songs; they provide her immense relief...Women learn the songs from their mothers, and elderly women who have known the songs longest, sung them year after year for decades, reflected upon and internalised them."

SECTION-V
AESTHETIC DEPICTION

A beautiful Garhwali woman wearing a *Nath* and *Bulak* village Kotigad.

Why have the rays of the sun paled
Gooddess Laxmi's beloved has emerged
Radiant like the sun (after her ceremonial bath)

SECTION-V

AESTHETIC DEPICTION

Songs describing the beauty of a woman

The image of the beauty of a woman etched in Garhwali folk songs encompasses a much broader creative representation of her being. The songs contain images of the woman beyond the description of merely her physical attributes. Beauty has a much wider connotation in these songs. While the references used to describe the beauty of woman are always the goddesses, metaphors are also drawn from nature. For example, the description of the woman after the ceremonial bath, is as follows:

Song 1

Why have the rays of the sun paled
Goddess Laxmi's beloved has emerged
Radiant like the sun (after her ceremonial bath)
Why are the waves in the ocean dancing !
Parvati's daughter is blooming like the full moon
after her bath,
That is why the waves in the ocean are dancing
How has the pure white Ganga become muddy
Sitaji's beloved has become so pure after her bath
That the Ganga appears muddy in front of her.

(App.I,p.318)

The reference to the goddesses Laxmi/Sita/Parvati, and the symbols from nature's bounty the sun/the ocean/the river Ganga, in describing the beauty of a woman reflect the deep relationship of the people with nature and the sacred. The imagery thrown up in the above song illustrates the point mentioned earlier that the decription of the beauty of a woman manifest in Garhwali folk songs is indeed beyond her physical attributes. Her face is not merely radiant but she is goddess Laxmi's daughter radiant like the sun, she is Parvati's daughter as beautiful as the full moon, she is

Sita's beloved pure like the river Ganga. There is sublime quality to the description of beauty etched in the songs.

Song 2

In the forest
Behind the snow covered mountains
The beautiful one, must be
Her face is like the moon
Amidst dark clouds
When will you come home 'fortune'
When will you meet me.
I will be happy only then
Your hair must be flying in the air
The bundle of grass on your head
Hides your beautiful face
You must be going to the forest
In the rain
To collect fodder
Oh my dear *bhagywati*
On whom fortune has bestowed its bounty
When will you come home ?

(App.I,p.318-19)

This song describes the beauty of the Garhwali woman, the metaphors used are from the natural environment -

'Her face is like a moon
amidst the dark clouds'.

The image of beauty encompasses her whole being. She is *'bhagyawati'* for him, fortune has bestowed its bounty on whom. Songs describing the beauty of a woman are not only sung by the husband, they can be sung by anyone interestingly these songs on beauty were not sung by women, but were sung by men in the villages where the research was conducted.

Song 3

She's wearing a beautiful green *saree*
And a red blouse

Her hair are combed very nicely
She asks her husband for tea and *pakoras*
And moves quickly in the *mela*
When she walks in the *mela* with her friends
Her green glass bangles
Look so beautiful !
On her fair arms.
Her long black tresses
Move as she walks along.

(App.I,p.319)

The following song was sung by the young man who participated in a group discussion at village Ranichauri in Chamba block:

Song 4

You are as beautiful
As stars shining brightly in the sky
The beauty-spot on your face
And the dimple on your cheeks
All add to your beauty
When your smile
It is like a thousand flowers blooming !
Your dark eyes
And unruly fair
Your soft hands and feet
And beautiful teeth
Indeed make you look like a 'queen of beauty'.

(App.I,p.319)

Again the imagery is closely linked to nature...'You are as beautiful, as the stars shining brightly in the sky'. The smile of the woman is linked to a thousand flowers blooming!.

The women in the gathering where this song was recorded did not show much interest in the songs describing, their beauty — "Garhwali women are beautiful naturally, but what of this beauty, when the whole day we have to work so hard ", said Kamlabehn from village Ranichauri :

"For us the two most significant symbols of beauty for a married woman are, the *maang* (parting) which is always filled in with bright red *sindoor* and the nose ring. The nose ring of Tehri Garhwal is famous *didi*..it is a work of art", said Vimlabehn of village Dargi.

In the songs the maang is described with reference to the width of the river.

"Your *maang* is as beautiful and as wide as the river".

The *nath* (nose ring) is considered a symbol of *suhag*. The one worn on the lower part of the nose is called *bulak*. In comparison to other ornaments worn by women the nose ring is referred to the most in the songs.

"Your beautiful *nath* has left a mark on your cheek".

According to Leelabehn from village Ranichauri, "The *nath* is never removed as long as the *Pati* — husband is alive".

The above examples illustrate that songs describing beauty also reflect socio-cultural aspects of the society. According to Ryal Guruji, a music teacher working with the NGO at Khadi, many writers have written extensively about the beauty of the woman of Garhwal. Tota Krishnana Garela was one such writer. The following lines, originally in Sanskrit give an idea of the kind of imagery he refers to in his text :

The sun's rays falling on the woman's face
The reflection of the sun's rays
falling on her swaying gold ear-rings
And the yellow wild flowers in the fields
Shine like the gems
creating a beautiful sight!

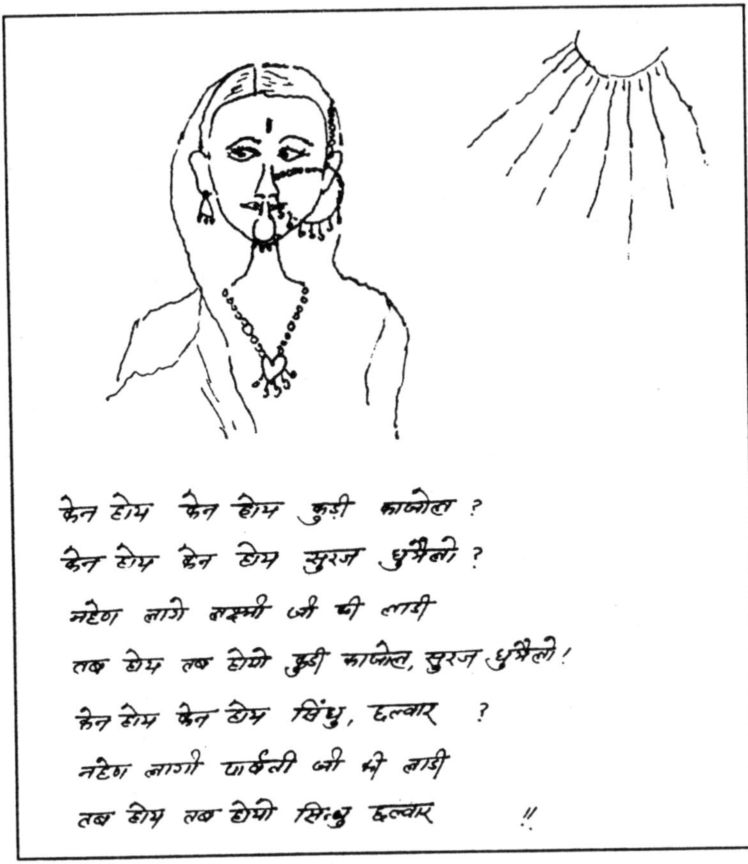

Fig. 4.13 : Song describing the bride after the ceremonial bath.

SECTION-VI
DISSENT, PROTEST AND SOCIAL CHANGE

Women of Village Kotigad protesting about liquor licenses issued, at a Mahila Mandal Meeting

Dear Sisters,
Come together, form a Mahila Mandal
And change the course of your life
How will you spend your life alone

SECTION-VI

DISSENT, PROTEST AND SOCIAL CHANGE

Folk art is an integral part of living. It is functional and spontaneous. It also reflects the constancy of belongingness and affinity in a cultural context. In the process of cultural change, innovation has a special role. The roots are unchanging, the process is continuous.

Change is characteristic of all cultures but the rate and direction of change vary considerably. The factors that influence the direction of such changes are the degrees to which a culture encourages as well as approves flexibility and the particular needs of a culture at a specific point of time.

Even when the cultural changes are supposed to be beneficial it may be difficult for an individual within a culture to accept the change because an individual is guided by certain norms and beliefs. Hence, for securing social transformation, change in the beliefs or value system of the individual is needed, thus making them more adaptive and responsive to organic development and growth.

Folk-lore causes change in the society as the society causes the change in folk-lore. Though this mutual relation between the two is inseparable, folk-lore is the product of society, society is not and cannot be the product of folk lore. Naturally so, influence of society over folk-lore is far greater than the influence of folk-lore on the society. Nevertheless, folk-lore is one of the many forces created by the society, but sometimes, this force acts so powerfully that the whole society directly moulded by it (Islam 1985).

Folk songs in India have served as vehicle of social communication and they have helped mobilizing public support for a cause. Folk songs are one of the most powerful propaganda media to direct the attention of people towards a particular programme.

A successful effort was made in Maharashtra to mobilize women and give them messages of social change through folk media. A group of fifty women toured some of the major districts of the state staging plays and singing songs on crucial issues related to women's lives; like dowry, reproduction, struggles of working women and other such themes. Songs written by women were either adapted to old tunes or given new content.

Nearly ten thousand people attended these programmes.

Songs are not static, they are dynamic and keep changing, with new content being added to express and reflect the concerns of the people in society. The songs reflecting dissent, protest and social change related to women's lives have been analysed under the following heads :

Social Issues

a. Alcoholism.
b. Education for Women.
c. Changing Status of a girl-child.
d. Dowry.

Change in cultural fabric — impact of modernisation

a. New Technology and change.
b. Changing customs and tradition.
c. Chamba town: a new face.

Environmental Issues

a. Dissent and protest related to exploitation of women in the forest.
b. Smokeless Chullah.
c. Natural Disasters.

Mobilising Women's Power

a. Creation of Mahila Mandals.

Protest Movements

In Tehri Garhwal the NGOs have played a significant role in mobilising the women's power, by the formation of Mahila Mandals at the village level, to address issues related to women's lives. As stated in the chapter on 'The Process/Methodology' two NGOs, one working in the Chamba block, and one NGO working in the interior valley of Budakedar were selected, for the collection of new songs composed by women on social issues.

Social Issues

Alcoholism

Song 1

Oh people of this world — what is in this world?
Do not drink alcohol !
Your house will be sold — do not drink
Your fields will be sold — do not drink
Your *thali* will be sold — do not drink
Oh people of this world — what is in this world?
Sit down to sing *bhajans*
And have good thoughts
Do not drink alcohol !

People who drink get into fights
They are found lying in the streets
Their wives and children carry the burden of
their deeds
They wash the utensils in the neighbourhood
And earn money for their sustenance
Oh people of this world
Do not drink alcohol
The world has been blessed
By people who have earned a name for themselves
People of this world,
What is in this world
Do not drink alcohol.

(App.I,p.321)

The Sarvodya movement which was initiated by Shri Beharilalji of Budakedar village, in Tehri Garhwal had a great impact on the life of the people in the villages surrounding Budakedar. A number of local shops making country liquor were closed down on the initiative of the women of the village, who had formed a Mahila Mandal with the support of the NGO Lokjeewan Vilas Bharati. Dharamdevi head of the Mahila Mandal at village Thati (Budakedar) said, that the above song had been composed by the women, because alcoholism was a serious problem they faced in their lives on a daily basis. When the men came home on holidays they would play cards during the day and in the evening they would consume country liquor and abuse the women. "The Mahila Mandal gave us a forum to express our concern and we all came together to tackle this problem".

According to her, singing songs was only one aspect of their action, they took out processions in the village singing slogans and motivating other women to support them. They were able to close down the local shop, as it did not have a government license, on their own initiative. Repeatedly singing these songs did have an impact, according to Dharamdevi, the idea was to focus the attention of both the men and women to the evils of consuming alcohol and above all create awareness amongst the women that together they could handle this issue more effectively.

In Chamba block also, with the support of the NGO Mahila Nav Jagran Samiti, women of villages Kotigad and Pipli took out processions on anti-liquor singing slogans and songs. In Oct./November 1994 women from ten villages in Chamba block approached the District Magistrate not to renew the license for the liquor shops. About two to three hundred women participated in the anti-liquor movement. They marched in a procession and closed the liquor shop at Chamba with a big lock. The shop is closed to date.

Education

Song 2

At dawn!
The women of the village
leave to cut grass
Vimla is a new *ghasiyari*
She climbs slowly the steep path
She is 12th class pass
She cuts her finger instead

After a few month
Vimla becomes skilled in cutting grass
She thanks her friends for their wisdom
Vimla now shares her knowledge with her friends
On the way to the forest
She teaches them to read and write
What a wonderful sight

This sharing has changed their lives.

(App.I,p.321-322)

The song about Vimla *Ghasiyari* (woman who cuts grass) makes a statement about sharing skills. Vimlabehn has lived in the foothills of Haridwar-Rishikesh. While she is educated till class 12, she does not have skills in the work roles to be performed by her after marriage. She learns the art of cutting grass from her friends and holds classes for them in the forest on the way back.

The song gives value to the traditional wisdom of the women and also points to the importance of imparting education according to the time, location and needs suitable to the women of the mountains. Running adult education centres for women would have no meaning, as the women would not be able to take time off and go there for education.

According to Ganga Prasad Bahugana, an NGO representative from village Ranichauri, " Earlier girls were not sent to school even if families were financially well off, because schools were located at great distance from the villages. Significant changes have taken place as far as the education of girls is concerned in Garhwal in the last fifteen years, because school have since been established at a shorter distance and parents have started sending their girls to school with a sense of confidence. All girls study till class 12 now, and the age of marriage for girls is between 18 to 22."

Benidevi's comment on education cited earlier in the section on father/daughter relationships is significant here too: " Education is the greatest asset of the young daughters-in-law and daughters of the family; while they have to perform the same work roles, they are able to plan their work better and have more time for leisure".

In the context of the above the following two songs, one on the status of the girl child and the other on dowry are also significant.

Changing Status of a Girl-child

Song 3

The *Vedas* and the *Puranas*
Deny the selling of a girl
By her father
A daughter is born from the same womb
As a son to a mother

But only the son is entitled
To the parent's property
Taking material wealth
In exchange for a daughter
Is a crime
Do not sell your daughter
As though she was a cow!
Stop doing this
And take blessings from your daughters.

(App.I,p.322-23)

The above song was sung by women from Ranichauri village, in the age group 45-60. The women who sang the song said that social customs which had degenerated or led to the down fall of women in the society, created an awareness about the ills of such practices, and songs were composed to denigrate such customs. Leelabehn, who sang the song is the wife of Ganga Prasad Bahuguna an NGO worker with Parvatiya Jan Kalyan Samiti in Ranichauri. Leelabehn and Ganga Prasadji are both outstanding individuals who have worked with the women's movement in Garhwal for over sixty years.

Folk songs as stated earlier are not static, they are dynamic and keep changing. The content encompasses in its gambit all contemporary issues related to the lives of the people in society. While a reference is made in the above song to the traditional custom prevalent in Garhwal called *Rada-Bada,* which meant taking money in exchange for the daughter from the boys family, the emphasis of the song is to focus the attention of the people in society to the status of the girl-child.

A daughter is born from the same womb
As a son to a mother
But only a son is entitled
To the parent's, property.

Bhavanibhai head of the remand home for boys in Tehri said, " All the important decisions of the household are taken by the men, viz., investing money, buying animals, and deciding the marriage of the daughter. Land is always in the name of men, on death it goes to the son and not to the women, even though they are the ones who work on the fields. 97 per cent women of Garhwal are farmers".

"Whether songs can create changes in such fundamental issues is difficult to say, but repeatedly singing them does influence the attitudes of people", says Leelabehn who composed the above song.

Dowry

Song 4

Dowry ! this great evil
Has become an issue of discussion
In every village, every town!
Home, fields,etc. are mortgaged
To pay the debt incurred to give a good dowry
Not only do parents feel happy at finding a good family
By giving dowry they spoil the life of the
daughter in her in-laws home
As the demands keep increasing!
Girls are compelled to commit suicide
Do not give dowry

Educate your girls
Help them stand on their own feet
Giving and taking of dowry is both a crime
Stop this *pratha* — custom
Shame to those, who sell their daughters
Kanya-daan is the *daan* of the Gods
Only devils (*rakshas*) have desire -
Do not give dowry
Stop this custom.

(App.I,p.323)

Linked to the status of the girl child is the issue of dowry which is reflected in the above song. This song was composed by the women of Hadamb village, Chamba block. Only recently since the last five years has the issue of dowry become significant in the context of the socio-cultural life of the people of Garhwal. Ramabehn, head of the Mahila Samkhya project, Tehri, said, " These influences have into our society by the migration of men into the plains. Television is also responsible to a large extent for bringing this material culture to our hill state".

At a meeting of NGOs working in Tehri Garhwal, held at Budakedar in March 1994, the researcher had discussions with many representatives (both men and women), as well as interacted with a group of over three hundred village women on the above issue. Lakshmi Rana representative of the NGO Jan Vikas Kalyan Samiti, Chirbattia, said that in families with strained economic resources this issue was felt more acutely. When the dowry was inadequate men often took on a second wife, and the first one was either compelled to commit suicide or live at the mercy of her brother and bhabhi. Lakshmi Rana herself was a victim of a dowry demand. She walked out of her marriage telling her father not to succumb to the demands of her in-laws family. Socially, ostracised by her kin group for a while. Lakshmi Rana turned her strength and potential to head the NGO at Chirbattia (her village). Today her NGO is particularly committed to rehabilitating girls who have been abandoned or ill-treated.

The last few lines of the above song link the social message, " Giving and taking of dowry is a crime", to the traditional custom of *Kanya-daan* which is the *daan* of the gods, while desire for material objects is linked to the devil or *rakshsas* of society.

Changing Cultural Fabric : Impact of Modernisation

Whenever old customs and methods of doing work are replaced by new ones, when there is change in the socio-cultural fabric of society, the transition becomes a significant event for those who witness the changes. This process or event gets expressed in folk tales, in myths, in ballads, in proverbs and in songs.

New Technology and Change

Song 5

Our traditional customs
and methods of doing work
Have been changed
With the advent of new machines !
Instead of flour mills run by water
There are electric mills to grind the grain
All the daughters and daughters-in-law of the
village go there now !
The *Atta* ground in a *chakki*
Was like butter
Today nobody goes to the *chakki*

They have been converted into chairs for sitting.
Dear friends, stop and think about all this -
do not run after new fashions only.
Our traditional customs
Are being replaced by new technology
by the new daughters-in-law.
The *gingyal* - pestle - has been burnt as fuelwood
There were traditional dances by the *bedas*
Today everybody only watches films
The young boys are rarely seen at home today
They all crowd the cinema halls.
The young woman used to wear long sleeved blouses
But today they walk around with half their arms bare!
The boys wear tight trousers
And can only sit on a sofa-set
Our culture was governed by *dharam-karma*
Today the young woman in the family
roam around with uncovered heads
They are so fashionable
Their *saree pallus* are flying in the air all the time.

(App.I,p.324)

The above song was composed by women in the age group 45-60. Interestingly the same song was sung in village Pipli, Chamba block, and in the Budakedar at a distance of 82 kms. It throws light on so many aspects of the life of women in Garhwal, which have changed in the last 15 years.

* Electric mills have replaced flour mills.
* The chakki has been converted.
* The *Gingyal* has been burnt as fuelwood.
* No traditional dances.
* Everybody watches TV/films.
* Less of *Dharam* and *Karam*.

An interesting discussion followed the recording of this song at village Pipli in the Mahila Mandal meeting. Sumadevi who sang this song said, "The electric flour mills have reduced the tedium of a work to a large extent, but the *gharat*, flour mills run by water had a special significance in our lives. We would all collect our grain and walk to the water mill.

There in the lap of nature we would sing songs, express our joys and sorrows. Often we would cook *chappattis*, make *chutney* from pudina leaves, growing nearby and would sit together and eat. Also the *atta* tasted much better than it does today."

Plate 17 : Women grinding rice using a long wooden stick called *Gingyal* — Village Sabli, Chamba Block.

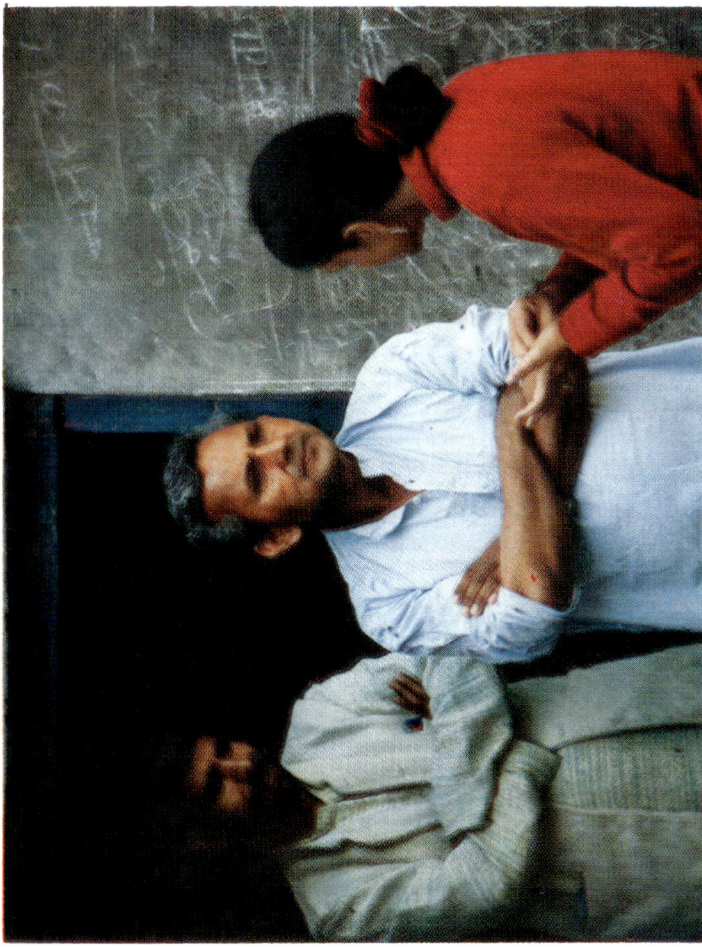

Plate 18 : Shri Behari Lalji, Secretary Lok Jeevan Vikas Bharati discussing the cultural context of songs, Village Budakedar.

Chamba Town: A New Face

Song 7 : Song describing Chamba

Chamba town, situated on the main road
Has beautiful little and big shops.
The students from the college near by
Gather in the streets
Their teachers urge them to study land
Not to smoke tobacco
And not to say unkind words to others
Chamba town, is a nice little town
Even the road to New Tehri goes from here!

(App.I,p.325)

Environmental Issues

Dissent and Protest related to Exploitation of Women in Forests

Getting fodder and fuel-wood for domestic consumption is a major task performed by the Garhwali woman. Her life is centered around going to the jungle twice a day; once for fuel wood in the morning and once for fodder. In areas where the forests have been taken over by the government, and where the jungles have been cut extensively because of construction of roads, this activity becomes even more difficult for her. She has not only to walk a longer distance, but interact with forest rangers and forest guards. This is not a particularly pleasant situation for her because the latter represent power and authority whereby exercising control over her life in a number of ways.

The following song by a *Harijan* woman in village Gonful, near Budakedar reflects some of these aspects.

Song 8

Dear Kamali
Why did you bring the wood of the Deodar tree
Cut by the timber merchants
They sell this wood in the market
And make large wooden boxes
Now they will beat you up.

Kamali, you made a big mistake
By consuming sweet meats
offered by these men
When you go home
Your husband will beat you Kamali
Nobody likes the idea
That you ate the sweets
offered by the timber merchants
Dear Kamali,
Why, oh why, did you do this ?

(App.I,p.325-26)

The patrol or forestguards try to lure the woman cutting grass by offering them sweets, Kamali is an innocent girl, she accepts the sweets offered by them; her friends in the above song try to warn her about the dangers of such an act. While songs are a pointer to what goes on in the society, what is significant here is that women have to cope with such exploitative situations even while they perform their daily tasks of survival.

In some songs the interaction between the forest stranger and the woman cutting grass is given a romantic connnotation:

Dear grass cutting woman
You are so beautiful
Whichever forest go to cut grass
Will become beautiful like you! (Nautyal, K., 1992).

Such romantic interactions or illicit relations between the outside agency and the grass cutting woman are not truly indicative of Garhwali society and culture, but they do exist as the songs reflect.

Since it is the woman who has to brave the forest alone on a daily basis she has to cope with the remarks of the patrol and the forestranger. Another interesting angle to the above situation is reflected in the following song :

Song 9

While cutting grass
You wandered off to an unknown field
On your strength and courage
And the forest rangers did no good to you

They confiscated the *daratis*
from all the women cutting grass on the hillside
Dear *ghasiyari*
The sound of your bangles resound in the forest
The sound lures people from here and there
Come I will go with you to the jungle
And you can cut grass with no fear of the 'patrol'.

(App.I,p.326)

A man from the family, in this case the *devar* sings the above song to his *bhabhi*, offering her protection from the presence of the outside agency. His reference to "did no good to you!" indicates molestation and harassment. The women at the *Shivir* in Budakedar where this song was recorded, said that the patrol did confiscate the *daratis* of the women cutting grass, to trouble them. B.P. Nautyal one of the resource personal at the seminar said in hindi, " We do not want that any employee of the forest department should say anything incriminating to our women". The word *"bhaun kuch"* encompasses a much wider meaning than just incriminating. B.P. Nautyal remarks initiated a lively discussion and this aspect of women's life in relation to the forest was deliberated upon at length.

Thus, many songs in Garhwal make reference to the exploitation of women by the forest rangers, representing the presence of the outside agency. At the *Shivir* in Budakedar this aspect of woman's life in relation to the forest came up for discussion. The Mahila Mandal representatives of about 10 villages around Budakedar suggested that the jungle around the village should be given to the care of the gram panchayat and should not be under the control of the forest department. This would minimise the dangers from outside agencies. Decisions regarding taking care of the jungle around the village would rest with the people of the village.

Smokeless Chullahs

Song 10

Dear sisters and friends
Do not stay behind times
Come forward and make a smokeless *chullah* in your home

Man has reached the moon

There is electricity in every village
And your *chullahs* are still the same old ones.
When there is smoke in the room
The eyes are constantly watering
The utensils get blackened with soot!
Dear sisters! it is time to change
Come forward, and make smokeless chullah
Your utensils will remain clean
You will consume less fuel-wood
It will be a pleasure to cook in the kitchen

Dear sisters! it is time to change
With the smokeless *chullah*
You can cook two things at a time
Your eyes will be saved from smoke
And you can eat your food in peace.

Do not delay dear sisters!
Come and learn the technique to make a smokeless Chullah
Dear sisters!
Come forward, do not remain behind times
And make yourself a smokeless Chullah!

(App.I,p.326-27)

The above song composed by the women of Manjyar village in Chamba block (just above Kotigad) aims to create awareness of the advantages of the smokeless *chullah,* because :

— Consumes less fuelwood;
— Can cook two things at a time;
— Utensils remain clean;
— Eyes are saved from smoke.

While the same messages have been propagated for many years now by government agencies and voluntary organisations, what is significant here is that the song has been composed by village women themselves, based on their own experience of using the smokeless chullah.

The Mahila Navjagran Samiti hold periodic training programmes for the making of the *Nada Chullah* in the various villages. The demonstration is given by a woman who has been using the *chullah* assisted by a trainer. Using simple charts, the construction as well as the advantages are explained to the women. Some of the other activities of the Mahila Navjagran Samiti in the villages in Chamba block are as follows:

1. Saving the forest/environment.
2. Water Harvesting Tanks.
3. Mahila Sanghatan.
4. Smokeless Chullah.
5. Sulabh Sauchalayas.
6. Anti-liquor campaigns.
7. Clearing the pathways.
8. Running Balwadis for children.
9. Training programmes for *Balshikshikas.*

Natural Disasters

***Song 11* (floods)**

Beyond the mountains of Harsil
The thick black clouds
Look like the black bangles on your arms
These clouds created torrential rain
And the mighty river Ganga flooded
Somebody's daughter
And somebody's daughter-in-law have been
swept in these floods
The Gujjars have lost their buffaloes.
The flat fertile land
Has been converted to undulating land
I see the saree of a woman floating
Down the river
Oh what destruction.

(App.I,p.327)

Songs are also composed on natural disasters and events that have a significant bearing on the life of people in the region. The two songs 11 and 12 were composed by the women after the devastation caused by floods in 1990, and after the earthquake that rocked Tehri Garhwal in 1992.

Song 12 **(on Uttarakhand earthquake)**

Dear God!
How did you turn your face
From Garhwal the 'land of Gods and Goddesses'
Today this land lies in silence!
After the months of Sawan and Bhadon
Come Asuj
And we were all waiting for *Deepavali*
At 3 o'clock one night
This treacherous earthquake came
The earth was shaking with its impact!
Within seconds
Fields, homes, entire families were buried alive
There was darkness everywhere
The town of Uttarkashi was devastated
Whoever saw this sight
Fell like jumping into the river and dying
Oh what a night!
Dear God!
Why did you get upset
With this beautiful land Garhwal
Today it lies stunned in silence!

(Composed and sung by the women of village Budakedar which was effected by the earthquake.) (App.I,p.328)

Songs reflect the significant contribution of women to the family and community life Garhwal, *"Aurat ki zindagi pahar jaisi kathor hai,* Ganga Prasad Bahugana and their character is also firm like the mountain".

Mobilising Women's Power

Creation of Mahila Mandals

Shashibehn who is heading the NGO, Mahila Mandal Nav Jagran Samiti located at Chamba, says "There is tremendous power in the village women of Garhwal. Before the Mahila Sangathan was started women used to say, meetings are held only by men for men, what will we do in a meeting. Now they fully participate in all the activities; and they compose their own songs."

The following two songs, were composed by the women of the Mahila Mandals of villages Kotigad and Pipli respectively:

Song 13

Situated at the edge of two gorges
Kotigad is the name of our village
Everyone worships the Lord 'Rama' here
The environment of this village is very nice
People belonging to three castes lives here
Brahmins, Thakurs(Rajputs), and Harijans
Predominantly it is inhabited by Rajputs
When there is a meeting in the village
All the sisters leave their work
And come to attend the meeting
This coming together is wonderful
It has given strength to our society
Shashibehn started this Mahila Mandal
She teaches us to mobilise ourselves
And solve our own problems
We have learnt a lot of good things
And made a difference in our society
The head of our Mahila Mandal is very active
She leads us and we all follow her
How wonderful it is to work together
Dear Sisters!
Keep the name of this Mahila Mandal flying high
Spread the light of knowledge from village to village
Involve all the daughters and daughters-in-law
Our village Kotigad, situated between two gorges is beautiful!
(App.I,p.328-29)

Song 14

Dear Sisters,
Come together, form a Mahila Mandal
And change the course of your life
How will you spend your life alone.

Let us come together
And address the problems facing our village

Plate 19 : Women singing songs on the importance of Mahila Mandals — Village Kotigad, Chamba Block

Sulabh Sauchalayas with assistance from Mahila Nav Jagran Samiti.

According to Gunadevi, head of the Mahila Mandal of Kotigad, "NGOs have played a tremendous role in creating awareness and empowering women in all the five districts of Garhwal". Shashibehn, head of Mahila Navjagran Samiti, said that the focus of their activities in forty villages of Chamba block has been on the following :

— creating awareness amongst women about their needs and problems;
— recognising their inherent potential/power to make a difference in their own lives;
— participation of women at all levels of activities, for meeting their needs and solving their problems.

The songs composed by the women clearly reflect this approach.

Song 14 was composed by Devakibehn, head of the Mahila Mandal at village Pipli, which is located at a distance of 3 kms. from New Tehri. In the song she traces the historical background of the formation of the Mahila Mandal in their village.

When construction on the Tehri Dam started, a new township came up in New Tehri. People were given land in lieu of their land in old Tehri and new houses were constructed to house the displaced population and the retinue of government personnel who were involved in the construction of this dam. As a result of this construction, the people of village Pipli (located on a slope below New Tehri) were affected as is reflected in the song sung by Devakibehn.

The night a large stone from the road above hit an army officer of the village and seriously injured him, it was the women who came together to fight this injustice. They marched in a procession to the office of D.P. Maurya at Tehri, to stop the construction of the road, or take necessary precautions so that the people of the village are not injured by loose stone hurling down the hillside. According to Devakibehn, " Women who were fighting and bearing the burden of all the hard work related to life in Garhwal, have come out to join the movement to create a difference in their lives. The men only join our protest on our request, they show no initiative on their own". The Mahila Mandal at Pipli is now four years old.

Protest Movements — The Andolan for Uttrakhand

The *Andolan* for a separate state of Uttrakhand, according to Vipinbhai started with the issue of Reservation. He said, "The composition of the caste structure in the Hill areas of Garhwal is : 98 per cent are Brahmins and Thakurs, while only 20 per cent are Harijans. It is unfortunate that the reservation suggested for 2 per cent of the population is 27 per cent. In order to fulfil the quota these numbers would filled by people from other districts of U.P.

"The Uttrakhand Kranti Dal people linked the issue of Reservation to their demand for a separate hill state by convincing the people that if they got the latter, their demand of Reservation will be looked into automatically. This appealed to the people and women and children jointed the movement in larger numbers. The participation of women in the *Andolan* and the

Fig. 4.14 : The Andolan for Uttarakhand

rallies and meetings held to discuss the Uttrakhand issue is of great significance".

According to Pauripoorananda Panauli, the women of Garhwal have braved the domestic and agricultural front for so many years in the absence of the presence of NGOs in this area, they have given a voice and the courage to link themselves to larger issues affecting the society in Garhwal.

Plate 21 : Discussing the issue of Uttarakhand with Dharam Devi — Village Budakedar.

He said," The women have always been self reliant in aspects of their lives, they have now come into the open to uplift their society ".

However, according to Vipinbhai, "This movement lacks directions and there is no one to guide this women's power. There should be small committees formed at each of the eight districts. These committees should voice the opinions of the people of that district. Then, an apex committee of eight representatives, one from each district should be constituted. One leader should be elected from the apex committee. His/her voice will then be the voice of the people".

The women showed great enthusiasm about this issue. At several Mahila Mandal meetings in the villages near Chamba in November 1994 and March 1995, the researcher was welcomed by the women with: " If we get a separate state for Uttarakhand, you will receive some credit for it". I was amazed at their always including me in issues relevant to their lives. Perhaps the documentation of their songs, their voices had become very significant to them.

However they expressed deep concern about the treatment of their sisters in Muzaffarnagar and the Katia shoot out near Mussorie. Slogans like " Beijing is close, but New Delhi is far.." were heard often at Mahila Mandal meetings. This could be attributed to the presence of NGOs in the area who received funds from international organisations.

Songs are life-centered, they are the pulse of a society, their dynamism is reflected in their content which has a movement, a continuity. As anthropologist Prof. S. C. Malik has said "Tradition is a continuous creation in the Now".

Garhwali Women working in the Fields — A View

5

SUMMING UP
Some Highlights

The main concern of the present study has been to examine the relationship of folk songs to the life of the women of Garhwal at both the individual level and collectively at the community level. The conceptual framework states that folk songs are to be understood as a matter of actual experience and of participation. It is this keen observation of the data at the participatory level which gives insights about the significance of folk songs, and also provides a sense of cohesiveness from within to the community. In terms of oral traditions, as reflected in folk songs, the study of women their images — was important because women are the carriers and active bearers of tradition. These folk expressions within a culture reveal to us women's lives, especially as they speak from their hearts; it tells us about the sheer joy of living together in the community, and many other aspects of interactive social behaviour.

Conceptual Framework : The Approach

The content analysis of the songs of the women of Garhwal clearly indicate that women use songs as a medium of expression, as their channel of communication, and they breathe life and meaning into the song. One of the most significant questions related to the methodological approach for this study was : How does the researcher investigate this area which gives us insights into their life? The answer became possible because the researcher got deeply involved in that culture because of her own participation in the women's lives, and conversely their participation in her life. This has been the core-methodology of this research, and one of its major contributions for setting up clear guidelines for new approaches to field research, and evolving new methodologies.

The very life of the women of Garhwal, implicitly and spontaneously shows a high level of ecological responsibility, i.e., not only to their environment but also to their family, household, social issues, and so on. It was possible to decipher all this in the multiple layers of meanings that were available in the songs.

This methodology has the ability to move behind the explicit, to the implicit form of knowledge which is embedded in the songs. It is in this sense that songs of women became a crucial and important source material for understanding the images and life of the women of Garhwal. It is this approach to the material evidence which therefore is central and not peripheral to their life and of course, central to this thesis.

The holistic perspective stated above is different from the prevalent 'objective' approach of the social sciences. This study stresses wholeness whereby all parts belong together, partake in each other. It is within this overall inter-connectedness that the idea of participation arises — each part, each one of us participating in the totality. It is in this way that the approach chapter forms the backbone of the way the material has been looked at. It provides some significant answers towards the understanding of those communities wherein tradition is passed on by oral means.

Highlight of the main Findings and Themes of the Study

The folk songs of any area provide its living history. The folk songs of Garhwal also in their manifest and latent representations weave a multi-coloured fabric of that society. Garhwali folk songs have various elements, dialects, and emotional enactments. But one feature which stands out is the portrayal of women in the songs. Whether it is songs invoking the goddess as a deity, or songs sung in celebration of various life-cycle events, or songs of longing and anguish — it is the woman who is the focus, the pivot. The woman does not merely give voice to the folk songs; she lives and experiences the song in her daily life, and in a way creates it. This symbiotic relationship between the experiencer and the creator is a very special feature of the folk songs of Garhwal.

The life of the woman in Garhwal is deeply influenced by the natural and socio-cultural environment. Born in poverty, her life begins amidst the hardships associated with life in the mountains. She is married off at a young age to a far away unknown destination — the man she marries is away, thus her emotional longing for her parental home gets intensified. Her extremely hard life in her new home, walking long distances to get fuel, fodder, water; the harsh treatment meted out to her by her in-laws all find expression in the form of a song. In fact the various aspects of her life and the emotions experienced by her find expression in a variety of songs reflecting pain, joy, love, longing, hope and pride.

In short, the main objective of this research has been to present this multifaceted image of the woman as reflected through the folk songs of Garhwal. Briefly, the different aspects highlighted are as follows :

— The analysis of the songs presented here in a summary has shown how rich this source material is in depicting so many aspects of a culture — the life of the women of Garhwal in this case.

— While the songs were categorised for analytical purposes, it is clear that the categories are not mutually exclusive but are linked in fact. The songs have multiple levels of meaning and present a holistic picture of the life of women in a society.

— The songs of the women of Garhwal have highlighted their life patterns, their emotions, their social relations, their world view, their integral relationship with nature and the ecology of the region and their significant contribution to agriculture in the hill communities. Their integral beingness and the presence of the sacred is also manifested in their songs.

— One of the major contribution of this work has been to show that appropriate methodologies need to become an integral part of social science research programmes which affirm, articulate and vindicate the idea of the methodology of participation. So far, the available linear methodologies have continued to reinforce the idea of fragmented understanding of traditional societies. Our approach requires a new form of perception, a new way of acknowledging the totality of the human phenomenon.

— It is clear that subjectivity as such and experience thereby is nothing secret and hidden. It is not anything mystifying that cannot be shared, understood and communicated. The reference is to creatively understand women's images in 'folk' songs with particular focus on the many faceted society of the Garhwal region.

— Thus, in the community under study, as has been illustrated by the content analysis of the songs in various sections, songs are a part of a living - lived experience, a tradition which is created anew in the Now, everyday. It is an expression of one's being, of one's experience in day-to-day life. While it is transmitted through generations by word of mouth, the creator or experiencer breathes new meaning into it.

— What, I experienced personally is the 'lived experience', an aliveness of the song and its words which alone speaks about the lives of the women. All this has been translated into knowledge through the written word, supplemented with audio-visual means. However, even this only slightly approximates to the experience felt in the field. It does not tell one about the sense of identification which the women feel with the song. The women were not mere passive receivers of another form of entertainment as in modern times. They were active participants and the researcher herself becomes a participant-observer in this sense because the lived experience invoked, evoked and provoked something inwardly. It was in this sense that the study of folk songs for understanding women's lives took on a significant dimension.

— This study has clearly shown that as interpreters of cultures, the knowledge of the 'self' and of the 'others' comes together in some subjective and creative understanding. In the natural flow of interaction, especially in music and dance and so on, there is something behind the words — a hum of another kind — which takes into account a large sensory inventory which cannot be frozen into the written word. The human approach to a cultural model therefore encompasses all 'experience', the feeling of something beyond language, that gives some meaningfulness and vibrance before being classified and explained away.

— The point that has been especially made is that in most field work reports the early experiences and feelings of the worker tend to be forgotten, at best confined to reflexive introductions. The content of culture, which we learn about through our experiences with others, is much more than what we can confine to texts — our learning is much more than a textual interpretation.

— The emphasis has been on the fact that all informative-descriptive knowledge has to be integrated within the experiential dimension with which both the researcher and the 'other' culture is involved in. Folk songs are thus to be seen as events, processes in a larger whole. This book illustrates as to how folk songs reflect a world view which shows the women-centredness of Garhwali society. In other words, folk songs are not mere songs but they enhance the understanding of a community and its life; these are powerful indicators for looking at the culture in general. This has been another way of contributing to the general production of knowledge in a humble way, throughout this research work.

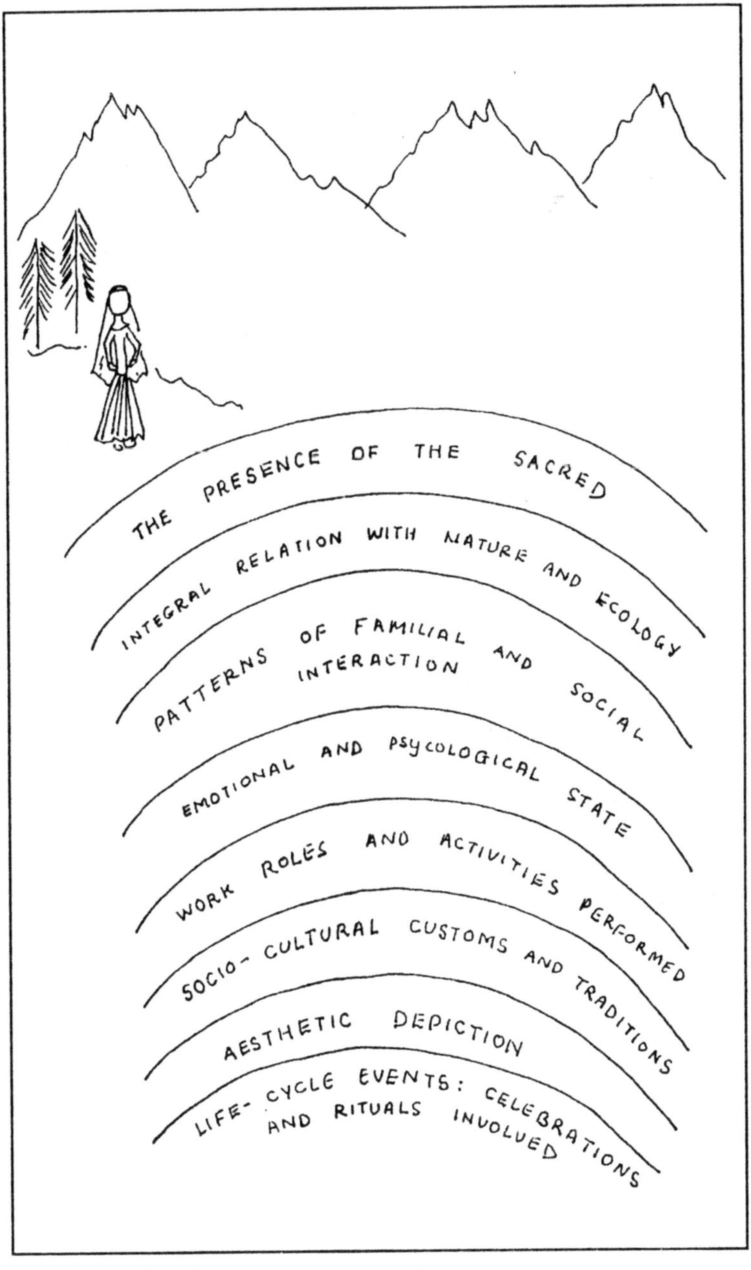

Fig. 5.1 : Multi-layered symbolism inherent in songs

The Song lives on .... Suma Devi village Kotigad, Chamba Block

6

EPILOGUE

Language, Culture and Communication

One of the most important components of human and animal identity is language. It is essential for all social interaction and behaviour, and is a part of cultural life styles since it allows for both communication and identification. Human language is not static, it changes along with other variables. It is the centre of human societies because language reflects patterns of thought; it being the output of the social and cultural conditioning fossilised as symbols and images. In this way it provides cohesiveness of any lifestyle, creating a cultural identity whereby it provides norms of behaviour to which members of a group can respond and identify; it creates a sense of confidence. Obviously, language is crucial for one's style of life, as an expression of originality, of the uniqueness of ourselves, as individuals and as a part of the larger society and even of the species (Malik, 1995).

No one will disagree with the above statement. This chapter highlights the context within which the songs have been viewed, i.e., emphasising communication in terms of integral listening, of the silence which forms the background of true human communication in oral traditions. This brief introductory background with regard to culture and language is essential, given the context of the dominance of the Western mode of communication widely prevalent all over the world today. Our stress in this research has been on the holistic functioning of an integral human being, where both silence and language are necessary. (Malik, 1989)

In many earlier pre and non-industrial small societies, the power of the unsaid was considerably of crucial importance. We know that a large part of communication was carried out taking into account this aspect of the functioning of the brain which in modern times has been lost in the use of mere expressive language, an internal and external *chatter*.

In Garhwal, as demonstrated by the interviews with the women, when the song of a woman takes off, it reverberates in the air, she feels free, because according to her, nature — prakriti — is listening, the whole

Fig. 6.1 : Listening to the Song ...."Nature is listening, the whole universe is listening."

universe is listening, the trees are listening, the birds and the babbling stream is listening. This clearly unifies her in a way with all the elements. She sees herself as a part of a cosmic order, her 'world-view' contains within it the 'other', the sacred. Is this not the answer to her rootedness, her centering which gets expressed in her very presence? On the contrary, modern man and his philosophies are grounded in only half a language, i.e., within any discourse the strength of listening is ignored. In fact what one takes to be a form of genuine dialogue, is a mere speaking without listening. There is actually no authentic listening taking place, as this has been referred to as 'warring monologues' by Fiumara (1990), who says what 'proper hearing' is,i.e.,there is no saying without hearing, no speaking which is not also an integral part of listening, no speech which is not somehow received.

In the general context of participant-observation, of a participatory universe and experiencing the other which has been emphasized throughout the book, there was one question which perplexed the researcher all the time. Apart from recording the songs, their words and contents, the meanings and the questions of when and why they are sung, a crucial question was the one about this 'dialogue' which was happening all the time, hearing the 'unsaid' in its silence. The togetherness, of the researcher and the women in their physio-geographical, socio-cultural environment; all of this communicated volumes to each other.

Participatory-Experience

A major task of this thesis has been to make explicit those moments of 'experience' which become constructs for knowledge, as revealed from folk ways of life. The movement of this research in this direction will indeed be a very significant contribution, I hope to the understanding of societies based on oral traditions. The various 'images' of the woman as reflected in the folk songs of Garwhal and as experienced by me, within the participatory-conceptual framework, moreover, provides one with a deeper understanding of the dynamics of cultural communication. Outwardly, the hard life — tedious, harsh, at times severe — of the woman, her moments of anguish and longing, her not so significant status in her home in terms of authority and decision-making, her lack of access to health care facilities, education and employment opportunities; all these recorded observations indeed bring forth certain negative images about her. And, yet, her very presence is, in a way unnerving, i.e., her presence has a powerful impact within her social setup and its ordering. It is the woman's integral being-ness, her rootedness, her centering in the relationship with the sacred which is what empowers her within this cultural configuration. It counteracts and overshadows the harshness of her life. She emerges as being all there; her biography merging in a way with her sense of identity. This deeper identity of hers cannot be located merely by asking questions; by setting up digital markers based on "who and what she is". All this can only be experienced simultaneously in empathy with her. This is why the songs of women mirror her life, and viewed holistically become crucial. She and her songs are no longer to be looked at as mere objective entities. These processes are interlinked in multiple ways with several other manifestations that form a very intricate part of the very fabric of her life in that community.

The significance of the need to look at songs as indicators of women's lives and their communication patterns is apparent. It is in this 'image' then that everything begins to unfold spontaneously, rhythmically creating movements and patterns that form a picture, an image of 'what is'. And, hopefully, this work has effectively translated this 'shared experience' into a knowledge which is of another order. This indeed was a great challenge for me.

One of the most rewarding experiences during field work in Garwhal was experiencing and understanding this 'openness' of the women to one another, and to me. This became possible when I dropped the preconceived notions and thoughts about every thing which were buzzing inside my head. It was a great learning experience when one allowed all that to be, and just 'listened', to the forest, the silence, the sounds, the hum behind the words uttered, the song that was being sung. In short, this is what true listening and communication is all about.

Integral Listening

The important point to note is this; an individual can speak only if one is listened to, rather than there being something one might say that one would subsequently attend to 'by means of listening'. It is easily seen how the mechanism of 'saying without listening' has multiplied and spread, to finally constitute itself as a generalised form of domination and control, ignoring ways of life capable of 'letting-lie-together-before'. It is totally ignoring a broad base of human communication networks that are deeply rooted in the cultural milieu characterised by oral traditions which represent a 'continuous creation in the now'.

Today, social scientists, especially folklorists are doing a re-thinking on how they are looking at cultures from this alternate approach within the context of oral traditions. For example, to examine events and processes whereby songs and women are not treated as 'objective' entities. This is why the emphasis here is on the idea that it this shared experienced which has to become an important aspect of general knowledge about human communities; and, to note that integral listening implies the beginning of open-ness and a true dialogue.

To experience the "Thou truly as Thou", an openness is necessary. But this openness exists ultimately not only for the person to whom one listens, but rather anyone who listens is fundamentally open, and shows concern spontaneously for everyone and everything around one. Without this kind of openness to one another there is no genuine human relationship, no belonging together (Friedman, 1995).

Field Work and Experience

Thus, field research as presented in this study, is both a product and a process — a process because it involves everyday interactions, comprehensive experiences and local knowledge; and a product because its result is a written text intended to encourage a scientific and universalistic understanding. Both are inherent in the task of learning from cultures, which in our case is to show the harmony between the two kinds of knowledge, i.e., the attempt to translate embodied practices into analytic categories. My task has been to show that it is in the methodologies of this study that a fusion is possible in these two situations — as is evident from the analysis of the songs. It is important to highlight local categories which are relevant for the participants and not initially impose one's own categories on the experience of those who participate in the various cultural expressions (de Rada and Cruces 1994).

Cultural reality in terms of sensation, feeling, thought and action cannot easily be represented except by dwelling in the world of experience which one attempts to render mutually intelligible, i.e. the task is to make field research to come to terms with life with its enormous variety of cultural forms especially nontextual ways of communication. In all this effort, the intuitive and commonsense feeling of the researcher plays an important role in this endeavour. This approach is very different from the majority of cases which dwell upon some natural 'objectivity' in their attempts at interpretation of other cultural reality 'out there', especially in terms of functional and structural interpretations which have stripped these investigations of their humanistic coefficients —the latter being considered as some forms of distortions of reality.

Today, the hardline between the observer and the observed has disappeared. But does this mean truth and fiction, experience and scholarly accounts is also not there? It is no longer true that mere field work descriptive accounts are mirrors of cultural reality 'out there' — it is not a true representational reality because the cultural conditioning of the researcher's culture has to be taken into account in these reflections. Given this situation, this thesis makes a significant attempt to evolve methodologies in general and specifically for purposes of getting involved in the social situation which he/she is studying. Thus by its very nature this is a significant departure from the methodologies evolved earlier.

Obviously, one cannot become the 'native', as seeing culture through the eyes of its subjects. But one can certainly broaden the scope of human discourse by seeing the interrelations of sets of symbols anchored to the text of the local culture. The shared experience of knowledge and the multifunctionality of knowledge becomes important in this approach. One could say it in another way, in this knowledge through experience, that human beings transcend the limitations of individual experience through interpreting expressions; and, this transcendence constitutes a process whereby experience structures expressions and expressions structure experience (Kempy and Burszta 1994).

Touchstones of Experience

Field work in all social sciences, is more than a provider of data for cross-cultural studies as many researchers seem to believe until now; it is not supposed to question basic premises of research. But I have attempted to show that today interdisciplinary field experience can be shared across disciplines. For example, social practice and experience together contribute towards a holistic understanding of cultures. Earlier approaches have failed to understand this aspect from its limited angle, when inner experience was not seen as a link between the psychological and the cultural dimensions.

Thus the three; social, linguistic and conceptual experience is the common ground for togetherness. The task for future research in interdisciplinary field then is to see how social practice, language and cognition interconnect, and to work out correspondences and correlations. In this way some of the essence of field research, and not just isolated exotic cross-cultural details, may enter the interdisciplinary discussion (Widlok, 1994).

From the viewpoint of this research, experience is the touchstone of good field work, a crucial evaluative concept so that researchers recreate experience — either their own or other people's so that it is directly accessible to readers. Ofcourse, akin to this is somewhat better done by poets, artists, musicians and so on. Other people's experience is after all mostly inaccessible, except in momentary and partial glimpses, but it is still a touchstone. One cannot create a total representation which totally matches a social fact, but one can recover something, note how that has changed and become aware of what it is that one is leaving out. Even a computer representation of a document is not the document itself, for example. It is important to see the linkages between events and social processes and structure, and not to see the boundaries as fixed. Events are important because they are part of experience, and attributable to social processes which allows us to seek explanation; something that many will deny. We often think of other people's experience as ineffable, ungraspable and inexpressible. But in many cases, in order to explain any social processes — change — we can make lifetime-based models, which emphasize the experience of decision-makers, the shape of sectors of their social world, which may have a fairly close approximation to how it was experienced (Davies, 1994).

Finally

Various routes from experience to social and cultural knowledge have been explored, presented and discussed in this study; questioning both local and anthropological concepts. This tour reflects different poles of experience; stressing process at the expense of structure, and knowledge as a creative field rather than as a solid construction. The 'objectivity' approach has been replaced by more sensitive forms of studying and by a much wider use of the senses in field work. The latter experience cannot be taken at face value because it must be studied in its sensational depth. In real life, knowledge, so often isolated as cognition in theory, is not independent of emotion. Emotions, consequently, belong to the realm of rationality. Individuals are not only defined by their space but are also its defining consciousness - thinking implies empathy and caring.

Just as culture is meaningful only to someone in particular, not in some emotionless state of reasoning which we share in some cross-cultural sense, the agent of scholarship is a living person, not just the mind. Field work is thus essentially an intersubjective experience; sensations, feelings, and emotions demand a certain degree of personal involvement — what it means to be in pain, hungry, joyful and so. In short, there is no way of understanding people except through one's own experience and power of imagination (Hastrup, 1994). Culture and society can no longer be studied from 'above' so to speak. We cannot know anything except by way of our own presence and questioning. Since knowledge is profoundly embodied, understanding can only be achieved by way of involvement — the lived experience of the researcher. Human rationality is profoundly imaginative; it is a capacity for ordering representations, for making sense of unprecedented experiences, and for acting upon them in meaningful ways. Meaning is not a fixed relation between sentences and objective reality, as objectivism has it. Meaning does not exist in itself within the fixed coordinates of an abstract place; it is always meaning for someone in a particular social space.

The desire for fixed standards in science has challenged the interplay between social processes and cultural knowledge. The main point of this study has been dignify subjective experience, not to deny reality; to appreciate imagination, not to disregard reason; to honour our differences, not to underestimate our common humanity. Within this view, there are no facts without value, no reason without emotion, and no knowledge without experience. In this way the particular conditions of knowledge (e.g. women's image in folk songs) also become shared experience amongst those who study, and will continue to study and learn from 'other' human cultures and societies.

Oral traditions are remarkable because they preserve incredible continuity which is preserved through the transmission of ideas, knowledge, religion and culture over the centuries, despite the absence of formal means of communication. This is what has allowed for the tremendous unity of tradition across the country. This is obvious despite regional variations and linguistic diversity.

Folk-lore, folk musical and dance traditions have been passed down through many generations, adapting to changing times, whenever necessary and yet retaining in their contemporary form, an extra-ordinary vitality.

Even in the modern context, folk songs continue to form a major component among the entertainment media of rural India in performing a communication function. They impart knowledge about the weather, health care and improved agricultural technologies. They are an agency of social control or socialization encouraging the moral values of the community. It is clear that in studying Indian civilization oral traditions is the key to the whole process of communication in contemporary times.

Thus, by highlighting the significance of oral traditions, particularly folk songs within the context of understanding the lives of women in a community, the importance of this study is that it has wider application both in the Indian as well as the global context wherever traditonal communities are being researched in an attempt to come to grips with the dilemma of tradition versus modernity.

APPENDICES

ORIGINAL GARHWALI SONGS

APPENDIX - I

SECTION I

SONGS ON THE ECOLOGICAL PRSPECTIVE

Song 1

"उत्तराखण्ड की सुन्दरता का वर्णित गीत"

स्वर्ग उत्तराखण्ड भूमि हिमालय स्वर्ग जैसू फूल ब्रहमी कमला - 2
स्वर्ग उत्तराखण्ड भूमि हिमालय स्वर्ग जैसू फूल ब्रहमी कमला - 2
गंगा हिमालय कू दर्शन छः भारी, हिमालय बद्री केदार ब्रहमी कमला - 2
ये हिमालय डांडी कांठी हिमालय देवदार ब्रहमी कमला - 2
गंगा जमुना की शोभा मेरी-2 हिमालय गौ मुख कू पाणी ब्रहमी कमला - 2
भोला भाला लोग रैंढा-2 हिमालय यूं कैलासू माजी ब्रहमी कमला - 2
रंग बिरंगा फूल खिल्यां छन-2 हिमालय बर्फीली चट्टान ब्रहमी कमला - 2
बादलों की ओर बणी छः-2 हिमालय बर्फीली हवान ब्रहमी कमला - 2
सन्त मुनियों कू पावन धाम-2 हिमालय तपस्या की भूमि ब्रहमी कमला - 2
देश-देश का भक्त लोग-2 हिमालय तीर्थ औंदा भूमि ब्रहमी कमला - 2
भादौं की फूलोरी केदान पत्ती-2 हिमालय चमकीलू छः धाम ब्रहमी कमला - 2
गंगा जमुना केदार नाथ-2 बद्री कू धाम ब्रहमी कमला !!

Song 2

सौन्दर्ययुक्त (पहाड़ की सुन्दरता का वर्णन)

हम छौं गढ़वाली हमारू गढ़वाल यू छः हमारू पहाड़
यू छः हमारी जन्म भूमि यू छः हमारू घरबार
सिरवाणी यैंच बद्री केदारनाथ यरव सी निकलदी गंगा की धार
य छः हमारी जन्म भूमि यू छः हामरू पहाड़
सेरा खेतूमा नाज की दाणी चूड़ी दाथूड़ी बजली छम छम
घास कू तैं जाँदी छन बेटी ब्बारी बौण मा ढम-ढम
हम छौं गढ़वाली हमारू गढवाल यू छः हमारू पहाड़

यू छ हमारी जन्म भूमि यू छ हमारू घरबार
गाँधी जी कू छः यू प्यारू देश चरखा काक्षिक देंदा उपदेश
यू छः हमारू श्रृंगार यू छः हमारी जन्म भूमि यू छः हमारू घरबार

Song 3

सौन्दर्ययुक्त : - (पहाड़ की सुन्दरता)

यू ठण्डू पाणी मेरा पहाड़ स्वामी नी जावा परदेश ।
केला कुलई छः मेरा पहाड़ स्वामी नी जावा परदेश ।।
देवतौं की भूमि मेरा पहाड़, स्वामी नी जावा परदेश ।
हरी भरी सारी मेरा पहाड़, स्वामी नी जावा परदेश ।।
ऊँचा हिमालय मेरा पहाड़, स्वामी नी जावा परदेश ।
घणा देवदारु मेरा पहाड़, स्वामी नी जावा परदेश ।
हिसर किन्गौड़ काफल मेरा पहाड़, स्वामी नी जावा परदेश ।
यू ठण्डू पाणी मेरा पहाड़, स्वामी नी जावा परदेश ।

Song 4

"गढवाल की सून्दरता का वर्णन"

मेरु गढ़वाल दीदौं कन्यू भग्यान - 2
केला कुलई दीदौं बाग बग्वान
डालियों का छैल दिदौं घूघती कू छोल
भालू हिलांस दिदौं का फूलों का झोल
सेयूं गढ़वाल दिदा खड़े उढाल
धरती माकु तैं हाथ जोड़याल - 2
डांडी काठयों ऐगी सूरज भगवान
औरु की चारु दीदा तू भी इन्सान
गाड गढनीयों बीच गाड़ी खमणोट
पुराडयों का बीच दीदा चूड़यों कू छमणाट - 2
धणा गौं कू दीदा सेन्टुलू प्रदान
औरु की चारु दीदा तू भी इन्सान - 2

घणा गौं कू दीदा सेन्टूलू प्रदान
बेटियों का रूप्या खान्दा तब देंदा दान - 2

Song 5

बारहमासा गीत

आयो मैनो चैत को, हे ददियों, हे राम।
उठीक फुलारी झुसमुस, लगी गैन निज काम,
मैनो आयो वैसाग को, सुख की नी आस,
ग्यों जौ का पूलों मुड़े, कमर पड़ीगी झास।
आयो मैनो जेठ ही, मक्को हवेगी मौत,
स्वामी मेरा घर नी, समझी रयूं मैं मौत।
मास पैलो बसगाल को, आयो यो अषाड़,
मैं पापीण झुरि-झुरी मरयों, मास रयो न हाड़।
मास दुसरो बसगाल को आयो स्यो सौण,
चिट्ठी नी पतरी ऊँकी कु जाणो कब घर औण ।
मास आयो भादों को डाँडू कुरेड़ी लौखी,
तेरी खुद स्वामी जिकुड़ी मा बिजली सी चौंकी ।
आयो मैनी असूज को बादल गैन दूरु,
जोन काँठों मा औंदी, जिया लाग बुरु ।
आई दिवाली कातिकी, चढे घर-घर टैकू,
यू दिन स्वामी का बिना ज्यू लगदू कैकू ।
आयो मैनो मंगसीर को हे बैठयों, हे राम,
स्वामी की खुद मा हाड़ रयो न चाम ।
पूष मास की ठंड बड़ी घर-घर कंपादी गात,
कन्हि होली भग्यान सी पति जौंका सात ।
लगी मैना माघ को गौं गौं छन ब्यो,
व्योली आँखी झुकैक ब्यौला से मिलदी स्यो ।
फागुण मैना आये, हरी-भरी हवैन सारी,
भी झूरी-झूरी मरयों एकुला बांदर की चारी ।

Song 6

बसन्त के महीने का गीत-ऋतु - गीत

बसन्त बहार माजि ढैड़ा फूल्याँ सार माजि
सचि बैठी रीतू बौड़ी ऐगी
पहाड़ों की धार माजि कोकिला पुकार माजि
नाचण नाचण होली लगी-नाचण लगी होली
मन बापूरा उड़ी-उड़ी बैठयाँ होला डाला डाला - 2
गुन-गुन की धून सुणिक आज स्वामी आला - 2
चल खुटी मजदार माजि काली गंगापार माजि - 2
मन की उमंग बौड़ी ऐगी - सचि बैठा रीतू बौड़ी ऐगी ।

Song 7

ऋतु गीत - घूघूती घूराण लगी

घूघूती घूरौण लगी मेरा मैत की - 2
रीतू बौड़ी बौड़ी ऐगी, ऐगे चैत की - 2
डांडी काठयों कू हिम गलीगे होलू - 2
मेरा मैत कू बौण मौलीगे होलू - 2
कब मेरा मैती औजी दिशा भेंट आला - 2
कब मेरा भाई बैणियों की राजी खुशी ल्याला - 2
तेबारी मा बैठया होला बाबाजी उदास - 2
माजी देखणी होली लगी होली आस - 2

Song 8

ऋतु 'सावन' का गीत

सुणा मेरा स्वामी जी, सावण आयो,
रूण झुण्या बरखा, घनघोर लायो ।
दौड़ी-दौड़ी कुयेड़ी, डाडों मां आयो,
कुरेड़ी न स्वामी, अंधियारो छायो ।

कुरेड़ी देखीक, जिऊ खुदी आय,
कनु पापी आँखी, आँसू भरि लाय ।

Song 9

ऋतु - गीत

करव होली मेरा डाँडी कांठी,
करव कुरेड़ी सौण की ।
आंलद का बीच छानीम होली,
भैंसी ब्याई सौण की ।
दूध टचाला और खीर पकाला,
गोंदकी खाला नोण की ।
करव होली मेरा डांडी ओ कांठी,
करव कुरेडी सौण की ।
सूरमा सितारू मैकू नी प्यारू
प्यारू छ मैकू मेरू गढवाल
करव होली मेरी डांडी अ कुरेडी सौण की
रूम झूम बरखा छूम-छूम होया
खुद लगी छ मैत की ।

Song 10

ऋतु गीत

आवा दीदी आवा भूली भैजी आवा
हरियाली खुशहाली का गीत गावा
रिमझिम रिमझिम जब सौण बरखलू
किसाण कू मन मोर तब हर्षल
खेत खलियाणुमा तब हरियाली आली
धरती माता की तब प्यास बुझाली
सात स्वरों मा गीत गावा - 2
डालियों का बीच या हिलांस बोलती

बाँज और बुरांश की डाली लगावा
हरियाली खुशहाली का गीत गावा ।।

Song 11

ऋतुपूरक (सौन्दर्य)

रिमझिमा कु मैनू यू सौण रसीलो रसीलो रसीलो ।
त्वैतैं मेरा सौं जोड़्या मैतैं ना लुकौ ।।
घास कू तैं जोला सुवा मली सारी मा ।
घास की गडोली जन धरी मुण्ड मा मुण्ड मा मुण्ड मा ।।
त्वैतैं मेरा सौं जोड़्या मैतैं ना रूकी ।
मली सारी लग्यूं छ देवी कू थौल ।।
वख आई होली दादी भूली गैल ।
बाबा मा बोली मांजी ना बोली ना बोली ना बोली ना ।।
त्वैतैं मेरा सौं जोड़्या मितै ना लुकौ ।
डाडयों की हवा उडली सरासर सरासर सरासर ।।
धोती कु पल्लू सुवा उड़ालो फराफर फराफर फराफर ।
धोती कु पल्लू जनु बांदी कमर मा कमर मा ।।
त्वैतैं मेरा सौं जोड़्या मितैं ना रूकौ ।।।

Song 12

सावन का महिना (ऋतु गीत)

ओस आलण सी भरेन सारी ।
बरखा लगी छ मूसलधारी ।।
घाटा बाटा भी टूटेन बतेरा ।
भक भरेन गाड गदेरा ।।
ओस आलण सी भरेन सारी ।
बरखा लगी छ मूसलधारी ।।
धरमा बैठी छन त्यौंकी बेटी ब्बारी ।
बरखा लगी छ मूसलधारी ।।

कनकै जौला मैतियों का डेरा ।
घाटा बाटा टूटी गैन बतेरा ।।

Song 13

सुन्दरता का वर्णन (वृक्षों के गीत)

डाडयों मा बुंराश फूली शैन ।
डांडी हामारी कनी भली सजणी छन ।।
डाडयों मा का फल पकी गैन ।
डांडी हामारी कनी भली सजणी छन ।।
चला गैल्याण्यों डाडयों जोला ।
डाडयों की समूण काफल ल्योला ।।
डाडयों मा अब बाँज मौलीगे होलू ।
बाँज की जड़्यों मा पाणी फूटीगे होलू ।।
चला गैलाण्यों काफल ल्यौला ।
बाँज मा पाणी फूटी तीस बूजौला ।।
डाडयों मा बुंराश फूलेन डांडी सजनी छन।
बुंराश तोड़्यान् पर डाड़्यों न मुडियान ।।
बाँज तुम लिजावा पर डाल्यों न तोड़्यान ।
घास तुम बाँटा पर कुलई नी काटा ।।
नितर हवै जाणु तुमन यूं पहाडू सी छाँटा ।
डाड़्यों मा बुंराश फूली गैन ।।
डांडी हमारी कनी भली सजणी छन ।।।

Song 14

वृक्षारोपण : - (पर्यावरण)

घणा जंगल की झपन्याली डालो झफन्याली डाली कू घेरू
डाली लगावा छोया फूटला गौं नीस सखाड़ा मा सेरू
घणा सेरा कू लसण प्याज घणू होलू जीरू
गढ़वाल हमरू देवतौं की भूमि त्यौमतें बतौला सेरू

गौं का अखाडी पिछवाडी झूमूली फल फलौं की डाली
डाली लगौला फल छकौला त्यौं डाल्यौं तै रखा जखाली
पारवती कू मैत छ परव हिमालय का कांठा
गंगा जी की लैर बगदी शिवाजी का जटा
घणा सेरा कू लसणप्याज घणू होलू जीरू
गढ़वाल हमरू देवतौं की भूमि त्योंते बतौला सेरू

Song 15

जंगलों के बचाव के लिए संदेश

ना काटा त्यौं डाल्यों ना काटा
दीदयौं डाल्यों ना काटा भूल्यौं डाल्यों ना काटा
डाली काटली त पाप लगलू
डोखरी न पूगड़ी कुछ बचलू
डाली काटली न माटी बगली
खेती हरयाली भी कुछ ही नी राली
गोरू भैंसी बाखरयों कु चारू
झपन्याली डाल्यों तैं फूलों कू सारू
पाला त्यौं डाल्यों तैं औलाद माणी
औलाद भ्वाल कू रूणी भी जाली
नाज औ पाणी यू डाली ही दयाली
ना काटा तौं डाल्यों ना काटा भूल्यों डाल्यों ना काटा ।।

Song 16

पर्यावरण सम्बन्धी गीत

ना काटा न काटा कोलईं की डाली ।
ना काटा न काटा यूं रखा जग्वाली ।।
दगन्यों मा छः पाणी सेरौंमा छ फूल ।
खिल खिलादूं बुँराश कू फूल ।।
यूं बांज बुंराश कू ठण्डू छ पाणी ।

ना काटा ना काटा यूं रखा जग्वाली ।।
पत्तियों मा छ दूध जड़्यों मा छ पाणी ।
पुंगडयों मा छ खाद छ खेती किसाणी ।।
या धरती छ सारी उपकार वाली ।
ना काटा ना काटा यूं रखा जग्वाली ।।
यूं डाल्यों कू देण छ माटू पाणी ।
सर्रर्सर बथौं छ झट बरखा बरवाणी ।।
यूं रौत्याली डाडयों मा छ यूंकी हरयाली ।
ना काटा ना काटा यूं रखा जग्वाली ।।
हिमन्त ऋतु बसन्त यूं सी औंदी ।
अषाड़ व सौंण की बरखा भी सूंसी होंदी ।।
यू रीतू बसन्त तैं छ बणौण वाली ।
ना काटा ना काटा यूं रखा जग्वाली ।।
गंगा जमुना कै छन सिरवाणी ।
पशु मन्खियों का ई छन पराणी ।।
ना काटा ना काटा कोलईं की डाली ।
ना काटा ना काटा यूं रखा जग्वाली ।।

Song 17

लोक गीत : वृक्ष की उपासना

मंगलमय हो जीवन प्राण मंगलमय हो जन-जन का ज्ञान
मंगलमय हो वनस्पति मंगलमय हो वृक्ष भगवान
मंगलमय हो वशुन्धरा मंगलमय हो देश हमारा
मंगलकर्णी गाँव-गाँव हमारा मंगलकर्णी हो जग ये सारा
वृक्ष मेरे माता पिता वृक्ष मेरे भगवान
वृक्ष मेरा संगी साथी वृक्ष मेरी सन्तान
वृक्ष मेरा धन वृक्ष मेरा तन वृक्ष मेरा मन
वृक्ष लगाकर हम करें इस धरा को सम्पन्न
मेरी माटी की देय से प्रभु जग जीवन निकल जाय - 2
मेरी माटी की देय में एक वृक्ष लग जाय

छूटी जो सेवा मुझसे - 2 वो वृक्ष सेवा कर पाय
मारो पाथर पीड़ा सहन कर देवे मारो पाथर फल दे देवे
अपने आप धाम सहन करे धाम दूसरों की करवि विश्राम
ऐसा ही गुण ज्ञान ले लेवे वृक्षों से इन्सान
ऐसा ही वरदान दे दो हम सबकी हे भगवान
हम भूख को सहन करते हुए-2 भूखों को भोजन देना न भूलें
हम प्यास को सहन करते हुए प्यासे को पानी देना न भूलें
संकट व दुखों को सहन करते हुए हम सेवा का भाव न भूलें
ऐसा ही ज्ञान लेवे वृक्षों से इन्सान
ऐसा ही वरदान दे दो जननी के जन-जन को हे भगवान ।।

Song 18

हिसर की सुन्दरता के बारे में

तेरी काली घाघरी पिंगला बुरका! तू त पिलौंदी रस का घूटका ।।
हिंसर तेरी छ जात हिंसर! बल सून छ वू बाण जख भी छ हिसर ।।
हिंसर तेरु मैंक्य करूँ विचार! नी होंदी किन्गोड़ भी तेरी चार ।।
तेरी काली घाघरी पिंगला बूरका। तू तू लोगू पिलौंदी रस का घूटका ।।
डाड्यों की छैं बल गदीन्यों की राणी ! त्वै देखिक औंदू मेरी गीचीमा पाणी ।।
हिंसर तेरी मैं क्या करूँ बढ़ाई जलेबी हो जनी जनी बालूसाई ।। तेरी काली ।
दूर बिटीनी तू घोर बूलौंदी घोर तेरा आवा तू काँडा चूमौंदी ।।
हिंसर तू छै बड़ी मजाकी ! कैन नी जाणी हाय तेरी या चालाकी ।।
हिंसर प्यारी नी खैच रोपली ! हाथ जोड़दू त्वैक छोड़ दी मेरी झगूली ।।
तिमलू बेडू किनगौड़ सरीका ! तेरा अग्वाड़ी सब लगदान फीका ।।
हिंसर तू छैं बड़ी दयालु ! औंदी जाँदी रैयी सालू साल ।।
तेरी काली घाघरी पिंगला बुटका ! तू त पिलौंदी रस का घूटका ।।

Song 19

गर्मियों की धूप (पानी की तकलीफ)

हड़ी कू धाम लैगी ओढंणी सुखी गैन बरीखी जा दयोरा - 2

सिल्वाणी सुखी गैनी कना बुरा हाल हवैन बरीखी जा दयोरा - 2
हमक पड़ीगी बण्ढा खाली रैगी हक जा धाम रूकी जा धाम - 2
सभी गौं की बेटी ब्वारी सभी छन पन्यारी हकी जा धाम - 2
मेरी बारी नी औंदी तू देखी जा भाली हकी जा धाम - 2
उकाली कु बाटू हिण माठू-माठू जागी रै दीढी जागी - 2
तुंरतुर्या छ पाणी बण्ढों की खैंचाताणी मरे जा बण्ढा भरेजा
दयौरा मामा पाणी की छ स्याणी नी छ खाणी फूटी जा छोया फूटी जा
हयूंद मैत जाण छ क्योकू, क्योकू थौ खाण फूटी जा छोया फूटी जा
हड़ी कू धाम लैगी ओढणी ऊबैन बरीखी जा दयोरा बरीखी जा
सिल्वाणी सुखी गैन कना बुरा हाल हवैन बरीखी जा दयोरा

Song 20

पाणी का तरास ऋतु गीत

ऐगी बसग्याल मांजी, दुरू हवैगी पाणी ।
तेई पाणी का बाना मांजी, छुरि जांदी घाणी ।।
पाणी की पन्यारी मांजी, पाणी की पन्यारी ।
उकाली कू बाटू मांजी, तुर-तुर्या धारी ।।
बुणी जाली माणी मांजी, बुणी जाली माणी ।
रूडी का दोफेरा मांजी, नी सारेन्दू पाणी ।।
नांरगी की दाणी मांजी, नारंगी की दाणी ।
पणधारी ढेकी पेंढा मांजी, सरग्वाणी पाणी ।।
कानि हवैन स्याणी मांजी, कानि हवैन स्याणी ।
रवाणू मिलि जांदू मांजी, नी मिलदू वाणी ।।
दैव लायी भोम मांजी, देव लायी भोग ।
स्वामी परदेश मांजी, गुरमुल्या जोग ।।
मूल्वाणी सूखीगैन मांजी, अब करव जाणी ।
रात-दिन रटणू हवैगी, हे पाणी ।।
भारत आजाद मांजी, भारत आजाद ।
पाणी की तरास मांजी, सदैं रली याद ।।

Song 21

मुंगरी पकी गैन खुदेड़ गीत

सौण भादौं का मैना ऐना मुंगरी पकी गैन ।
गौं की दीदी मूली सभी मैत्वाड़ा ऐ गैन ।।
मुंगरयाड़ा मुंगरी पकीन,
सन्क्वाली पंछी रवैगीन।
रात रीक दिन बांदर खारू करी गैन ।।
सौण भांदौं का मैना ऐन मुंगरी पकी गैन ।
गौं की दीदी मूली सभी मैत्वाड़ा ऐ गैन ।।
ओड़ाल ओडाम गैन,
रतव्याणी धरमा ऐन,
नाक चदयूं यनू-जनू लाभ जीती ऐन ।।
सौण भांदौं का मैना ऐन मुंगरी पकी गैन ।
गौं की दीदी मूली सभी मैत्वाड़ा ऐ गैन ।।
सारी चौंरयौम कारवड़ी लगीन,
स्कूल्या छोरा खैगीन ।
मुगरयाड़ा मा खाली खड़ा मुंगरेढा रैगैन ।।
सौण भांदौं का मैना ऐन मुंगरी पकी गैन ।
गौं की दीदी मूली सभी मैत्वाड़ा ऐ गैन ।।

Song 22

वृक्षासेपण (पर्यावरण)

मनखी कू जब चोलू छूटलू डोल्यौं डाल्यौं मा पंछी बणी जालू
फूदकी फूदकी मै फाग्यों जौलू ना काटा ना काटा यू डाल्यों ना काटा
डाडयौं डाल्यौं मा कविता गौलू मनखी कू जब चोलू छूटलू
डाल्यौं डाल्यौं मा यू गीत गौलू हे डाली गुणवान हे डाली भगवान
सुर्र-सुर्रया बथौं डाल्यौं कू बरखा बत्वाणी औंदी पत्तों मा यू दूध छ डाल्यौं कू
जडयों मा छ पाणी भूखौं तै खाणू देंदी टीसों देंदी वाणी
फल फूलों न भरी छन डाली कन लगदेन स्वाणी

सभी कुछ डाली हम सैं देंदी नी करदेन क्वी गाणी
पाला पोसा यूं डाल्यौं सणो औलाद अपणी माणी
यू डाली गुणवान यू डाली भगवान, धरती मा जब डाली ऐन देणा का खातीर सब सूखसैन
यकी जगा मा खड़ी डाली युग युग बीतेन मारा दुंगा की बदला मा फल देदेंन
अफू खेंदी यू डाली धाम और देंदी यू डाली आराम यू डाली गुणवान यू भगवान
निराशौं की आशा ये डाली पंछीयों कू बसेरू
निराशौं की आशा ये डाली बटोयों कू डेरू
यूं डाल्यों का छैल लगी छ तपस्यों न ध्यान
यूं डाल्यों का छैल पाई तपस्यों न ज्ञान यू डाली गुणवान यू डाली भगवान
यूं डाल्यों का छैन रैन राधा जी व श्याम
यूं डाल्यों की गैल रैन सीता जी व राम
डाल्यों डाल्यों लगी धाम डाल्यों डाल्यों राम राम कू छ विश्राम
मनखी कू जब चोलू छूटलू डाल्यौं डाल्यौं मा पंछी बणी घूमलू ।।

Song 23

लोक गीत (वृक्ष)

बचपन बीतीगी बीतीगी जवा
लम्बी हवैजा मेरी अपणी कहानी
जीवन कू धाम ढली चलीगी
हे पापी प्राणी त्वै रात हवैगी
गीत लगा चाऊ कविता
गंगा यमुना आख्यों पर ऐगी
सारा जगत मा करूणा फैलेगी
एक बार सारी दुनिया तैं रोवेगी
तब जन्म लेली बुद्दी वाली
खाली जगा पर तब होली डाली
सारा जगत मा फैलली हरियाली
तब जैक होली जन-जन की खुशहाली ।।

SECTION II

SONGS ON CELEBRATION - LIFE CYCLE EVENTS

मंगल गीत

Song 1

सगुनी कागा बोललु सगुन की बात
त्वैई दयौला कागा दही भात पूड़ी,
रूप की ठोंरणी तू चौं दिसौं सगुन भेज ।।

Song 2

सुणियाला ब्रहमा जी तुम चौक पुरियावा ।
गज मोतियान से चौक पुरियावा ।।
तुमरा घर यो कारिज वीरयो ।
ये कारिज सुफल फल्यान् ।।

Song 3

मंगल गीत (वैवाहिक)

स्या होली स्या होली तेरी भौजी सुहागीण ।
ज्वीन त्वैतैंय तीलू तेल चढाई ।।
स्या होली स्या होली तेरी चाची सुहागीण ।
ज्वीन त्वैतैंय हल्दी पीली चढाई ।।
स्या होली स्या होली तेरी बडी सुहागीण ।
ज्वीन त्वैतैंय लाडी दही सफेद चढाई ।।
स्या होली स्या होली तेरी माजी सुहागीण ।
ज्वीन त्वैतैंय लाडी आचमन चढाई ।।
स्या होली स्या होली तेरी मौजी सुहागीण ।
ज्वीन त्वैतैंय लाडी वीलू तेल चढाई ।।

Song 4

मंगल गीत

पैर पैर मेरा यूँ कपडौं
तेरा बाबाजी लैन टालखी भोलै की
मांजी न तेरी पिटारी साजी

Song 5

मंगल गीत

पैर पैर लाडी मेरी, रेशमी कपड़ी,
पैर पैर लाडी यूँ गहणो
बाबाजी लेन हस्ती लादी सोनू,
घोडा लादी सोनू ।।

Song 6

मंगल गीत

आई गैन आई गैन जनती का लोक
शिबजी ऐन पार्वती बिवौण
आई गैन आई गैन शिव की असवारी,
शिवजी ऐन पार्वती बिवौण
बिष्णु ऐन लक्ष्मी बिवोण, बर्मा ऐन सावत्री बिवौण

Song 7

संस्कार-गीत

बैठा-बैठा बैकूजी तमाखू गुड़यामू
बैठा-बैठा बैकूजी बिछाणु बिछायूं
तमाखू भरूयूं छ बैठा-बैठा बैकूजी
पान सूपारी ल्यावा बैठा-बैठा बैकूजी
बैठा-बैठा बैकूजी तिलग लगावा
बैठा-बैठा बैकूजी सजली तिबारी
बैठा-बैठा बैकूजी भोजन करयाला ।।

Song 8

मंगल गीत

खोली देवा खोली देवा घौड़ पड़दा ।
देखण देवा कन्या को रूप ।
हमारी कन्या च गौरी स्वरूप
तुमरो बनड़ा श्याम स्वरूप, चमार सी कालो ।

Song 9

गोत्रोचार (मांगल गीत)

बेटा रे बेटा, गोबर लेटा, बोल बेटा गोत्र अपणो
माजी तेरी चमारों की जायी, पिता छ घुनारों को बेटा
बोल बेटा गोत्र अपणों ।
बेटी ए बेटी, चन्दन लेटी, बोल बेटी गोत्र अपणों
माजी तेरी माजी लक्ष्मी स्वरूप, पिता छन बिष्णु स्वरूप
मामा जी होला मामा जी होला बरमा स्वरूप
मामी जी होली तेरी सावीत्री स्वरूप,
बोल बेटी बोल गोत्र अपणु ।

Song 10

कन्यादान (वैवाहिक)

खूब देणु बावाजी दिल छोडी दान ।
दी देण बाबाजी दिल छोड़ी दान ।।
दी देण बाबाजी गऊ कन्या दान ।।
दी देण बाबाजी चांदी सोनू दान ।
दी देण बाबाजी दिल छोड़ी दान ।।
खूब करणी बाबाजी पौणौं की सेवा ।
यू जनम सूखपैला वे जनम मेवा ।।
खूब देणू बाबाजी दिल छोड़ी दान ।
दी देण बाबाजी दिल छोड़ी दान ।।

Song 11

मांगल गीत - कन्यादान

मैं दीनी बाबा जी कन्या कू दान - 2
मैं दीनी बाबा जी रोजी-रोजी कू दान - 2
ब्बे बाबू देला गौ कन्या कू दान - 2
चाचा चाची देला सोनू चाँदी दान - 2
मै दीनी बाबाजी भाई कू बाँट
हमारा गोत्रियों की तू कनी जन्मी
क्या हमारा पितर स्वर्ग हवै जाला
दानियों मा दानी जगदीश पंवार - 2
दानियों मा दानी सीस काटी दीनी दान - 2
दानियों मा दानी राजा हरिशचन्द्र - 2
जी जरा करी लगदू गौ कन्यादान ॥

Song 12

मांगल गीत

जबारी बर-ब्यौली फेरा फेरदान
पैली फेरू फिरी लाडी कन्या छः कुवाँरी
दूजू फेरू फिरी लाडी कन्या छः कुवाँरी
तीजू फेरू फिरी लाडी कन्या छः मां की प्यारी
चौथू फेरू फिरी लाडी कन्या छः बाबा की प्यारी
पांचों फेरू फिरी लाडी कन्या छः कुवाँरी
छटौं फेरू फिरी लाडी कन्या हवै चूकी विराणी
सातौं फेरू फिरी लाडी कन्या सासू की छ ब्वारी ॥

Song 13

मांगल गीत

औंदी किलै नो ढोल देंही
भई जा तू भैर
औन्दू छौं मैं औन्दू छौं मैं
गैल्याण्यों मिलदू

औंदी किले नी ढोल देंही
मौत हवैगी देर
औन्दू छौं औन्दू छौ मैं
माजी मिलदू
औन्दू छौं औन्दू छौ मैं
भैज्यों तै मिलदू
औंदी किलै नी ढोल देंही
कि मौत लयाली देर
औन्दू छौं औन्दू छौं मैं
बाबाजी मिलदू

Song 14

विदाई गीत

काला डांडा पाछ काली छ कुएड़ी
मैं मेरा बाबाजी मखुली नी जांदों।
मैं मेरा बाबाजी डैर लगली ऊँ खोलू
यखुली यखुली मांजी कनु कैक धौलु ।
अनगईं घौलो बेटी त्वै सकल जनीत
त्वै तैं मेरी धिया लाडी, येखुली नी मेजू ।
अनगाईं घौलो बेरी यैं, त्वै दास और दासी,
पिछनैं घौली त्वै तैं गायों का गुढयार ।
त्वै तैं मेरी धिया ब्बै, यखुली नी भेंजू ।
अगनाईं घौली लाडी मैं गुप्त भंडार,
पिछनैं घौलो लाडी, भैंस्यों का खरक,
भैंस्यों का खरक लाडी बा,रयों की तांढी,
त्वै मेरी लाडी सांकी येखुली नी मेजूं ।

Song 15

बधु गृह प्रवेश (मांगलीक)

शुभ दिन शुभ घड़ी आई सुहागण ।
हम घर हम घर आई सुहागण ।

अमरित सिंचदी आई सुहागण ।
मोतियों परोखदी आई सुहागण ।
शुभ दिन शुभ घडी आई सुहागण ।
चौछोड़ी माणिक दिपकदो सुहागण ।
चौ दिशी चमकण लैगी सुहागण ।
कोठड़ी दिपकण लैगे सुहागण ।
हम घर हम घर आई सुहागण ।
शुभ दिन शुभ घड़ी आई सुहागण ।

Song 16

जन्म का गीत

जा धौं भौंरा माँजी का पास हमारी
जा धौं भौंरा कुशल-मंगल बोल आई ।
जा धौं भौंरा बाबाजी का पास हमारा
कल्याण बोल आई कुशल-मंगल सुणाई ।
धियाँण तुमारी मैं बोलणी भौंरा,
जा धौं भौंरा भाई जी का पास हमारा
जा धौं भौंरा कुशल मंगल सुणाई ।
बैण तुमारी मैं बोलणी भौंरा ।
जा धौं भौरा माँजी बोल आई ।
धियान तुमारी माँजी लाल तोड्यो
धियान तुमारी माँजी रण जीत्यो
जा धौं भौंरा माँजी का पास हमारी ।

Song 17

जन्म का गीत

तू होलो मेरो तपस्या को जायो ।
तेरी जिया ब्वैन खटु कैन कर्म,
तेरी जिया ब्वैन नीम लैन धर्म ।
तेरी जिया ब्वै तीर्थू का नौं छुबडुल्यों नहेंणें,
देवतौं का नौं वींन धारू ढुंगी पूजीन ।

तू होलो बाबा डाँडों कू उधौऊँ,
तू बणलों बाला कुल की जोत ।

Song 18

चूडाकर्म (माँगलीक)

नाई रे नाई तू मेरो भाई - धर्म को भाई ।
मेरा लाडा पीड़ा ना लाई, पीड़ा ना लाई ।
त्वै दैलु नाई मैं पाँऊ खडाऊँ हाय जुगत,
त्वै दैलु नाई मैं कानों कुण्डल, शाल-दुशाला,
त्वै दैलु नाई मैं जरिद कपड़ा, रेशमी पगड़ी,
मेरा लाडा तू पीड़ा न लाई, नाई रे नाई ।

Song 19

लड़की पैदा होने पर

नौन्याल जब होलु हमारू,
सबु सणी स्यू सुख देलु न्यारू ।
घूसड़ी धूसड़ी स्यू बदलु अग्वाड़ी,
आलु स्यू लग्यू पकड़ी क दाड़ी ।
न्यौन्याल घूघू चदलू जबारी,
मूकी मैं टैकी प्यौलु तबारी ।
प्रसुति कु दिन भी झट ऐगी,
ओबरा जनानों कू भी ठट् लैगी ।
क्वी भैर औन्दा क्वी भीतर जांदा,
कभी क्वी कै तैं कभी क्वी कै तैं भटयांदा ।
राणा की भी आस लगी छ भारी,
प्रगट होन्दा छन सी वबरी ।
जयसिंह राण तब भैर औन्द,
वय हवी, क्य हवी, मन छवी होन्द।
कर्जातु वब्रे बिटि सबू कु हवे,
भारी पिछोड़ी 'बेटलु' ही हवे ।
राणा न सुणी जब सी या बात,

अपणी कपाली तिन लाई हाट ।।

Song 20

मंगल संस्कार गीत

फूल गुब्बारों न पांलगी झकाझोर बणीगी - 2
दीदा बैठीगी पांलगी मा पौणा नाचण लगीगे - 2
सुबेर कन्यादान मां घपरोलु मचीगे
मारखूडया गौंडू दिदा सिंग मा अैगी
क्वी पौण ओबरा लूक्यां क्वी बैठया डिडांली
दीदा बैठी रोण लगी पकड़ी कपाली
बारात पैटद पैटद रूमक पड़ीगी
दीदा बैठी पांलगी मा पौणा नाचण लगीगे ।
वनी अध्यारां मा बल नी दिखेणी बाटू - 2
वनी टूटी छः जगा मा पलंगी कू लाठू - 2
फूल गुब्बारों न पालंगी झकाझोर बणीगे
दीदा बैठीगी पालंगी मा पौणा नाचण लगीगे
दीदा बैठी तिबारी माँ पौणा बरखा न भीजे गौन
दीदा बैठी पालंगी मा पोणा वरखा न भीजे जैन
फूल गुब्बारों न पालंगी झकाझोर बणीगे
दीदा बैठी पांलगी मा पौणा नाचन लगेन ।।

SECTION III

SONGS DESCRIBING SOCIAL RELATIONS

खुदेड़ गीत

Song 1

माँ होली जौंकी खुदेड़ गीत

मां होली जौंकी मैत बुलाली, मैं कू बुलालु माँ,
मेरी आंख्यों मा आँसू माँ ।

हे माँ तु मेरी बचीं जू रैंदी, मैं मैत बुलौंदी माँ,
मैं समझौंदी बुंझौदी माँ ।
भाई होला जौंका बैण्यों मा जाला, मैत बुलाला माँ,
हे माँ मैं कू बुलालु माँ ।
माँ होली जौंकी मैत बुलाली मैं कू बुलालु माँ,
मेरी आंख्योंमा मा आंसू माँ ।
माँ बाप की मैं एकलौती बेटी, गरीब घर माँ
मैन लीनी जनम माँ ।
दगडयाणी सभी थौलू जांदीन, क्वी मैत्वाड़ा जांदी माँ,
मेरी आंख्यों मा आंसू माँ ।
माँ होली जौंकी मैत बुलाली, मैं कू बुलालु माँ,
मेरी आंख्यों मा आंसू माँ ।
स्वामी जी मेरा परदेश गैन, औंदी नी चिट्ठी माँ,
कई सालों बिरी हे माँ ।
कनु कै बितौलु यी जिन्दगी मैं, छऊं दुखी मौत माँ,
करव हर्चीगी मौत माँ ।
माँ होली जौंकी मैत बुलाली मैं कु बुलालु माँ,
मेरी आंख्यों मा आंसू माँ ।

Song 2

खुदेड़ गीत

ऊँची डाड्यों तुम नीसी हवै जावा
बाबा जी कु म देश मैंते दैखण देवा
घूघती घूराली मांजी हिंलास बासली
आग भबरांदी मांजी बाडुली लगली
फूली गैं बुरांश मांजी मौली गै बाँज
जैका मैती होला माजी ऊ जाला मैत
निरमैती मैते मैत नी बुलौंदा
कारदू दिन मैं माँजी रोंदू रोंदू ।।

Song 3

खुदड़े गीत - (परिवारजनों को सम्बोधित)

मेरी प्यारी घुघती जैली मेरी मांजी तैं पूछी ऐली ।
मेरी प्यारी घुघती जैली मेरी मांजी तैं पूछी ऐली ।।
मेरी सभी दगडयानी मैत गैन मेरू भेढवालु क्वी नी ऐन ।
मेरी प्यारी घुघली जैली मेरी मांजी तैं पूछी ऐली ।।
मेरू भेढवालु कुई नी ऐन मेरा भुला भी छोटा रैन ।
मेरा बाबाजी भी बुढ़या हवैन मेरा भुला भी छोटा रैन ।।
मेरी प्यारी घुघता जैली मेरा मांजी तैं पूछी ऐली ।
सी सभी दगड़यानी मैत गैन मेरू भेढवालु क्वी नी ऐन ।।
जब कभी मैं मैत जांदू मांजी की लाई रोटी खांदू ।
मेरी प्यारी घुघली जैली मेरी मांजी तैं पूछी ऐली ।।

Song 4

खुदेड गीत - (ससुराल मे स्त्री द्वारा)

बासी जा कफू मेरा मैत वाज, मेरी मांजी सुणली ।
तेरी मौण सुणी मेरा मैजी मैम पठाली ।।
बासी जा कफू मेरा मैत वाज, मेरू मैजी सुणलु ।
मांजी की दिनी समुण च्युड़ा मैकु ल्याजु ।।
बासी जी कफू मेरा मैत वाज मैजी सुणली ।
मेरू रैबार सुणीक मैकु ख्वाजा का बुखणा कुटली ।
बासी जा कफू मेरा मैत वाज, मेरी मां सुणली ।
लेण कु मैतें मेरा बाबाजी भेजली ।।
बासी जा कफू मेरा मैत वाज मेरू बाबा सुणलु ।
सुणीक बाबाजी मेरा मैजी मैम पढालु ।।

Song 5

खुदेड़ गीत

बौड़ी-बौड़ी ऐगी माजी ऐगी पूस मास
ऊंची-ऊंची डाडियों मा फूली गैलू बुरांस
फूली-फूली गै होली ग्यौं जौ की सारी

मैत आई गैई होली गौं की बेटी ब्बारी
मैं डांडा बुलाली जब मेरी मांजी
मेरी जिकुड़ी मा कुरेड़ी सी आली माजी
सासू गाली देंदी मै बापू की मारी
बासी खाणौं देंदी बोली मारी मारी
ऊँची-ऊँची डाडयों मा फूली गैन बुरांस
घूघती बासदी मा घूघती हिलांस
लाल हवैई गैन माजी काफूल की डाली
गौं की बेटी ब्बारी मांजी खाली करली ।।

Song 6

नी जाँदू सैसर

राती घनघोर मांजी राती घनघोर
सैसर नी जांदू मांजी दी डांडा पोर
बामण की पोथी मांजी बामण की पोथी
नी जांदू सैसर मांजी नी बणौं धोती
बासती मलेऊ मांजी बासती मलेऊ
सैसर नी जांदू मांजी नी बणौं कलेऊ
बीड़ी कु बण्डल मांजी बीड़ी कु बण्डल
नी जांदू सैसर मांजी नी मगौ सैण्डल
बासती सेंटली मांजी बासती सेन्टूली
नी जांदू सैसर मांजी नी बाँध मेतूली ।।

Song 7

खुदेड गीत

सैसर का डांडा मांजी लगदी डार
खूदेंदू प्राणी मांजी तेरा बिगर
जागी भी रंदी मांजी क्वी बेटी ब्बारी
निर्भागी निरमोही मांजी तरव की घस्यारी
गौड़ी भैंसी तौंकी मांजी रामदी चौक
बांजी पड़ी जाली तौंकी खराण्या शौक

घणा घणा जंगलू मांजी रीकू की टोली
छट छूटदी मूंड मतीन घास गड़ोली
ऊँची-ऊँची डाडयों म मांजी फूल्यां बूरांश
बाशद नी सूण्यों मांजी घूघती हिल्वांश
लाखड़ा नी होला मांजी क्वीला जगान
मेरा दिल की प्यारी तैं दुख नी दयान
घासीला नी होलू माजी डालौ रेडयान
मेरा दिल की प्यारी तैं दुख न दियान
घर मा बैठी रौन्दीन मांजी नणद जेठाणी
जब औलू घासन मांजी तब ल्यौण पाणी ।

Song 8

खुदेड गीत

पौड़ी छ सैसर मांजी पाली छ गाऊँ
जांखण्ड मामा काटे सुशीला छ गाऊँ
बुरू खोजी बुरू खोजी माजी त्वैन जवाई
दारू प्याण की मांजी जूं की आदत छाई
मैन यन बोलण मांजी त्वैन मैं मराई
चौदा बरस की शुशीला मांजी दूर ब्यवाई
दारू पीक ऐन मांजी बार बजी रात
रोण तैं मेरी पकाई मांजी तौन खाण भात
हाथ छडी उतारी मांजी खापरा सभालों
पल्या भीतर गैन मांजी ल्येन थमालो
थमाली देखीक मांजी मैन समझी मजाक
तेरी शुशीला रैयों मांजी छोटी अजाक
ही चोटी लगैन मांजी तेरी सुशीला हताक
पैली की चोटन मांजी कमर टुटीगे
दूसरी चोटन मांजी सिरड़ी उडीगें
दयूरजी यना रवैन माजी मुखडी मोडिक
बोरया पर बन्द करयों कमर तोडीक
रोपणी का खाला लगी पाणी कराऊ

दयूर जी भट्यान्दा मेरा सुशीला बऊ
छै मैना बीतीक माजी आली बग्वाली
छोटी भूली बिमला तैई मैत बुलाली
मेरी खुदन रोली मांजी रोण ना देयी
मेरा बांढा कू दूध मांजी ति तैं पिलैयी
सुशीला नऊ की छोरी भूल्यों होई न काई
सुशीला नऊ की छोरी भूल्यो अभागी होई
गैल की गैल्याणी आली थौलु कू मैत
तेरी सुशीला बची छोंदी ऐ जांदी सैत
गैल की बिमला माजी मैत मा होली
तेरी सुशीला भरव माजी रैगी मखुली
मै बैठी रंदू माजी रवीण डालो छैला
मैं यखूली छौंऊ माजी क्वी नी छ गैल ।।

Song 9

खुदड़े गीत
बाँसूरया मैजी

लड़की	कै गवाँ कु होलु त्यू बाँसूरया मैजी –2 हे भैजी मेरी खुद मीटै दी हे मेरा भैजी ।
लड़का	नी रोणू वैणी फोंजण आंसू –2 करी देण भूली मरदू वालू साँसू हे भूली मेरी
लड़की	किलै बाबा न इण्टर पढाई किलै बाबा न पहाड़ मा विवाई हे मरा भैजी मां बाप सदानी कैका नी रदां भाई भौज कैइका अपणा नी होंदा –2 हे मेरा भैजी
लड़का	नी रोण भूली नी फोजण आंसू कर देण भूली मरदू वालू सांसू हे मरी भूली –2

Song 10

मेरी कमला ज्वान हवैगी

मेरी कमला जवान हवेगी तू

तेरी शादी कर दयौला पहाडू मा - 2
मैं हाथ जोड़दौं पिताजी
मेरी शादी नी करण पहाड़ मा
पहाड़ी लोग खराब होंदान -2
नांगी खूरयों न काम करदान -2
तूमको हाथ जोड़दों बाबाजी
मेरी शादी नी करण पहाड़ मा
पहाड़ी लोग खराब होंदान
रात रात तक शराब पिंदान -2
कन कैक मै रात उठलू -2
कन कैक मैं कोदू पिसलू -2
पिताजी का मैं हाथ जोड़दौं -2
माजी का मैं खूटौ पड़दू -2
मेरी शादी नी करण मा पहाडू मां
मेरा सैण्डल रड़दा पहाडू मा -2
मेरी धोती फटली काडौं मा -2
मेरा हाथ जोडिया पिताजी
मेरी शादी नी करण पहाड़ मा
पहाड़ शादी होली त मैन फाँस खाण
मेरा हाथ जोड़िया पिताजी मेरी शादी नी करण पहाड़ मा
कन कैक मैं धाम मा जौलू
कन कैक मैं घास काटलू
मैरी शादी नी करण पहाड़ मा -2

Song 11

खुदेड़ गीत - बाप, बेटी की र्वाता

जा जा बेटी नागणी बजार दैज देलु रूप्यों हजार
तख त बाबा क्या रवाणू खाणू बाबा क्या लाणू
लांदा बेटी पछन्डू खांदा बेटी रझंगोरा कू फांणू
ना ना बाबा कतै नी जांदू बाबा कतै नी जांदू
जा जा बेटी भपूरा दैज दैल्यू रूप्यों हजार

तख त बाबा क्या खाणू खांदा बाबा क्य लाणू
लांदा बेटी आंगूडी खांदा बेटी कोढा की बाड़ी
तखत बाबा कतै नी जांदू बाबा कतै नी जांदू
जा जा बेटी नागणी बाजार दैज देल्यु रूप्यों हजार
तखत बाबा क्या खाणू खांदा बाबा क्य लाणू
खांदा बेटी कड़ाली लांदा बेटी ऊना की चोली
तख त बाबा कतैनी जांदू बाबा कतै नी जांदू

Song 12

खुदेड़ गीत - (ससुराल में)

ना देंदा बाबाजी जी चौ डांडा पोर ।
ना कदू भैजी रूप्यों कू जोर ।।
बाबा नदिन्यों मैं चौ डांडा पोर ।
भैजी न करी रूप्यों कू जोर ।।
माजी मौस्याणी थैं गुसरे सासू ।
मैत का बाटा देखी औंढान आँसू ।।
किलै दिनी बाबा मैं चौ डांडा पोर ।
किलै करी भैजीन रूप्यों कू जोर ।।
दयूराणी जेठाणी छन लड़ीकू वाली ।
गुसेर सासू मैं देंदी गाली ।।
भैजीन किलै रूप्या खैन ।
मैतै नो मेरी माजी यख चैन ।।
मैत नी बुलाई याद करी करी ।
रोणू छौं मेरी माजी तेरी याद करी ।।
ना देंदा बाबाजी चौ डांडा पोर ।
ना कदू भैजी रूप्यों कू जोर ।।

Song 13

खुदेड़ गीत (एकाकीपन)

कनै कनी बाबाजी कुटणी पीसणी
कनै देणी बाला तैं दूदी हो

सासू छ खराब मेरी
यत देदीं मरौण्या बुद्दी हो
यत दीन्यों बाबाजी बुढया जवैंक
यत दीन्यो सहोर दूरु हो
गैल की गैल्याणी करदी मजाक री
मेरा गला लगदी छूरी हो
यत जाणी बाबाजी छाला डूंगादू
यत लाणी बुटा कू दाऊं हो
स्वामी जी मेरा नजर नी आया
न त आया हमारा गाँव हो
जबरी रौं बाबाजी छोटी लौंडरी
तबरी थौं प्यारी तेरी हो
अब तब औण बाबाजी तेरा घरमा
जब आली मरजी मेरी हो
औंदी दे सासू बासी कोदवा
रूखू सूखू भातेंदू खांदू हो ।।

Song 14

खुदेड़ गीत

पिपला डाली निस मांजी तुरतुरया धारी
मेरा त सैसर माजी दु:ख छ भारी
दै दूध करवन खाण सैसर जैक
उकाली का बाटा जाण लाडू टेकिक
करयां होला भूलि तेरा कर्मू का जाग
रोण नी मेरी भूलि हैंसदा लोग
सूरसूर जगदू भूलि गाड कू पाणी
तेरी दगड़ धोखा हवैगी मैन नी जाणी
कोलई डाली ऐंच भैजी घूधति घूराँदी
मैत की याद औंदी भैजी जिकुड़ी झराँदी
ड्यूटी पर भूली मैत रोज जाणु छौं
तेरी याद औंदी भूली मन मा रोणुछौं

तेरायनि लिख्या रैनी भूली कर्म का जोग
लोगुमा नी रोण भूली हैंसदा लोग ।।

Song 15

स्वामी की याद का वर्णन
खुदेड़ गीत

सौण कुरेड़ी फुर्र-फुर्र उड़दी यूं डांडी काद्यों मा
तुम बिन स्वामी पट मौरी जोलू यूं गैरी गदन्यों मा
मैती नी औंदा किलै नी औंदा ब्वै बाबू भी नी छन
बौ मैजी मेरा परदेश गैन भीण्डी दीन हवै गैन - 2
सौण कुरेड़ी फूर्र-फूर्र उड़दी यूं गाड गदन्यों मा
तुम बिन स्वामी पट मरी जौलू यूं डांडी काठ्यों मा
लुकारी चिट्ठी सरासरी ऐन राती दिन
हमारी चिट्ठी घर नी आई भीण्डी दिन हवैन - 2
नी आला स्वामी पट मरी जोलू यूं गैरी दगदन्यों मा
सौण कुरेड़ी फूर्र-फूर्र उड़दी यूं ऊंची नीसी डांड्यों मा
तुम बिन स्वामी पट मेरी जौलू यूं गैरी गदन्यों मा ।

Song 16

खदेड़ गीत
पति-पत्नि

तु छै मेरी प्यारी गंगा निरदयी समान
छौं मन सी रोणु मैं दगड़या न मान
कुठारी का खाना चन्दा कुठारी का खाना
तू गई न गई चन्दा काफूला का बाना
गुलेर की गारी चन्दा गुलेरी की गारी
द्वी हजार मेजदू चन्दा आज घर बारी
भूजी जाली राई चन्दा भूजी जाली राई
ताजदान सईं चन्दा समलौण रैई
पाणी की परात चन्दा पाणी की परात
बीस गीत औण चन्दा तेरी बारात ।।

Song 17

विविध गीत

किलै बाजी मूरली हो बैणा ऊँची नीसी डाडयों मा ।
तेरी घूर घूर सूणी मैं लगदू उदास ।।
स्वामी मेरा परदेश मैं लगांदू आस ।
भूमि का भूमिया देव धारी दयान ध्यान ।।
स्वामी मेरा परदेश राजी खुशी घर ल्यान ।
बाखरी चदौलू हे देवी मैं तेरा मन्दिर मा ।।
स्वामी मेरा परदेश ऊँ सै राजी खुशी राखी मा ।
देवी भगवानी मेरा रखियाली लाज ।।
स्वामी मेरा परदेश छन मैं छौं यखूली आज ।
चुनरी चढ़लौं हे माता मैं तेरा मन मा ।।
कुशल मंगल मेरा स्वामी घर लेई मा ।
किलै बाजी मूरली हो बैणा ऊँची नीसी डाडयों मा ।।

Song 18

खुदेड़ गीत - पति पत्नी

पत्नी — औंदा सौकार जब कई फेरी
स्वामी जिकुड़ी झूरांदी मेरा
पति — नी रोणू प्यारी नी कनू सोक
तेरा रोयान हैंसदा लोग
पत्नी — यनु समझै थों मैं बाबाजीन
नथूली देलो मै तोला तीन
पति — दुनिया का मन मा पाप हवैगी
हिन्दू धर्म कू यू नाथ हवैगी
पति — कूड़ी पूगड़ी लेक प्यारी त्वैक
बेणवाश हवैगी मैकू आज
पत्नी — ना बोला स्वामी तूम येनी बाणी
मेरी आख्यों मा छूरदू पाणी ।।

Song 19

लड़ाई जांदू राधा (पति-पत्नी संवाद)

पति — मेरा कपडौं मा राछा लै देणी पाणी
मैं लडाई जांदू राछा फिर कभी नी आणी
पत्नी — हाथ खूटा धोलाया स्वामीजी रसाई बणी छ
सच सच बतावा स्वामी जी करव लड़ै लगी छ
पति — घूण्डू-घूण्डू कू कीच रे राधा घूण्डू-घूण्डू कू कीच
लड़ै लगों छ राधा बौडर का बीच
पत्नी — तेल की कड़ाई स्वामी जी तेल की कड़ाई
तुम रावा घर स्वामी मैं जौलू लड़ाई
पति — बटे जाला ढांव रे राधा बटे जाला दाऊँ
तू लड़ै जैली राधा लोग धरला नाऊँ
पत्नी — धार मकी तोण स्वामीजी धार मकी तोण
तुम लड़ै जैल्या स्वामीजी मैन कनई रौण ॥

Song 20

खुदेड़ गीत

तुम त हवैला प्यारा स्वामी दिल्ली सैरू मा
सैरू सैरू जाँदा होला कारू कारू मा
हम घास काटदौं स्वामी धारू धारू मा
पैदल हिरणु स्वामी गारू गारू मा
हाथी खुटयों का बेहाल फटी फटी की
पाताल बैठिग्यों स्वामी घटी घटी की
बदली करावा स्वामी कोटद्वार मा
मैं मिलण औलु स्वामी हरिद्वार मा ॥

Song 21

रामी बौरण — का गीत

बाटा गोड़ाई क्या तेरू नौ छ बोल बौ राणी करव तेरू गौं छः ।
रौतू की बेटी छौं पाली गौ छ सेढू की ब्वारी छौं रामी नौ छः ॥
बटोई जागी ना पूछ मैकू केकू पूछदी क्या चैंदू त्वैकू ।
मेरा स्वामी न छोड़यों मैई घर निरदयी हवै गैन मैई पर ॥

ज्यूंरा का घर नी जगा मैकू स्वामी बिछोय होयूं छ जैकू ।
बटोई जोगी बारा साल हवैन स्वामी जी मेरा घर नी ऐ। ।।
चल बौ राणी छैल बैठी जौला अपणी खरी उखमी लौला ।
जागी हवैक भी आँखी नी खुली छैल बैढली तेरी दीदी भूली ।।
स्वामी सी तेरी अब नी होण भेंट करव रंदान गौं का सरपंच सेठ ।
जोगी न गौं मा आलेख लाई भूखू छौं भेजन देवा माई ।।
रामी तैं रवेतू से बुलौण लैगी झट और ब्बारी घर मा साधू ऐगी ।
झट औ ब्बारी झट कैक घर मा साधू छ भूखू ऐक ।।
रामी रस्वाड़ा मा मिसेगी जोगी माजिम बतोण लैगी ।
मालू का पात मा धारी भात भात मैं तेरा नी लांदू हात ।।
मात नी खांदू मैं खांदू रोटी ब्बारी न तेरी गाली दीनी खोटी-खोटी ।
खांदेंई जोगी व खाई लेयी मी खांदी जोगी त बाटा जैई ।।
रामी तैं स्वामी की याद ऐगी बैठीक घणमण रोण लैगी ।
मैई छौं माता तुमारू जायो आज नौ साल मा घर आयो ।।
रामी स्वामी तैं देखण लैगी मांजी हिया मा चिपकैक रोण लैगी ।
स्वामी तैं गाली दीनी मैन मौत किलै नी आई होली मैकू मौत ।।
चुपरा प्यारी नी रोण त्वैन भगवान भजन मा मन लाई मैन ।
नी रोऊ प्यारी ना हो नाराज अब घर ऐग्यों मैं आज ।।

Song 22

सास बहू का गीत

तेल कड़ाई जनु लायो साग,
तनी मेरी सासू ब्बै तनी भेरू भाग ।
रेड़ी जालु धोलू माकरा बणूमां,
ऐक घर क्या ली जौलु ।
रोली कु मलेऊ घर कू बगत हवैगी,
गडोली संलेऊ ।
कुटला की कूट सैडा बण घूमी,
माजी न पूली न मूट, घर क्या लिजौलु ।
लुहा कु तसालु हल्दी कु रंग थौं,
हयै चुकी मसालू, घर क्या लिजौलु ।

Song 23

स्त्री का दुःख (खुदेड़ गीत)

हाथी फटीनी खुटि वीडेनी मन ज्यू बोल्दू रोण कू
सासू भेजदी घासीला मी तैं बाटू देख्यूं नी बौण कू
खाली गदन्यौन घास मी ल्यौंदू भैंसौं कू तैं हरीऊँ
दूध खांदी बगत बोल्दी सासू तेरा बुबाकु धरयूं
मेरी सिकैत लाड़िक मा लगौंदी मार खलौंदी घर ऐक
हाथी कटीनी खुटि तीडेनी मन ज्यू बोल्दू रोण कू

Song 24

सास बहू का गीत

कनै कनी बाबाजी कुटणी पीसणी
कनै देण बाला तैं दूदी हो
सासू छ खराप मेरी,
यत देंदी मरौण्या बुद्दी हो ।
औंदी दे सासू बासी कोदवा
रूखू सूखू भातेंदू खांदू हो ।

Song 25

सास बहू का गीत

मेरी जिकुड़ी मा कुरेड़ी सी लौंकी
सासू गाली देंदी मैं बाबू की मारी
बासी खाणौं देंदी मैं बोली मारी-मारी
ऊँची डाडयों मा फूली गैन बुराँस
लाल हवै गैनी माँ काफूली की डाली
गौं की बेटी ब्बारी माँ खाली लून राड़ी

Song 26

सास का आन्तक (पारिवारिक गीत)

निकरण सासू त्वैन दिन रात झगड़ा ।
मैन भागी जाण स्वामी जी का दगड़ा ।।

स्वामी मेरा घर आला बैठीक रेल मा ।
सासू तू फूकणी मैन मट्टी का तेलमा ।।
स्वामी मेरा घर आला अग्वाड़ी की सटिमा ।
सासू आग लगाव मैन तेरी पीठ मा ।।
स्वामी मेरा घर आला मैं दिल्ली घमलू ।
त्वैते मेरी सासू मैं खेत मा भेजौलू ।।
दयूर जी खूब चैंदा दयूराण मयालू ।
तेरू त मेरी सासू हम द्वी फूटबौल बणौला ।।

Song 27

आलासी बहू
"आधुनिकता से भरपूर औरत"

खडी उठ धौं ब्बारी नकूल ख्याल
दस बजीगी दिन की तू आंखी खोल्याल
कूरणक देण ब्बारी मा भीतर लुकदी
चश्मा लगैक आखों मा खित-खित हंसदी
भैर औदों ब्बारी जरा धाम देख्याल
दस बजीगी दिन की तू आंखी खोल्याल
घास कू जांदी ब्बारी ठंडू माढू हिरदी
बणम जैक ब्बारी छसियारों का जूं टिपदी
क्यकन यन ब्बारीकू कन फूटी कपाल
दस ब्जीगी दिन की तू आंखी खोल्याल
अंग्रेजी ब्बारी बोल्दी हवेयर इज भाई बाच
छोरा भी मेरू सीधू सादू पकडौंदू तीं तास
काजू बादाम खैक ब्बारी बणी छ लाल
इस बजीगी दिन की तू आंखी खोल्याल ।।

Song 28

"बाजू बन्द गीत"

घर कू बगत हवैगी घर क्या लीजाण ली घर कब जाण ले दगली घूमौ
घर क्या लिजाण ना घासिला होई मेरी मैन घर कन कैक जाण दौ रूमैला बौ

हे नी होलू पज्यार मैणा घर घूमा बाटी ऐली मिमल लीजैन्यार दौ दुदयाल बौ
रीतू ऐगी बौड़ी मैली भैस्यों न क्य खाण दौ रूमैला बौ
झगुली कू मैल भग्यानी विचारी कदी बाजारू की सैल घर जौला बौ
पाणी कू कजार करवी किलै जाण जौला नई टिरी बाजार दौ चलाया बौ
तमाखू की सोड़ टैग्स्यों की लैन लगी नई टिरी की रोड़ दौ घरबारया बौ
अगेला का बासी कखन घूमण जाणी बणूा रैबासी
कागजू का तौऊ तुमारी खबर लेण औंदी गाड़ बौऊ ले घर जौला बौऊ ।।

Song 29

"बाजू-बन्द गीत"

गैल्या गौड़ी देली दूध ले प्यारी ढबकौ की मैं लगदी खुद रणी कनै दौ
मैली गौडी कू चरांत लगी जांदी खुद बैणी बैठयूं तेरू परात सची समझौ
यारी बाखरी बजीदी औणू मैलीबार भारी खुद लगदी डबरींगी दौ
यारी दरी मा पौणक मैं लगदी खुद बैठी ज्यू बोदू रोणक त्वै बैणी का संऊ
यारी तिमलू कू पात व्यूं भूलौं बिगर मेरी मैं लगदू हात रणी कनै दौ
बैणी बोई धाली चीण पट मरी जाण मैली त्वै सैली का बीन सची समझौ
गैल्या सोलू दाणी प्यार द्वीया बच्या चैंदा प्यारी होंदी रली भ्यांर बींगी ली जा दौ
बैणी छोली घाली माठा करवी-करवी बीती बैणी होया हम कठ्ठा त्वै बैणी का सौं
मैली लाल चड़ी गोंदू सोंगा की मिलापी मैं भी तनू बोदू दौ ली सणी बौ
हे माजी भूजी गेंहू धाण दिन को क्रोद बैणी त्वै मजीं लगाण दौ री बाना बौ
गैल्या फांसी मा का कीडा नीं सकदू काम करी हाथूपैरू पीड़ा त्वैमा बोदू बौ
मैली डाली कू हरिल बुझौण्या बुझाये गैल्या ना बुझू शरील फडौं समझौ
यारी मूजी त भंगजीर कुछ बाबान दीनी कुछ तकदीर बींगी ल्यान बौ
बैणी कटेरी मा प्याज बैणी कनै रोण यख बाबाजी की लाल यन बींग बौ
यारी झंगोरू झब्लु बाबाजी की लाल प्यारी त्वै रौण पड़ेलु बींगी ल्यान दौ
हे मां मूजी जालू मास एक दिल करदू बैणी डाली खाण फांस सची समझौ
यारी घूघता की धोली सांगों की छलाया गैल्या तू तनू ना बोली रण कनै दौ
बैणी झगुली कू पल्लू यना कना चैंत बैणी मरणू होंदू भलू यन समझै
यारी झंगोरा की घाण तू लगदी भौज मैन काल भारी मर जाण दौ बिग्याल बौ
हे बौ झंगोरा कू न्यार कना कै टुट्लु माजी मांग कू यू प्यार डर लगी बौ
मैली औलौं कू अचार मैन दुनिया देख्याली पर क्वी नी तेरा चार हे गैल्याणी दौ

बैणी घूघता की धोली मैली यी दुनिया माजी यनु क्वी पंछी नी होली सची लांदू बौ
यारी घूघता कू धोलू त्यारी चारी गैल्या प्यारी कनै कनै होलु दूरया बाना बौ
गैल्या साबण कू गाज कनी करी खौलु मांजी बु पुराणू राज दौ रूमैला बौ
यारी दुकानी की पीन कैमा लाण खैरी डब क्वी अपणू नीन बींगी ल्यान दौ
मैली ग्वाल की मुराश केकू करी बाबा त्वैन मैकू यू दूराश सची समझौ

Song 30

बाजू-बन्द गीत

कागजू का तौऊ मेरी प्यारी छुमा
बल्या पाखा धाम लग्यों छ बल्या पाखा औऊ
तौली पकी दाम हे मेरा ढयूर मैं लगदू धाम
भूजेलू बडयोंकू मेरी प्यारी छुमा
त्वै पाणी पिलौलू मौजी बाज की जड़यौं कू
झंगोरा की दंयो हे मेरा प्यारा दयूर
मैं न्योंदू पल्या कारव मैम घसिला नी होयी
लसपसी खीर हे मेरी प्यारी छुमा
छापा मा छपौलू गैल्या तेरी तस्वीर
बरण कू काज हे मेरा प्यारा दगड़या
घर कू बगत हवैगी क्या लिजौलू आज
घुछता की छोली प्यारी मेरी छुमा बौ
छुआ छुमा सभी बोदा कनी छुमा होली ।।

Song 31

दीपावली का गीत
खुदेड़ गीत

ये दिन का बीच मैन रोटी खाई उबाणी
सैसरी होन्दा यन खराब मैन नी जाणी
कातिक का मैना आई माजी बग्वाली
ढूला मैजी तैं रैग्यों मा जग्वाली
दिवाली का दिन मांजी रोटी खाई उबाणी
गौला लग जांदू माजी नी माणदू पराणी

लूकारी काड़ाई माँ चूला मा चड़ीगी
लोण रोठी खैक तेरी बेटी भूखी पड़ीगी
यू गीलू झंगोरू माजी अद उमालू फाणू
देखि याली मांजी मैन मंख्यों कू खाणू ।।

Song 32

खुदेड़ गीत (परदेश में)

पूगडयों का बीच मा फल फूल
रौत्याली डाडयों मा घसियारी होली
घास काटढी गीत लगांदी
हाथू मा छुणक्याली ढासूड़ी होंदी
पुगण्यों का बीच मा पूगडयों का बीच
सेरौं का बीच मा घास काटदो अ गीत लंगादी
हाथू मा छुणक्याली दाथूड़ी होंदी
तीं धार पोर गोर चराणा
तीं गौड़ी की बाच्छी रामणी होली ।।

Song 33

खुदेड़ गीत

रयाँसू की दाल रयाँसू की दाल
मेरू प्यारू छ टिरी गढवाल
किलै बाबाजी न पढायों लिखायों
किलै चाचाजी न हल्या कू विवायों
हल्या का पिछाड़ी क्या ढिंका गणेन
कलम की हाथ्यों मा छाला फूटेन
रयाँसू की दाल रयाँसू की दाल
मेरू प्यारू छ टिरी गढवाल
किंगरी की जर किंगरी की जर
शराप पड़यान त्वैकू चाचा तू थौं रेंजर
रयाँसू की दाल रयांसू की दाल
मेरू प्यारू छ टिरी गढवाल ।।

Song 34

खुदेड़ गीत (ऋतुयुक्त)

सौण की अंध्यारी रात घनघोर ।
ना बास ना बास हे पापी मोर ।।
नींद लगी मैं झकझोर ।
ना बास ना बास हे पापी मोर ।।
सौण की अंध्यारी रात घनघोर ।
ना बास ना बास हे पापी मोर ।।
रूण झूण-रूण झूण बरखा लगीगी ।
मैसण मैत की याद आइगी ।।
काखड़ी मूंगरी पकण लगीगे
मैण मैत की याद आइगे ।।
भैंसी दूदयाल गौड़ी ब्याई छ:
मैत बिटिन माजी की चिट्ठी आंई छ:
सौणा की अंध्यारी रात घनघोर ।
ना बास न बास हे पापी मोर ।।

Song 35

खुदेड गीत (मायके में न आ सकने के कारण)

सबेर उठीक मेरी मांजी आय गमजाई ।
अपणु प्राण मेरी मांजी अफू ही समझाई ।।
काखडी की राई मांजी काखडी की राई
मेरी जगाा पर मेरी मांजी फूक डाली लाई ।।
तोडी जाली टांटी मांजी तोड़ी जाली टांटी ।
मेरा बांठाकु खाणु मांजी भुलौंमा बांटी ।।
शेरा की तुवार मांजी सेरा की तुवार ।
त्वैम जब औलु तब आली मुखड़ी मा अन्वार ।।
बिछै जाली दरी मांजी बिछैं जाली दरी ।
मेरा बांढा कु खाणु मांजी दुंगा मति धरी ।
अब बुरांश फूली गैन त्यूं डाडयों जौला ।।

भूजी बणाई तरकारी मांजी भूजी बणाई तरकारी ।।
कनै औंण भैजी न मैम मेरू भैजी रौंदू डयूटी सरकारी ।।

Song 36

खदेड़ गीत (पति-पत्नि)

नत रंत रैबार भेजी नी देढां चिट्ठी घर बण सी सैत मेरी किस्मत फूटी ।
सारा लग्यूं रौंदू स्वामी चिट्ठी का बाना पोस्ट मैन जी होरू पूछणक जांदू डाखाना ।।
हे जिहोरू चिट्ठी भी आई छा हे जिहोरू चिट्ठी भी आई छा ।
क्वी नी सुणदु मेरी भैसी भगवान रूढी घरबण सी सैत मेरी किस्मत फूटी ।।
तनु ना बोल प्यारी मेरी किस्मत फूटी कौन की नौकरी छ नी मिलदी छूट्टी ।
चमचम व राजू अब दूध नी फेंदू देली मा भऐक पिताजी भटयांदू ।।
हे पिताजी तुम कख चली गया हे पिताजी तुम कखी देखेदांनी ।
औड़ लंगादु ऊ रात मा उठीक घरबण सी सैत मेरी किस्मत फूटी ।।
लाल स्याही लेखिक त्वैक आलू तार मेरा राजू की माँ तू हवै ना लाचार ।
जिकुड़ी मा लैगी गोली जब कनु छौं डयूटी फौज की नौकरी छ नी मिलदी छूट्टी ।।
नत रंग रैबार भेजी नी देढां चिट्ठी घरबण सी सैत मेरी किस्मत फूटी ।
तनु ना बोल प्यारी तेरी किस्मत फूटी की नौकरी छ नी मिलदी छूट्टी ।।

Song 37

खुदेड़ गीत

उड़िजा कागा बादलु बीच मेरी मांजी मा मेरू रैबार लिजा ।
चौक अग्वाड़ी चुलु की डाली ज्वीं नीस बैठी होली मेरी मांजी ।।
उड़ीजा कागा बादलु बीच मेरी मांजी मा मेरू रैबार लिजा ।
सोना न तेरी चोंच मणौलु चाँदीन तेरा पंख गड़ौलु ।।
रैबार देदेयी मेरी मांजीमा बाबाजी मेजी मैते लोण कू ।
उड़ीजा कागा बादलु बीच मेरी मांजी मा मेरू रैबार लिजा ।।
उड़ीजा कागा बादलु बीच मेरा बाबाजीमा मेरू रैबार लिजा ।
बाबा मा बोली कागा अफू आन नितर मैं लेणक मैजी भेज्यान ।।
उड़ीजा कागा बादलु बीच मेरी मांजी मा मेरू रैबार लिजा ।।

Song 38

विविध गीत (शौर्ययुक्त)

झगोरा कू बोट गणेशी झंगोरा कू बोट ।
मी जांदू लडै गणेशी छोड़ मेरू कोट ।।
साग की कड़ै सिपैजी साग की कड़ै ।
तुम खा घर सिपैजी मैं जांदू लड़ै ।।
त्वैकू न्यारा सौऊ गणेशी त्वैकू मेरा सौंऊ ।
तू जैली लड़ै गणेशी लोग धरला नौंऊ ।।
कू बगोति बरड़ी सिपैजी कू बगेति बरड़ी ।।
धार जाण जौलू सिपैजी तुमारी ब्बै करड़ी ।।
जूड़ी मार फन्द सिपैजी जूडी मार फन्द ।
जा मेरी प्यारी सिपैणी घर तू छै आसामन्द ।।
धारमा की तोण सिपैजी धारमा की तोण ।
मेरा पेट जनन्यू चजू तुम जन होण ।।
हंसुली गढै गणेशी हंसुली गढै ।
नौनु होई जालु सिपैणी अंगरेजी पढै ।।

Song 39

"आलसीपन का विविध गीत"

ज्यादा नी होण मेरी ब्बारी धुमण्या ज्यादा नी होण मेरी घुमण्या
झट छोरान मनीआर्डर करी चली जांदी डाखाना ज्यादा नी होण
चम्बा बाजार घुमणक जांदी पेट पीड़ा का बाना
पेट पीड़ा का बाना तेरी खुटी घुमण्या ज्यादा नी होण मेरी ब्बारी घुमण्या
छुपछुप गैल्याण्यों दगड़ करदी व करार
चला गैल्याण्यों घुमणक जौला नई टिरी बाजार नई टिरी बाजार तेरी खुटी घुमण्या
ज्यादा नी होण मेरी ब्बारी घुमण्या – ज्यादा नी होण मेरी ब्बारी घुमण्या
मन रंगमत तेरू ब्बारी कुमण्या ज्यादा नी होण मेरी ब्बारी घुमण्या
लाल रंग का सैंडल पैरदी, वसन्ती रंग की साड़ी
थौल मेलों मा ब्बारी मेरी पैरो जांदी अग्वाड़ी
काम काज की डर ब्बारी सांदी लुकण्या ज्यादी नी होण मेरी ब्बारी घुमण्या – 2
गौं करवी पंचैत आज ब्बारी करवी जा जाणी
छोरा छ मेरू सीधू सादू ब्बारी वणी सयाणी

ब्बारी बणी सयाणी मेरी ब्बारी घुमण्या ज्यादा नी होण मेरी ब्बारी घुमण्डा - 2

Song 40

बाजूबन्द गीत (लड़का एवं लड़की)

लड़का — हे लाडी ग्यौं जौ का ये खील
हे लछी न्यारू मन लैगे हे लछी तेरी हरसिल
हे लछी न्यौन्यालु जाटू की हे छत तेरा हरसिल
लड़की — हे गौल्या हिसर कू गोन्दा हे गैल्या हिसर कू गोन्दा
हे गैल्या त्वै जना कति लोग बल यख माया लाण ओन्दा
लडका — हे लछी हैंसी गाड़ी पैसी हे लछी हैंसी गाड़ी पैसी
हे लछी तेरा बिना है लछी अब नी रयौंदू मैसी
हे लछी न्यौन्यालु जाटूकी हे लछी नी रयौंदू मैसी
लड़की — हे गैल्या बुणी जालु माणू हे गैल्या बुणी जालु माणू
हे गैल्या हम बाखखयों कू हे गैल्या टेकू ना ठिकाणू
लड़का — हे लछी सिंया की सिंयाली हे लछी सिंया की सिंयाली
हे लछी भली माया लायी हे लछी लोड़ ना लठयाली
हे लछी न्यौयालु जाटू की हे लछी तोड़ ना लठयाली
लड़की — हे गैल्या कोट कू बटण हे गैल्या कोट कू बटण
हे गैल्या माया लाणी सौंगी हे गैल्या निभैणी कढण
लड़का — हे लछी बाखूरी का गौंणा हे लछी बाखूरी का गौणा
हे लछी ज्वानी पाई त्वैन हे लछी फिर बौड़ी नी औण
हे लछी नौन्यालु जाटूकी हे लछी फिर बौड़ी नी औण
लड़की — हे गैल्या बुणी जालु खेस हे गैल्या बुणी जालु खेस
हे गैल्या छै मैना हरसिल डाडोंमा छै मैना रिसीकेस
लड़का — हे लछी ग्यौं जौ ये खील हे लछी ग्यौं जौ का ये खील
हे लछी ग्यारू मन लैगी हे लछी तेरा हरसिल
हे नौन्यालू जाटूकू की लछी हे लछी तेरा हरसिल

Song 41

बाजूबन्द गीत

क — भैजी माचिस की तीली मैं मौत दिन हवैगी मै माजी नी मिली खुद लैगी बौ

ख — खल्याणी की दांदी खुदेणी मौसम बैणी मैं खुद लैगी जांदी ले घर आली बौ

क — झल्ल कू यू रीक ले हे मेरी माला तू खुदेंद कीक ये रूमैला बौ

ख — खोती मा की या धाण उलारया पराण मेरू कु बुझालू खुद लगी बौ

क — भैजी सिन्दुर की डब्बी आपणी माजी मा भेजी उड़ी जौं क्या अभी दौ रूमैला बौ

ख — बाड़ी खैंडी तौला हे मेरी रूमैला माला सरासरी औला खुद लगी बौ

क — भैजी टमाटर की क्यारी वो हे मैं खुद लैगी भैज्यों की मचदौं की न्यारी कनै ऐलु बौ

ख — नी खुदेण त्वैन माला हेरा गुला त्वै मिलण आला माला तेरा भुला हे रूमैला बौ

क — हे भैजी खल्याणी की दांदी वो ऋतु बौड़ी औंदी खुद लगी जांदी कनै रौण बौ

ख — रयांसू की रौड़ी डांडयों का उरांश उड़ी ऐगी ऋतु बौड़ी मेरी बाना बौ

क — कागजू का चाक वो बाबाजी नी देंदा जाणा बिदेशी छ लोक वो कनै शैलु बौ

ख — वालसू का छाना मांजी छोडी अपणी त्यौं विदेश्यों का बाना माला विदेश्यों का बाना

क — भैजी कागजू का चाक बाबाजी की इज्जत छ वो बचौण नाक कनै रौलु बौ

ख — भैली चूड़ी कांच विदेश्यों की बोली होंदी प्यारी जन हरसिल की लांच मेरी बाना बौ

क — भैजी गुलर की गारी वो आंख्यों न डरौंदा ल्वाक धम औंदा मारी कनै शैलु बौ

ख — शैला तोड़ी बौला हे मेरी माला बौजी सला एक जौला दौ रूमैला बौ ।।

Song 42

बाजूबन्द

थफुला का थरी तेरी याद औंदी गैल्या खुदे खुदे भारी
झंगोरा की दांऊ जा पापी सौण प्यारा मादौं औऊ खुद लगी बौ
चांदी का बटण विदेश्यों की गैली भाभी दिन कन कै कारण
बासी जालु मोर भैजी बैठयां होला मेरा मां होरू का घोर
हिसरी कू गौंदा परदेशी लोग माजी निदर्यी होंदा हे लगुली बौ
बटण का काज पंछी होंदू उड़ी जांदू प्यारी माम आज भैजी मेरा औ
रेड़ी जालू धौलू बाकरा बणूमां ऐक घर क्या लिजाण बौ
रोली का मलेऊ घर कू बगत हवैगी गडौली सलेऊ घर जौला बौ
कूटला की कूट सैडा बण घूमी माजी न पूली न मूट क्या लिजौलु बौ
लूवा कू तसालू हन्दी कू रंग थऊ हवै चुकी मूसलू सच्ची बोदू बौ ॥

Song 43

बाजूबन्द गीत (जंगल में गाया जाने वाला गीत)

लड़का घूधती की धोली है पाखा की घस्यारी कै गवां की होली ।
लड़की झंगोरा की दाँव तेरा नजदीक गैलया, गैल्या मेरू दऊ गांव ॥
लड़का पकी जाला खैणा कै गंवा की है तू यनि मयालु मैणा ।
लड़की झंगोरा की दाँव तेरा नजदीक गैल्या, गैल्या मेरू छऊ गाँव ॥
लड़का घूधती की घोली त्या बाजूबन्द लाण वाली कै गंवा की होली ।
लड़की पाणी की परात गौं कू नौ बतौलु छोरा मेरी गैल औऊ ॥
लड़का पाणी भरी भर घर जाण कु टैम हवैगी चल गैल्याणी घर ।
लड़की घूघता की घोली मेरी जिया मांजी कै जगामा होली ॥
लड़का रोठी खाई आधा मैं खुद लगीगे गैल्या तेरी अब जादा ।
लड़की झगुली कु मैल मैं खुद लगीगे गैल्या औंदू तेरी गैल ॥

SECTION IV

WORK ROLES AND ACTIVITIES PERFORMED

Song 1

(औरत के काम का वर्णन)

सबेर उठीक मोल गाडणी

चायी कु बूंद पेणक नी देणी सुण ल्या बाबाजी
बासमती सूधी मैन कुटिक ल्योण
खाण कू कोद की रोठी मैकू देण सुण ल्या बाबाजी
बासमती सूधी मैन कुटिक ल्यौण
खाणकू गीलू झंगोरू मैकू देण सुण ल्या बाबाजी
बसग्याली मैना रूणझूणा पाणी
नांगा खूटियोन कन जाण धाणी सुण ल्या बाबाजी
धोती कटिगी घूण्डू घूण्डू मा
बरखा लगदी नांगी मूण्ड मा सुण ल्या बाबाजी
भैजी कु बोली तू मैम ऐई
मेरा हाल तू अपणा आँख्यों देखी जैई सुण ल्या बाबाजी
भैजीन करी रूप्यों कू जोर
बाबा ना दीन्यौं चौ डांडा पोर सुण ल्या बाबाजी ।।

Song 2

खदेड़ गीत

अनपद छौं मैं नी छ ध्यान - 2
भवासी पार लगावा भगवान - 2
परधेस मति छ मेरी सारी
मेरी नाऊ तैं तू पार कैरी
पूस का मैना की जाडी की बार - 2
घास तैं जाण धमिली धार - 2
आयी अषाड़ रोपणी लाण - 2
सुबेर उठीक पुगड़यों लाण - 2
य चिट्ठी मेरी पौछे देण
भायों सी मैन आशीर्वाद लेण
नी आला स्वामी नी आला घार - 2
डाखाना जाण सबेर कन तार - 2

Song 3

खुदेड़ गीत (कठिन काम का वर्णन)

लगदू धाम लगदी तीसा झट पसीना चूभदा कीसा

चैत बैशाख ऐन गैन गैल्याणी औलुकु मैन गैना
चैत बैशाख ऐन गैन मेरा भैजी मैम नेन
नी रोण छोरी पूसा ऐ जालू भैजी त्वैतैं मैत ली जालू
लगदू धाम लगदी तीसा झट पसीना चूभदा कीसा
माजी पिताजी मेरा मैं याद ऐना गैला की बाडूली गौला मा रैन
छोटा भूला भतीजा मैं याद ऐना त्यौंकी खूद बिसरौण कना
लगदू धाम लगदी तीसा झट पसीना चूमदा कीसा

Song 4

काम का गीत

रेडी जालु धौलु बाकरा बणुम ऐक,
घर क्या लिजौलु ! घासीला नी हवै !
टोली का मलेऊ घर कु बगत हवैगी,
गडौली सलेऊ ! घर जाण ले !
कुटला का कूट सैडा बण घूमी माजी,
न पूली न मूट ! क्या लिजौलु दौ !
लुवा कू तसालु हन्दी कू रंग छऊ,
हवै चुकी मसालू ! चल घर औ !

Song 5

औरत की विवशता (काम का बोझ)

कू ल्यालू न्यार कु ल्यालू पाणी घर आया मैमान यन मनख्यों मा ।
कू जालू पन्यार कू ल्यालू भरी पाणी घर आयां मैमान यन मनख्योंमा ।।
कू बिछालू दरी यना मनख्यों मा ।
कू हेरलू घरबार यन मनख्यों मा ।।
कू धाण कू जालू कू देलू न्यार पाणी ।
कू पीसीक ल्यालू मेरू घटवाड़ी यना मनख्यों मा ।।
दयूराणी मेरी मैत की ख़ुदयारी ।
जेठाणी मेरी नौन्यालू की दुदयारी ।।
कू ल्यालू न्यार कू ल्यालू पाणी घर आया मैमान यन मनख्यों मा ।
सासू की मार जेठाणी की गाली यना मनख्यों मा ।।
औरों की खचक मैकू बार-बार यना मा कुहेरदू घरबार यना मनख्यों मा ।।।

Song 6

खुदेड़ गीत

हे सीलू घस्यारी सीलू बटणु का काज - 2
तेरी नौनी छ छोटी सीलू यखी रैजा आज - 2
खल्याणी कु दांदू सीलू खल्याणी कु दांदू
घास की बगत सीलू मैं घासीला जांदू - 2
कुटला की कुट सीलू कुटला की कूट
दिवरी का ढंगार सीलू तेरी छुटगी मूट - 2
दयी की दयाल सीलू दयी की दयाल
तब जैली घासक सीलू पैली रोटी खयाल - 2
खल्याणी कु दांदू सीलू खल्याणी कु दांदू
मेरू शरील छ नखरू मैं रोटी नी खांदू - 2
थेपी जाली रोटी सीलू थैपी जाली रोठी
पैली दूध दियाल सीलू तेरी नौनी छ छोटी - 2
लेखी जाली पाटी सीलू लेखी जाली पाटी
दिवरी का ढंगार सीलू तेरी लगेन छाटी - 2
हे सीलू घस्यारी सीलू तेरी लगेन छाटी
चवनी की मेखी सीलू चवली की मेखी
हे गौं की घस्यारयौं तुमन मेरी सीलू भी देखी
आलू भरीं धाणी सीलू आलू भरी धाणी
हम ऐगे या घर सीलू गंदिलू थैं ल्यौणी - 2
सूधा लाया कोणी सीलू सूधा लाया कोणी
गौं का घस्यारा सभी ऐगा सीलू तेरी नौनी छ रोणी ।।

Song 7

दुख भरा गीत

हे नौनी हे नौनी तू रोंदी केक
उदासी तेरा मन या औंदी केक
उभागी प्रतिभा छौंऊ मैई
मैत भी हरची मैकू तैंई
आंखों मा आंसू जना मोती झलकण्या

ओंस की बून्द जना भ्वां मा परकण्या
बटोई भैजी ना पूछ मैक
केकू पूछदी क्या चैन्दू त्वैक
बटोई भैजी न पूछ यनी बात
दिन क्या दोफरा मैकू रात
जीवन बितैयाली रूखू सूखू
काल भी नी रै पख मैकू
मैती भी दुश्मन यना हवैना
हात रंगेन मेरा जन ल्वेना
खून चूसीक त्यू हवैन मोन
पंत बिगाडयाली मेरू त्योंन
अपणू बिराणू क्वी नी मेरू
कूजणी कथैं अब डेरू मेरू
मैती न खीती छः मेरू कुई
जीवन बीतीगी अब रोई-रोई
सुणबैं नौन्ना तू मेरी बावी
पापी पाखण्डयों की पख जाणी
गंगा गोमती छन द्वीई बैणी
ये पाप धौणकू होली दैणा

Song 8

औरत-आदमी का संवाद

वै देश जौला भण्डारी झमको,
जै देश मेला मा खेती झमको ।
जै देश चुलखंदा पाणी झमको,
जै देश मी हौंदी गाणी झमको ।
जै देश कोदा कु तेल झमको,
जै देश लइया की बाड़ी झमको ।
जै देश घिडंवा पदान झमको,
जै देश सेंटुलो दमैया झमको ।
जै देश घुघुती गिवेर झमको,

जै देश कागा डुलेर झमको ।
जै देश जौला भण्डारी झमको,
जै देश जौला भण्डारी झमको ।

SECTION V

SONGS DESCRIBING THE BEAUTY OF A WOMAN

Song 1

औरत की सुन्दरता का वर्णन

केन होये केन होये कुंडी काजोल
के होये केन होये सुरीज घुमैलो
नहेण लागी लक्ष्मी जी की लाड़ी
तब होये तब होये कुंडी काजौल, सुरीज घुमैलो ।
केन होये केन होये सिन्धु, छल्वार ?
नहेण लागी पार्वती जी की बेटी,
तब होये तब होये सिन्धु छल्वार ।
केन होये केन होये ये धौली घुमैली
नहेण लागी सीता जी की लाड़ी
तब होये तब होये धौली घुमैली, सुरीज घुमैली ।

Song 2

सौन्दर्ययुक्त (औरत की सुन्दरता)

हयूचली डाडयों पिछनै होली बांद मुखड़ी ।
बादल्यों का बीच होली जन चांद टुखड़ी ।।
बतौ मेरा भाग त्वैन कब घर जाण ।
कब दिखेली कब मिलली कब आलु प्राण ।।
फर फर हवा मा होली लटुली उडाणी ।
रूण झूण बरखामा होली घास कू जाणी ।।
फर फर हवा मा होली लटुली उडाणी ।
घास की गडोली होली मुण्ड मा थामणी ।।

बतौ मेरा भाग त्वैन कब घर जाणी ।
यीं बरखा का झवीड़ों मा मैन घर कनै जाणी ।।

Song 3

सौन्दर्ययुक्त (लडकी की सुन्दरता का वर्णन)

जब जांदी कौथिग सुमणी सैल्यों दगड़ी बैठली ।
हरिया साड़ी लाल बिलोज मथबेंडू मुण्ड बांधली ।।
ल्यावा स्वामी चाय पकोड़ी अफू अगनै सरकदी ।
हरिया साड़ी लाल बिलोज मथबेंडू मुण्ड बांधदी ।।
जब जांदी कौथिग सुमणी सैल्यों दगड़ी बैठली ।
हरिया साड़ी लाल बिलोज मथबेंडू मुण्ड बांधली ।।
जब जांदी कौथिग सुमणी सैल्यों दगड़ी पैटली ।
गोरी गोरी हाथ्यों मा सुमणी काँच की चूडी पैरली ।।
जब जांदी कौथिरा सुमणी सैल्यों दगड़ पैटली ।
लम्बी लम्बी लटुली तैंकी पीठ पिछाड़ी लटकली ।।
हरिया साड़ी लाल बिलोज मथबेण्डू मुण्ड बांधली ।।।

Song 4

विविधा गीत (औरत की सुन्दरता)

रूप कीं रजज्यानी भग्यानी कनी छैं
धार मकी गैणी दिखेंदी जनी छै
चौंठी मकु तिल तेरू घबराप्या दिल मेरू
हंसदी बगत गल्वाड़ी मा पिल पड़दू तेरू
फूलों की सूंठ बिगरैली जनी छैं
रूप की खज्यानी भग्यानी कनी छैं
लटली घुंघरयाली तेरी आखें रतन्याली तेरी
हाथ खुटा गंदक्याल मांस दांतूड़ी क्या बोलो बात
डाडियों कू हयूलांर दिखेंदी जनी छैं
रूप की खज्यानी भग्यानी कनी छैं ।।

Song 5

सौन्दर्य युक्त

कै गंवा की होली छोरी तिमलू दाणी
मठु मठु हिरण तेरू कै गंऊ जाणी
लाखों मा विधाता जी न मुखड़ी पछाणी
बान्दू मकी बान्द जनू तिमलू दाणी
पछूंडी देख्याल जरा मुक बतै दी
चांद मुखडी कु दर्शन करैदी
जिंदगी छ छोटी छोरी माया लगैदी
गैणा भी नी पैरयां तभी भली दिखेंदीं
मरी जाण मिटि जाण नी रण यख
माया लगै देण छोरी मन मा जैक ।।

Song 6

लड़की की चंचलता के बारे में

कै गौंऊ की होली यनी चबराट्या छोरी
आंखी तींकी काली जनी मुखड़ी छ गोरी
कालेज मा पड़दौं सिरिदेवी छ नौऊ
परधान की नौनी सिलकोटि छ गौंऊ
मोल मोल छोरा जन टेमरू की दाणी
यन सजी धजीक त्वैन कै गौंऊ जाणी
सिरिदेवी मिथून जनी भई या जोड़ी
अब हवैगी छोरा रात अब हवैजा तू गोल
मोल मिलणकू ऐ छोरा चम्बा का थौल

SECTION VI

SONGS OF DISSENT, PROTEST, SOCIAL CHANGE

Song 1

शराब का गीत (उपदेशात्मक)

संसार का लोगू संसार मा क्या ।

संसार का सुर्रा-शराब ना प्या ॥
सत्संग का बीच मा खराब ना हवा ।
संसार का लोगू संसार मा क्या ॥
झोपड़ी बीकीगी शराब ना प्या ।
डोखरी बीकीगी शराब ना प्या ॥
थकुली बीबीगी शराब ना प्या ।
संसार का लोगू संसार मा क्या ।
संसार मा सुर्रा-शराब ना प्या ॥
संसार का लोगू सत्संग बैठा ।
संत्सग मा रैक कुछ ज्ञान सीखा ॥
संसार का लोगू संसार मा क्या ।
संसार मा सुर्रा-शराब ना प्या ॥
उत्पाद करदान शराब पिंदारा ।
गौली गुएण्डी मरदान शराब पिंदारा ॥
शराबी का नौना हमेशा रौंदा ।
दुनिया का विस्तर मुण्ड मा उठौंदा ॥
शराबी की जनानी हमेशा रौंदी ।
लुकारा घर-घर जैक भाण्डा मठौंदी ॥
संसार का लोगू संसार मा क्या ।
संसार मा रैक शराब ना प्या ॥
गली गुएण्डी मरदान शराबी ।
दुनिया मा मेरा भयों या छ खराबी ॥
सत्संगी लोगू ना दुनिया थाम्याली ।
संसार मा रैक नौ भी कमाली ॥
संसार का लोगू संसार मा क्या ।
संसार मा सुर्रा-शराब ना प्या ॥

Song 2

बिमला घस्यारी

होंदू सबेर नकूल खां दीन ।
गौं की घस्यारी घास कू जाँ दीन ॥

बिसुणी म बात बैठीक लाँदीन ।
सयाणी घस्यारी कू बोल्यूं मांदनी ।।
प्यारी बिमला छ नयी घस्यारी ।
देखिक बण भूलिगे होस्यारी ।।
होन्दू.....................घास कू जाँदीन ।।
उकाली कू बाटू, हिरदी ठमा ठम ।
खूटयों कि पौजी, बजदी छमा-छम ।।
बिमला घस्यारी छ बारवीं पास ।
आंगली कटी गी नी कटेई घास ।।
होन्दू.....................घास कू जाँदीन ।।
कुछ मैनों का बाद बिमला घस्यारी ।
घास कारण म पैगी होस्यारी ।।
बिमला बोल्दी छ मेरी दीदी भूल्यौं।
तुमारा गुणौं तैं मैं कभी ना भूलौं ।।
होन्दू सबेर नकूल खाँदीन ।
गौं की घस्यारी घास कू जाँदीन ।।
प्यारी बिमला समझौंदी सबू तैं ।
नाम लिखणू सिखौंदी सबू तैं ।।
पढ़ी लिखी नारयों मनु काम करा दौं ।
अनपढ़ नारयों तैं, लिखणू सिखा दौं ।।
होन्दू सबेर नकूल रंवादीन ।
गौं की घस्यारी घास कू जाँदगी ।।

Song 3

विविध-गीत

बेदू पूराणू सब माँछ यू साप
बेटी बिकौणी अति छोर पाप
नान्याल जै गर्भ न जन्म लेन्द
जैजाद कू मालिक नौनू ही होन्द
नौनी कू पर्मोल हजार होन्द
अनर्थ अब यू होण लैगी

गौडी सी कन्या यख बिकण लैगी
बेटी बिकौणी अब छोडी देवा
नौन्यों कू हिस्सा कू आशीर्वाद लेवा ।।

Song 4

दहेज (उपदेशात्मक)

दैज की चर्चा जगा जगा बणीगी ।
कमर कू शूल बरमण्ड मा चड़ीगी ।।
जोड़ी जूगती सी जू पैसा कमाई ।
भूखां तीसा रैक स्यू उधार भी ल्याई ।।
घरवार गिरवी दहेज का बाना ।
दहेज भीकट पर भई जमाना ।।
नौनी भी भाइयों बड़ा घर बेवाई ।
दिखेण दर्शनू कू भी खूब जवाईं ।।
अपणा बूरा हाल छोरी कू छ तराष ।
कम दीनी दैज सैसरियों की ठणास ।।
देंदारा लेंदारा कैकु भी नी चैन ।
कैकी बिकी कूड़ी क्वी बोदगौं मा गैन ।।
दहेज का बाना रख जीवन नीराश ।
बड़ी बड़ी घटनौं कू यख छ वास ।।
कुई आड़ी फूकेंदी क्वी गंगा देंदू फाल ।
कैन खाई फांस कैन फोड़ी कपाल ।।
ना देवा दहेज नौन्यौं पढावा ।
जै घर मा चैन वै घर बेवावा ।।
ना देवा दहेज ना देवा दहेज ।
यीं परथा रोका ना करा तेज ।।
मोल लीक खडी ना करा यीं बीमारी ।
मनखी चैन्दु देख्यूं नी देखा तिबारी ।।
कन्यादान छ देवतों समान ।
दहेज की इच्छा राक्षस करदान ।।

Song 5

नया जमाना

चुपख्यली बणीगे सची उखल्यारी आज
भांती भांती की मशीन्योन कनु खोई साज
गाड गदीन्यों घट लग्यां छ अब हवैगी चक्की
कुरण पिसणक बेटी ब्बारी जांदीन तखी
घटकू पिस्यूं आटू छऊ जन मखन
जांदरी सिले गैन भायों देखण करवन
जांदरी जगा बेटी ब्वारीयों न फुर्सी बणाली
गिजालों का छिलका बणै आग ताप्याली
पैली जमाना बेडों नाच अब छ फिलम
छोरा छोरयों कु घर मा रैणु हवैगे जुलम
पैली जमाना सबुकी देखा मैरा आंगुड़ी
कटुवा बिल्वाज अब नांगी पाखुड़ी
छोरों की देखा अब छयीं पटपटी पैंट
बैठण भी किलै तौन बिना सोफा सैट
पैली जमाना रीतिरीवाज धरम करम
बेटी ब्वारयों की नांगी मुडली नी छ शरम
अब देखा बेटी ब्बारयों की नयी-नयी शान
साड़ी का पला बेटी ब्बारयों का गीचौं किरयांन
सभी भाई बन्दु ना लगा गीचौं बुज्याड़ा
यांसी जादा नयु फैसन कतै नी गाड़ा
चुपख्याली बणीगे सची उखल्यारी आज
भाँती-भाँती की मशीन्योन कनु खाई साज ॥

Song 6

पौराणिक गीत (संस्कृति)

करव लुकी होला रीती रीवाज पुराण ।
अब नी सुणेन्दा ऊपण्डों का पांवाणा ॥
करव गैवा अंगूडी वा टालों कू लवाणू ।
हरची कूलैं डाली झंगोरा कू वू खाणू ॥

करव गैन कुठार बू दाबला वू पुराण ।
अब नी सुणेन्दा ऊ पाण्डों का पंवाणा ।।
करव गै ऊ जांदरी वू उखल्यार कू कूटणू ।
करव गै वू बेटी ब्वारयों कू रतब्याणी उठणू ।।
बांजा पड़ीगैन घट वू गिंजाला पुराण ।
अब नी सुणेन्दा ऊ पण्डों का पंवाणा ।।
पैली लांदा थैं लोग खैरी छोटी बड़ी अपणी ।
करव गै ऊ चौखबा डिंडालों की कछड़ी ।।
करव लुकी गैहोला दाना उ सयाणा ।
अब नी सुणेन्दा ऊ पाण्डों का पंवाणा ।।
पैली थौंऊ बेढों नाच हरची ऊ रिवाज ।
करव गै ऊ देवी देवता हरची वा शक्ति आज ।
करव गैन ढाक ढकिरया ऊ लोग पुराणा ।।
अब नी सुणेन्दा ऊ पण्डों का पंवाणा ।
करव लुकी होला रीती रीवाज पुराणा ।।
अब नी सुणेन्दा ऊ पण्डों का पंवाणा ।।।

Song 7

औरतों ने खूद बनाया है

चम्बा सैर भलू बसीगी काणताल की रोड़ मा - 2
छोटी दुकानी बीच बाजार बड़ी दुकानी छोड मा - 2
चम्बा कु कालेज बोदू अवादौं छोरों लिखा पड़ा - 2
सड़की पर घूमी फिरीक बीड़ी तम्बाखू ना फूका - 2
सड़की फणा घूमी फिरीका बूरी बात ना सीखा - 2
पन्वाड़ी कू पान खयाली कस पड़ीगी धोती मा - 2
पन्वाड़ी कू पान बिकिगे सिकरेरयों की बत्तियों मा - 2
चम्बा सैर भूलू बसीगी नई टिरी रोड़ मा - 2 ।।

Song 8

विविध गीत (कमली पर दर्शाया गीत)

बीटा तोडी दलका कमली, वीटा तोडी दलका

त्वैन कन चोरीन कमली चिरात्यौं का छिलका
बकसू का खाना कमली, बकसू का खाना
त्वैन मारी मार कमली, छिलबटयों का बाना
मांजे जाला भड्डू कमली, मांजे जाला भूड्डू
त्वैन कना खाई कमली, चिरात्यौं का लड्डू
पाणी भरी छार कमली; पाणी भरी धार
जब ऐली धार कमली, त्वैन खाण मार
पाणी भरी धार कमली, पाणी भरी धार
तेरू जवैईं कमली आज, आणु वालू छ धार
मांजे जाला भड्डू, कमली मांजे जाला भड्डू
कना सुन्दर मणेन्दा कमली चिरात्यौं का लड्डू ।।

Song 9

विविध गीत

हे मेरी घस्यारी बौ दाथूड़ी का छणका बजौ
वीराणी सरीम गै तागत की धौंस मा
गाँव वालों न लूटीयाली इज्जत छ खाक मा
सर रर पतरोल छुटि बन्द बण घसियारी
लुटि हे मेरी घस्यारी बौ दाथूड़ी का छूण का बजौ
सर रर पतरोल छुटि बस खाला घस्यारी
लुटि हे मेरी घस्यारी बौ दाथूड़ी का छूणका बजौ
मैं तेरी गैल छौं हे मेरी घसियारी बौ दाथूड़ी का छूणका बजौ
सर रर पतरोल छुटि डांडा बिटि घसियारी
लुटि हे मेरी घस्यारी बौ दाथूड़ी का छूणका बजौ ।।

Song 10

बिना धुवी की चूली (पर्यावरण गीत)

दीदी-भुल्यौं अब तुम ना, खा पिछाड़ी।
बिना धुआँ कि चुली बणौण मा अवा अगाड़ी।।
सांइस कु जमानू ऐजी, मनखी चांद मा जैगी,
गौं गौं या बिजी ऐगी, तेरी चुली स्या तनी रैगी।।

धुवां होंदू ज्यू खुदेंदू जगदी नीआग।
आक्ष्यों या अंसधारी चूंदि पकदू नी साग।।
दीदी भुल्यौं अब तुम ना खा पिछाड़ी।
बिना धुवां की चूली बणौण अवा अगाड़ी।।
तीं भीतरी धुवां अति, हौंदी खराब मति,
भड्यों की होंदी कुगति, चुला बणौण की ऐगी मैं रीति।।
चुली बणावा बिना धुवां की, रैली सफा हांडी,
लगला म लाखड़ा रस्वैमा, सजली भांडी।।
दीदी भुल्यों अब तुम ना खा पिछाड़ी।
बिना धुवां की चुली बणौण मा आवा अगाड़ी।।
निर्धूम चुली बणैल्या, चीज द्वी कट्ठी पैल्या,
आंख धुवां सी बचैल्या, रोठी द्वी सुख सी खैल्या।।
ना करा देर बिना धुवां की चुली लगावा।
चुली लगाला सिखैली, वाल, ये धुवां अगावा।।
दीदी भुल्यौं अब तुम ना खा पिछाड़ी।
बिना धुवां की चुली बणौण मा आवा अगाड़ी।।

Song 11

विविध गीत

काली चुड़ी काँच माँ काली चूड़ी काँच
हर्सिला का डांडा मा बादल की लांच
मेरी गंगा मा बादल की लांच।
लणि काटी द्वारी माँ लाठी काटी द्वारी
कैकी बगी बेटी माँ कैकी बगी ब्वारी
एंछी गाड़ी पैंछी मां ऐंछी गाड़ी पैंछी
कणी डूबण लगी मां गूजरू की भैसी
छाला दूध लस्सी माँ छाला दूध लस्सी
कनी डूबण लगी माँ सैणु उत्तरकाशी
काटी जालू धोल माँ काटी जालू धोल
कैकी बगी छोती माँ कैकी बगी सौल।।

Song 12

भूकम्प (उत्तरकाशी का)

होला विधाता जी कना रूठी गैन क्यछ तेरू विधान रे
गढ़ कू गढ़वाल देवलों की भूमि कनी पड़ीगी रे सुनी
सौण बीती जनु, भादौं बीतीगी चैत सी बीती असूज रे
सी लोग बिज्यां थान भगवान औंदा बग्वाली दीन रे
संगरांती कातिग तीन गति की रात तीन बजी की वा बात रे
सभी सुनीन्द सेंयां भगवान ऐगी स्यू पापी भूचाल रे
गीड़ गीड़ थर थर भर धरती कांपिगे तूफान जनी भौण रे
सुणी नींद मा सबून भगवान गाड़ी डर की डेकणी रे
टुटु कुड़ी सारी दबगी कुटुमदारी टुटेन बिजली का खम्बा रे
सारी दुनिया मा अंध्यारू छायूं कू बची होलू भग्यान रे
उत्तरकाशी का घामक गाँव हे लोगू सुण्याला हाल रे
नी रै तख आज भगवान क्वी पाणी देंदारू रे
यीं टीरी लमगौं या बागी भरपूर पिपलोगी सारू भैगू रे
खण्डवार हवैगेन कुड़ी सारी कैकित मरी मवासी रे
क्वीदीन गंगोरी सारू मानपुर कीशनगढ़ मा नेई रे
देखिक दब्यां मुरदा भगवान छाती मा लगी तीर रे
कैकी टूटी हाथी भौतौं की छाती आँखी फूटीन कपाली रे
जैंन भी देखी हालत त्यौंकी गंगा जी मा दीनी फाली रे
होला विधाता जी कना रूढयां आज क्य छ तेरू विचार रे
गढ कु गढ़वाल देवतौं की भूमि सारी पड़ीगे सूनी रे

Song 13

सौन्दर्या (ग्राम की)

द्वीई खायौं का बीच मा बह्यू कोटि गाड़ छ नाम
सुणा याद रख्यां दीदौं यख छ सोना कू धाम
पूफू पूफ्याण चाचा भतीजा रंदा यख छ समाज
राम जी कू नामं लेंदा कनि रौनक छ आज-आज
नीगी रावत और पुण्डीर तीन छन जात
और छन ठाकूर रंदा ये गाँऊ माज

कनि रोनक छ यख कोटिगाड़ छ नाम
सुणा याद रख्यां भैज्यों यख छ तैलू घाम
जब गाऊँ मा मिटिंग होंदी-2 सभी बैणी काम छोड़दी-2
माता बैणी सबी औंदी-2 कनू प्यारू लगदू तौंकू समाज
राम जी कू नाम ल्यौला कनि रोनक आज
शशी बैण गँउ मा ऐन-2 कनि अच्छी शिक्षा तीन दीनी-2
माता बैणी जगराण ह्वैन-2 गाली गलोच अब नी रैन-2
कनू प्यारू छ बैण्यों तौंकू समाज
राम जी कू नाम लेंदा कनि रोनक आज
हमारू अध्यक्ष धाकड़ छ भारी-2 करवी घपला होंदू
त चलदू अखाड़ी-2 माता बैणी सबी दौड़दी अग्वाड़ी पिछवाड़ी
तब लगदू प्यारू तौंकू समाज रामजी कू नाम ल्यौला... आज
यूं मैला मण्डल तैं तूम ऊँचू रखावा-2
शिक्षा कू प्रकाश तूम गौं गौं मा फैलावा-2
बेटी ब्वारयों तैं अच्छी शिक्षा दिलावा-3
तब लगलू प्यारू तौंकू समाज-2
रामजी कू नाम ल्यौला कनि रौनक आज-2

Song 14

महिला मण्डल

हे दीदयों हे भूल्यों मैला मण्डल बणौला
अपवू जीवन कन कैक बितौला-2
अपणा हाथ की रसीद बणौला
जिला अधिकारी तैं गौं मा बुलौला-2
अपणा गौं की अत्याचारी दिखौला
जिला अधिकारी तैं गौं या बुलौला-2
बेली सारी बिटिन मोअर की रोड़
गौं का ऐंच मा टेंरूसूं कू तोड़-2
हे भाई बन्धो उण्डू फूण्डू हेरयाला
अपणा गौं का अत्याचारयों देख्याला-2
तीन सूत कू पाणी खतम करयाली

मोट्या घूघतन अत्याचार करयाली-2
हे भाई बन्दों क्य कल हमन
सएि अत्याचारी करयाली तुमन-2
पिछल्यारी का घूघतन जू जेल भोग्याली
तेई अन्याई घूघतन अन्याई करयाली-2
दस लाख की नैर खतम करियाली
प्यापार वालों न या नैर खयाली-2
हे भाई बन्दौं उण्डू फूण्डू हेरयाला
अपणा गौं का अच्चाचारयों देख्याला-2
मथली सारी हमारी ढूगौंन भरयाली
लेबर वालों ना गन्दगी करयाली-2

Song 14 Contd :

जल निगम के कार्या (व्यंयग से पूर्ण)

जल निगम वालों न अत्याचारी करियाली
डिग्गी तोड़िक फैणैय धरियाली
मुण्डैण कु पाणी खत्म करयाली
जल निगम वालों ने लैटरिंग बैठाली
हे भाई बन्धु क्य करयाली तुमून
पाणी का बदला क्य प्यणी हमून-2
जल निगम वालों न पाइप तोडियाली-2
लेवर वालों न रू पैप दियाली
पैप तोड़िक फणै म धरयाली
लेवर वालों न आंतक मचाली-2
सारी जिन्दगी फौज मा बिताली
घर बैण्कि दूँगा की लगाली
हे भैजी तेर दूंगा की लगीगी
तै दिन विटी मंडल बणीगी-2
धरमा आजीक तरखीबू चलेगी
हे भैजी धरमा पर दूंगो की लगीगी
धरमा गोरख्याणी न भीतर लूकाली

अपण गोरख्या भैरमा मराली-2
छोटा मोटा ठेकेदारों न बाटू तोडियाली
गौऊ की धौण मा दायूली ठोक्याली-2
हे भाई बन्दू करव जाणी हमन
सारी जिन्दगी होण बरबाद तुमन-2
दारू पीक बरबाद नी होण
अपणू जीवन बरबाद नी करण-2
दारू पीक जीवन खोयेन्दू
बेटी क्बारीयों क भौं कुछ बोलेन्दू-2

Song 15

नकोट शहरी की रोड

अहा नकोट की लेन मोटर चली खाँ-खाँ
नकोट की लेन मोटर चली खाँ-खाँ
चीणी जाली सीड़ी बल चीणी जाली सीड़ी
कठूड़ भग्याल सौडा देखा सवारियों की भीड़ मोटर चली खाँ-खाँ
सर्र: सर्र सिरंयारू औणु गजा डांडा खार
सीशों करयाला बन्द यख जुखाम की डार
नकोट की लेन मोटर चली खाँ-खाँ
गैंड अग्वाड़ी देखा कना छन दौंड
हौरन दियाला जरा चिड़याली का बैंड
नकोट की लेन मोटर चली खाँ-खाँ
खाड़ी जाजल अब ऐगी फकोट
मंसूरी जाँदारा बूढया बुढ़डी छूटी गैन नकोट मोटर चली खाँ-खाँ
गाड़ी हौरन दयाणी काईबाई नी करयान्
आगरा खाल का ताता छोलों न गीचों ना फूक्यान्
नकोट की लेन मोटर चली खाँ-खाँ
गाड़ी पौंछगी अब सैणा ऋषिकेश
धूलू माटू झाड़ियाला ढालूवा का ढेस-मोटर चली खाँ-खाँ
नकोट की लेन मोटरं चली खाँ-खाँ।

Song 16

जख देखा खाली जगा वृक्षारोपण (पर्यावरण)

जखभी देखा खालि जगा तख लगावा डाली।
भिनम की हो बाँज की हो, चौड़ीपती वाली। जख भी . . .।
गौंका अग्वाड़ी-पिछवाड़ी, क्वी जगा खाली नी रौ।
घासक तैं दूरू न जा, औ भूली डाली लगा।।
पेंणका पाणींकि अब, पट सुखिगी खाली। जख भी . . .
धारू गाडू डांडि-काठ्यों, डाल्योंकि हरियाली हो।
आमकी हो अखोड़की, बादाम की डाली। जख भी . . .
गौं गऊँमा जैंनभी जख, चुलु डाली पाली छ।
खांणक तैं लांणक तैं, तेल देण वाली छ।
जखभी देखा कंडि उखेड़ा, लिप्स्टि की डाली।
माटु खोंदी पाणी पेंदी, पूंजिपती वाली। जख भी . . .
डाली लगौंणी बचौंणी, आज बड़ो धर्म छ।
गौं का अग्वाड़ी-पिछाड़ी, फल-फुलुकी डाली हो।
दुनियाँ का खातीर अग्वाड़ी, बड्डु भारी शुभकर्म छ।
गौं गऊँका मिलि जुलिक, यों रखा जग्वाली। जख भी . . .।

Song 17

लोक गीत

पार की बीड़ा कु छैं घस्यारी
मालू रे तू मालु ना काट
मालू काटली त पाप लगलु
वार डांडयों की मैं छौं घस्यारी
मालू रे तु मालू काटण दे
भैंसी ब्याई छ थोरी हवैई छ
मालू रे तू मालू काटण दे
मैं तेरी स्याली तू मेरू भेना
मालू रे तू मालू काटण दे
मैं तेरू भेना तू मेरी स्याली
मालू रे मालू ना काटि

दीदी कुछ बाछी प्यारी
मैंकु छ भैंसू प्यारू
मालू रे तू मालू काटण दे
वीं भैंसी सैण ढौंड हैरा दौं
मालू रे तू मालू ना काटि
मालू काटलि त पाप लगलू
मालू रे तू मालू ना काटि।।

APPENDIX - II

वार्तालाप :
सुमा देवी से वार्तालाप। स्थान-पीपली गाँव

पहले के लोगों का काम था सुबह भोर में उठना, नाश्ता करना व एक साथ मिलकर जंगल में जाना व लकड़ी काटना और जंगल से कच्ची लकड़ी काटकर लाना। सूखने के बाद लकड़ी जलाने के काम में लायी जाती थी। कहीं तो गाँवों में अभी भी इस प्रकार का रिवाज दिखाई देता है। उन दिनों सबको अपनी-अपनी ओड़े (काठगुल) होती थी जो कि बीते हुए बरस की होती थी। कठगुल अपने घर के आगे होती थी। काँटे कि जो लकड़ियाँ होती थी उनके काँटे साफ किये जाते थे तथा उसके पश्चात उसे लकड़ी के साथ एकत्रित किया जाता था। लोगों का काम सुबह उठना था पानी लाना तथा आटा की पिसाई करते थे। आटा की पिसाई भी दो तरह की होती थी। एक तो महिलायें सुबह उठकर अपने घर के अंदर जो चक्की (जांदरी) होती थी उसमें पीसती थीं तथा दूसरी प्रकार की पिसाई घराटों में जो कि पानी से चलती थी उसका एक ही मालिक होता था जो आटा पिसाई के बाद आटा ही लेता था पैसे नहीं। गाँव के कई लोग इकट्ठा होकर वहां जाते थे तथा कभी कभी तो रात को उनका नम्बर आता था तो वे अपने पीसे हुए आटे में से कुछ आटा निकाल लेते थे जिसकी की वे रोटी बनाते थे रोटी वे तसाले में बनाते थे। तथा पानी के किनारे से पोदीना लेकर रोटी के साथ चटनी बनाकर बड़े चाव से खाते थे वह भी एक प्रकार का पिकनिक था। वहां पर जो सुविधायें हैं गीत गाये व समय व्यतीत किया। हर कार्य का समय होता था। मान लो शादी विवाह या अन्य बड़ा कर्म है तो कहां से पीसेगा इतना। पिसाई व कुटाई का भी दिन होता था। इस दिन गाँव की महिलायें इकट्ठी होकर आटा पिसने आ जाती थी उस दिन उनका खानी भी वहीं पर होता था इसको सामूहिक कार्य कहते थे। एक दिन मसालों की कुटाई व पिसाई का होता था। इस प्रकार सामूहिक कार्य करने का अपने आप में एक मनोरंजन था ।सारे कार्य समुहों में होता था।

वार्ता : ''भवानीदत्त जी से''

अगर तुमसे हमदर्दी होती तो तुम्हारे पैर में जूता होता, सिर पर छाता होता क्योंकि वहां तो ओले गिरते हैं तथा बारिश भी होती है। तुम्हारे सर पर छाता

नहीं है तथा पांव में जूता भी नहीं है। यहां की स्त्रीयां गांव भर में नंगे पैर जाती हैं और पुरूष लोग जब यहां से वहां जाते हैं तो उनके पैर में जूते होते हैं तथा लम्बे-लम्बे जुराब होती हैं। उनके पास छाता भी होता है और वह यदि दुकान तक भी जाये तो सज-धज कर ही जाता है, वह जहां भी जाये वह प्रत्येक घर में जा सकता है उसके लिए सबके मकान खुले हैं लेकिन औरत बेचारी क्या करे वह किसी के घर में नहीं जा सकती क्योंकि उसने जेवर पहने हुए हैं जिन्होंने उसे अपने घेरे में जकड़ा हुआ है। वह इस घेरे से बाहर नहीं जा सकती उसे भय है कि अगर कहीं बाहर निकलेगी तो उसके जेवर कोई छीन लेगा। तथा भय भी होता है कि उसके साथ बाहर कुछ अहित न हो जाय। यहां औरतों पर हमदर्दी नहीं रखते हैं आदमी अपने आप शराब पीते हैं और ताश खेलते हैं, वे औरतों को अच्छे कपड़े भी नहीं पहनाते, धोती बिलोज उनकी फटी हुई होती है। मर्द लोग उनके बारे में कुछ भी नहीं सोचते थे। वे जंगल में अकेली जाती हैं, घास काटती हैं लेकिन मर्द लोग घर में ही बैठे रहते हैं। जंगल में काँटे होते हैं रीछ होते हैं, बाघ होते हैं लेकिन और क्या करे उसे तो जंगल से घास लाना ही है। इन सब बातों का अर्थ यह होता हे कि औरतों से मर्द लोग इतना प्यार नहीं करते यहां तक कि उनसे कुछ भी काम करने को कहते हैं।

''गढ़वाल में वृद्धा गोमती से वार्तालाप'' व उसके जीवन में कठिनाईयाँ

इस वार्ता में गोमती नामक महिला है जो वृद्ध हो चुकी है अब वह पैंसठ (65) वर्ष की है तो वह अपने बीते हुए जीवन के बारे में कह रही है कि जब मैं जवान थी तो मैं सुबह 4.00 बजे प्रात: उठ जाती थी उठकर गोबर साफ करती थी, उसके बाद पानी के लिए जाती थी जो कि तीन या चार बार लाना पड़ता था। तब जाकर रात खुलती थी, इस बात को सब लोग जानते हैं उसके बाद ढंगोर (मडुवा) कूटती थी। झंगोरा कूटने के बाद खेतों में जाती थी तथा वहाँ से 1.00 बजे वापस आ जाती थी उसके बाद ही खाना खाती थी। उसे जिस समय पानी भी नहीं था उसी समय पानी भी लाना था क्योंकि बिना पानी के और काम भी रूक जाते थे। पानी लेने के लिए जब जाती थी तो घर के बर्तन भी साफ करने के लिए पानी के धारे (स्त्रोत) में ही ले जाती थी तथा वहीं पर पेड़ के नीचे दो मिनट आराम करती थी। पानी भरने के बाद बर्तन पानी लेकर पापस घर आ जाती थी तब तक चौक में झंगोरा कूटने के लिए रखा रहता था। एक ही टाइम के कूटने

से पूरा नहीं पड़ता था क्योंकि उस समय परिवार बड़े होते थे लेकिन घर में जो बहू होती थी उसको अधिक काम करना पड़ता था। झंगोरा या सारी (धान) कूटने के बाद मवेशियों का गोबर दूबारा साफ करना पड़ता था तथा दूबारा खेतों में काम करने जाना पड़ता था तथा साथ के साथ घास भी काटना पड़ता था। वह कहती हैं कि मैंने अपने जीवन में बहुत कठिनाईयाँ झेली हैं। मुझसे ज्यादा शायद ही किसी ने इतनी कठिनाईयाँ खा (झेली) रखी हैं। हमारे यहां से बनाली पन्द्रह मील दूर है जहाँ मुझे घास के लिए जाना पड़ता था पैर में चप्पल भी नहीं रहती थी नंगे पाँव जाती थी व घास काटकर लाती थी। लोगों को किसी-किसी को सुख था लेकिन मुझे कोई सुख नहीं था तो मैं दु:खी होकर गीत गाया करती थी उस समय जिसको दु:ख रहता था वह गीत गाता था लेकिन जिसको दु:ख नहीं रहता था वह नहीं गाता था। जिस समय मेरा लड़का हुआ उस समय मुझे नए गेहूँ की रोटी खाने के लिए मना कर दिया कि लड़के की तबियत खराब हो जाएगी उस समय मैं मडुवे की रोटी खाती थी उसमें भी मुझे ही मेहनत करनी पड़ती थी क्योंकि मडुवे को मैं ही पीसती थी और उसके पीसने के बाद दो रोटी बनाती थी तथा उसी को खाती थी। इस प्रकार से मैंने अनेक कठिनाईयों का सामना करते हुए अपना जीवन बिताया।

वार्तालाप

गंगाप्रसाद बहुगुणा से। स्थान : रानीचौंरी (टिहरी)

गढ़वाली लोक गीतों में लोंग पक्षियों पशुओं से वह बादलों आदि से बात क्यों करते हैं खास तौर पर औरतें ही ज्यादा बातें पशु पक्षियों से क्यों करती हैं?

ऐसा ही आपने कालीदास की रचना मेघदूत तो पढ़ी होगी उसमें लिखा है कि एक यक्ष होता है जिसको कि इन्द्र देव ने देश निकाला दे दिया था, तब वह अपनी पत्नि को याद करता है और बादलों से कहता है कि हे बादल तुम मेरी पत्नि के पास जावो व उसे संदेश देना कि उसका पति यक्ष का हाल समाचार इस प्रकार है व ऐसा हो गया है, यह कल्पना यहां पहाड़ी क्षेत्रों व पर्वतीय क्षेत्रों में है क्योंकि उनको पशु-पक्षियों पेड़ पौधों व रितुओं से लगाव है ऐसा इसलिए है कि वे प्रकृति के बिल्कुल नजदीक है इसलिए व अपनी भावनाओं को व्यक्त करते हैं जैसा कि यह है मेरी प्यारी घुघुती जैली, मेरू मांजी कू संदेश लेली। यहां जो पक्षी घूघुली है तो यह यहां के लोगों के बिल्कुल निकट है। यह कबूतर

जाती का पक्षी है जिसका नाम घूघुली है। इसके बहुत गीत हैं यहां पहाड़ों में।

गढ़वाल की स्त्री शायद जो अपने विचार महसूस करती है इसलिए वह अपने विचार इंसानों से ज्यादा पशु पक्षियों, पेड़ पौधों व वनों से व्यक्त करती है, अपनी बात को अपनी अभिव्यक्ति को वह पेड़ पौधों व बादलों के द्वारा करती है। वैसे भी पुराने लोगों का कहना है कि कबूतर व कौआयं जो पक्षी हैं, संदेश ले जाने का कार्य करते थे क्या ये सत्य है?

हाँ, राजा लोगों के पास ये होते थे लेकिन ये कल्पनायें इनके अंदर नहीं हैं बड़े-बड़े राजा लोग कबूतर कुत्ते दुनिया भर के जानवर पालते थे व उनको सिखाया जाता था।

इस प्रकार जो है न कि वो पक्षियों को अपनी सहेलियां मानते हैं। सहोयोगिनी अपना दुःख नहीं बाँट सकते, जेसे घर के आंगन में सास है जेठानी है ननद है उनके सामने अपनी जो भावना है वह कह नहीं सकते और जंगल है तो पह आपको जवाब नहीं दे सकता शायद यह मेरा अपना सोचने का ढंग है।

देखिए काल्पनिक दृष्टि से देखिए न वन में जब सीता का हरण रावण करके ले जाता है तो राम वन के पशु-पक्षियों व जंगल से पूछता है कि -

"हे खग है मृग मधुकर श्रेनी तुमने देखी सीता मृग नयनी।"

तो राम जो है वृक्षों, जानवरों से पूछता है इसलिए कल्पना तो पहले से ही चली आ रही है।

जैसे राम ने कल्पना करता है वैसे ही गढ़वाली महिलाओं ने कल्पना की है गीतों में देखिए ये तो हमारी कल्पना है तथा उन्हीं कल्पनाओं के आधार पर हमारी महिलायें गाती हैं, जैसे कवि ने कल्पना की है गीतों में, कालीदास ने कल्पना की यक्ष व बादल में।

एक चीज और भी है कि जितने गढ़वाली लोकगीत मैंने सुने हैं तो उनमें जंगल का बहुत महत्व है लोकगीतों में इसका क्या है? क्या ये हमारा क्षेत्र हमारी संस्कृति को उजागर करती हैं? अगर क्षेत्र को माने जहां घर बने हैं, जहां हम रहते हैं तो वन का महत्व अधिक क्यों आता है इन गीतों में ?

वन का बहुत महत्व है इन गीतों में ऐसा है कि वनों पर ये गाँव आधारित हैं वन हैं तो गाँव हैं और यदि वन नहीं है तो गाँव भी नहीं है तथा वनों से इनका लगातार सम्बन्ध है, बचपन से ही स्त्रीयां सुबह वन को जाती है, पशुओं को ले जाती हैं, चराती हैं व उसके बाद घर वापस ले आती हैं। अपनत्व ही इनका वनों

से जुड़ा हुआ है और वनों से सम्बन्धित गीत हैं लगाव भी है क्योंकि सारा जीवन ही वनों पर आधारित है गाँवों का।

ऐसा है इस गीत को धार्मिक गीत भी बोल सकते हैं भक्तिगीत भी इसको बोल सकते हैं। इस गीत में यह बोलते हैं कि देवता किसने रचे हैं, पार्वती की रचना किसने की है, गणेश जी को किसने बनाया है, किसने चार थनों वाली गाय की रचना की है, किसने दो थनों वाली माँ की रचना की है, दो थन की माँ होती है न और चार थन की गाय, इन सबकी किसने रचना की है। हे प्रभु भगवान किसने पंचनाम देवताओं को रचा है, पंचनाम देवता होते है न, पंचनाम जो है तो बद्रीनाथ है उसमें पाँच देवता हैं। हे प्रभु जी इनकी रचना किसने की है, मैं आपसे पूछ रही हूँ कि देवता किसने बनाये हैं ये वह भगवान से विनती करती है कि ये सारे देवता किसने बनाये हैं, वह कहती है कि यह सारी रचना किसने की है। तो इसको आश्चर्य है एक औरत को कि पूरी पृथ्वी के बारे में पूरे संसार के बारे में। यह ईश्वर को धन्यवाद दे रही है कि हे ईश्वर यह पृथ्वी, पशु पक्षी, पर्व ये सारी चीजें जो आपने रची है वह कैसे कैसे बनाये। चार थन की गाय बनाई तथा कैसे-कैसे इनके आकार बनाये।

गाय और माई गाय के साथ उसने तुलना की है माँ की जो कि एक स्त्री का प्रायवाची भी है, गाय के चार थन होते हैं तथा माँ जो है वो दो थन वाली है और देखों इनके शरीर से दूध निकलता है। तथा जिसने यह पृथ्वी बनाई है तो वह तो बड़ा महादान है क्योंकि भूमिदान तो सर्वश्रेष्ठ दानों में से है जो कि तुमने मनुष्य को दे दिया है, जो चीजें तुमने रची हैं दुनिया में, उसके लिए तुमने पृथ्वी की रचना की है, तो कितना बड़ा दान तुमने कर दिया है। कितने प्रकार के प्राणियों को तुमने जन्म दे दिया है वह इस गीत में ईश्वर को धन्यवाद दे रही है

अच्छा ये गीत महिलायें कब गाती हैं?

किसी पर्व में जब महिलायें दर्शन के लिए जाती हैं तो उनको बड़ा आश्चर्य होता है कि किसने यह पर्व बनाया होगा।

पर्व क्या होता है?

पर्व यानि धार्मिक, मजहब, त्यौहार, उत्सव आदि।

ये गीत कब गाये जाते हैं?

दीपावली में, होली में, बसंत पंचमी में ये गीत गाये जाते हैं जो कि भक्ति गीत हैं जिनको की किसी भी त्यौहार में गा सकते हैं।

इधर (गढ़वाल) में जो लोकगीत होते हैं वे किने प्रकार के होते हैं?

गढ़वाल में लोकगीत अलग प्रकार से बंटे हुए हैं, जो कि किस्म-किस्म के हैं जैसे कोई कारूणिक है, प्रकृति से सम्बन्धि है और आजादी से भी सम्बन्धित हैं, किसी घटना पर भी हैं जैसे कि किसी को बघेरा (बाघ) उठाकर ले गया, कोई पहाड़ से गिर गया, कोई नदी में गिरकर बह गया हो कैसे कैसे यह उनके साथ घटित हुआ यह सब लोकगीतों में गा देते हैं सौंदर्य गीत भी हैं और एक जो कि संदेश देते हैं उसका भी गीत है, देशभक्ति के गीत हैं, धार्मिक गीत हैं तो गीत तो बहुत प्रकार के है इसमें ऋतु गीत भी हैं। ऋतु गीत में बहुत लम्बा सा मुझे याद नहीं है लेकिन थोड़ा सा उदाहरण मैं आपको अवश्य दूंगा। वैसे बहुत सी महिलायें इसको क्या बोलती हैं जैसे कि ऋतु है मान लो वर्षा ऋतु है इसका गीत इस प्रकार है जो कि लोकगीत है:-

रूण झूण बरखा का छूम छूम छोया मैकू सूझीं छ रोण की।
आलण का बीच छान्यौं मा बोदी भैंसी ब्याई छ सौण की।।
रूण झूण बरखा का छूम छूम छोया मैकू सूझीं छ रोण की।
दूध वचाला खीर खाला गोंदगी खला नौण की।।

इस प्रकार के लोकगीत आपको मिलेंगे! इसका अर्थ है कि वर्षा ऋतु का मौसम है और हल्की-हल्की बारिश की बूंदे पड़ रही हैं तथा श्रोत जिनको की छोया बोलते हैं जिसके कारण मुझे रोना आ रहा है कि अच्छा लग रहा है। छानी बोलते हैं सिषनेबल मकान जिसमें कि ऋतु परिवर्तन होने पर गढ़वाल के लोग अपने मवेशियों को ले जाते हैं। यह एक प्रकार का मकान ही होता है जो घर के मकान से छोटा होता है इनमें भैंसों व अन्य जानवरों के छप्पर के कमरे बने होते हैं तथा रहने के लिए बरामदा भी होता हे। यहाँ गढ़वाल में पशुपालन ज्यादा है इसिलए कुछ मवेशी छानियों में रख देते हैं तथा इसलिए वह स्त्री यह कह रही है कि छानी में भैंस ब्याही होगी और इसके घरवाले जो कि छानी में हैं इस भैंस का दूध निकालेंगे इसको गरम करेंगे उसके पश्चात् वे खीर बनायेंगे और बचे हुए दूध की मट्ठा करेंगे जिससे कि मक्खन (नौण) निकालेंगे और मक्खन की डली खायेंगे ताकि आलण (हरे-भरे) में मजे-मजे से रह रहे होंगे।

वार्तालाप श्री प्रताम शेखर से
उत्तराखण्ड जन जागृति संस्था। स्थान : खाड़ी जाजल (टिहरी)

संपूर्ण क्रान्ति स्वर्गीय जयप्रकाश नारायण जी के समय से चली आ रही है। उनके लिए हम लोगों ने भी कार्य किया। सन् 1970 में जब उत्तर प्रदेश

सरकार ने वनों की कटांत पर पाबन्दी लगाई और हमारे लोगों का जंगलों में लकड़ी काटना बन्द हो गया उसके पश्चात् हमने सोचा कि अब क्या करना चाहिए लेकिन कंटात बन्द करने के पश्चात् भी जब बनों का कटांत पूर्णतः समाप्त नहीं हुआ, तब हम लोगों ने चिपको आन्दोलन के कुछ सदस्यों का सहयोग लेकर एक संगठन बनाया व माना कि हम शेमुल घाटी को चम्बा व नरेन्द्रनगर विकास खण्डों को अपना कार्यक्षेत्र मानते हुए तथा यहाँ पर जो भी कार्य करेंगे उसे उत्तराखण्ड जनजाती संस्था के नाम से उसके पर्चे छापकर इस संस्था का गठन करेंगे, व किया भी जिसको कि करीब करीब 10 या 12 वर्ष हो गए हैं। इस संस्था को हमने पूर्णरूप सन् 1983 में दिया तथा तब से यह संस्था लगातार अग्रसर है तथा इस क्षेत्र के विकास का कार्य कर रही हे। इस सस्था के प्रारंभ होने के समय जो सदस्य या व्यक्ति हमारी संस्था के लिए कार्य कर रहे थे उनमें हमारे मित्र श्री विजय जगहार जी इस संस्था के सीचव थे तथा मैं इस संस्था का अध्यक्ष था तथा आज भी हूँ। हम संस्था वाले अपना मूल लक्ष्य विशेषकर स्त्रीयों व बच्चों को मानते हैं क्योंकि पहाड़ों में स्त्रीयाँ व बच्चे अधिक संख्या में मिलते हैं कारण उनके आदमी अपनी रोजी-रोटी कमाने के लिए विवश होकर पहाड़ों से पलायन करते हैं। स्त्रीयों व बच्चों के बाद वृद्ध लोग भी ग्रामों में मिल जाते है। संस्था के गठित होने के शीघ्र पश्चात् हमने कार्य किया वह था पर्यावरण की जानकारी अपने भाईयों व बहिनों तक पहुँचाना इसके लिए हमने पाँच भाईयों व पाँच बहनों का नारा जो चिपको आन्दोलन को दिया था उसको अपना ध्येय व लक्ष्य मानते हुए काम किया जिसके लिए हमने (1) होडप (2) फिओन (3) फिलोट (4) फर्टिलाइजन तथा (5) फाइवर इन पाँच प्रकार की पौधशालाओं की नर्सरी से हम लोगों ने विभिन्न प्रकार के पौधे बंटवाये जो कि हमने गांव-गांव में वितरित करवाये जिनको की बहुत कम दामों में तथा कहीं-कहीं पर तो हमने इस पौधों को मुफ्त में भी वितरित किया। महिलाओं के संगठन बनाये तथा उनको सलाह दी कि आपके पास दो प्रकार की भूमि है एक तो वह जिस पर खेती होती है तथा दूसरी प्रकार की वह जो बंजर पड़ी हुई है पहले प्रकार की भूमि तो पैदावार की भूमि है तो उसकी जो मेड़ (बीटा) है उन पर भी पृक्षारोपण करो व अन्यों से भी करवाओ तथा बंजर भूमि पर भी घने वृक्ष लगवाओं तथा अन्य प्रकार की जो कि पंचायत के अधिनिस्त आती है तथा यह सामुदायिक भूमि है हमने उस पर भी पेड़ लगवाये। हमारी संस्था ने जरदार गाँव में वनीकरण का कार्य किया जो कि संस्था के द्वारा किया गया तथा गाँव

में व्यक्तिगत वृक्ष दिये गये। डैंकण व भिमल अत्यधिक मात्रा में वितरित किये गये कारण ये वृक्ष कम समय में जैसे 2 या 4 सालों में संपूर्ण वृक्ष बन जाते हैं। इससे हमारी महिलाओं पर कार्य का बोझ कम पड़ा। इनको जंगल न जाना पड़े व जंगलों की सुरक्षा हो सके। महिलाओं का जो काम करने का समय था वह सुबह 8 बजे से 12.00 बजे तक खेतों में रहती थीं तथा इस दौरान उनके बच्चे गलियों व गाँव के मौहल्ले में घूमते फिरते थे काई बच्चा गिर रहा है तो किसी के गिरने से चोट लग जाती है इसके लिए भी हमने लगभग सभी गाँवों में बालमन्दिर विद्यालय भी खोले हैं जिसमें कि बच्चा अपनी पढ़ाई भी करे व गली मुहल्लों में घूमने से भी बचे। यह भी हमारा अपने आप में एक ध्येय था जिसे भी हमने लगभग पूर्णरूप दे दिया है। हम लोगों ने गाँव में जो दूसरा अत्यंत महत्वपूर्ण कार्य किया वह था वह था शौचालयों को बनवाना क्योंकि यह भी एक अत्यन्त आवश्यकता है आजकल के वातावरण को देखते हुए हमारी माताओं व बहनों की शौच इत्यादि जाने में कई कठिनाईयों का सामना करना पड़ता है क्योंकि अब न तो घने जंगल हैं जिनमें कि वे आराम से शौच का त्याग कर सके इसलिए हमने शौचालयों के निर्माण पर विशेष ध्यान दिया और यह कार्य भी धीरे-धीरे उन्नति के मार्ग पर चल रहा है आजकल आपने भी देखा होगा कि लगभग प्रत्येक गाँव लोगों के निजी व संस्था द्वारा निर्माण किये हुए शौचालय हैं, इससे प्रत्येक नागरिक को सुविधा प्राप्त हुई। शौचालयों के निर्माण के पश्चात् हम लोग यह भी सोच रहे थे कि हमारे पहाड़ों में टीकाकरण भी नहीं हो पाता है। बहुत सी मातायें व बहने टीकाकरण के अभाव में प्रसव के दौरान अपनी जान तक गंवा बैठती है कारण कि उनको समय पर टीका (जो कि नियमित) होना चाहिए प्राप्य नहीं हो पाता व उनको प्रसव भंजन हो जाता है। ऋतुओं की वजह से हमने उन्हें इन्डोर (घरों के भीतर) में उन्हें परिशिक्षण दिया जिसकी विशेषता है प्रसव के समय की परेशानियों का निदान। इन सब बातों को ध्यान में रखकर हमने उनके स्वास्थ्य का भी ध्यान रखा। हमारे पहाड़ों में जल संरक्षण की भी परेशानियाँ हैं, वर्षा ऋतु में हमारे मकानों की छतों में से पानी कमरों में आता है जिसके निदान के लिए भी हमारी संस्था कार्य कर रही है।

यूरो सिमेट का कार्य भी हमारी संस्था कर रही है। महिलाओं में संगठन का कार्य भी जारी है। महिलाओं से शराबबन्दी की ट्रेनिंग दी जा रही है। सन् 1988 में हमने इस कार्य को प्रारंभ किया था जो कि जरधार गाँव से प्रारंभ हुआ। रामपुर के लिए हमें Vaish Land Development की ओर से अनुदान मिला था।

APPENDIX - III

"भौगोलिक एवं ऐतिहासिक पृष्ठभूमि"

गढ़वाल की भूमि

हिमालय के पाँच खण्डों में से एक खण्ड केदार खण्ड को भी माना जाता है। यही केदारखण्ड आधुनिक गढ़वाल है। गढ़वाल की भूमि में देवी व देवताओं का पवित्र स्थान है। इस भूमि में ऋषि मुनि रहते हैं यही उनका पवित्र स्थान है। यह प्राचीन भूमि इलावृत, ब्रह्मपुत्र, उत्तराखण्ड, रूद्र-हिमालय, चुल्लु-हिमवंत आदि नामों से ख्यात रहा है। हिमालय गढ़वाल की भूमि है, हिमालय के दो खण्ड शास्त्रों में विशेष रूप से पावन माने जाते हैं - (1) बद्रीकेदारखण्ड व (2) कैलास मानसरोवर खण्ड। गढ़वाल की भूमि को जब दूर से देखो तो अति ही सुन्दर व रमणीक प्रतीत होती है। गढ़वाल भूमि में सीढ़ीदार खेत व सुन्दर-सुन्दर वृक्ष देखने पर मन हर्षित होता है। जब इस प्रदेश में सुबह सूर्य की किरणें पड़ती हैं तो वे किरणें इस प्रकार चमकती हैं मानों सारे पर्वतों ने स्वर्णाहार पहना हो तथा सूर्य कि किरणें पड़ने पर हिमालय पर्वत ऐसा दिखता है मानों सागर के सारे मोतियों को एकत्रित करके हिमालय पर्वत पर ड़ेल दिया हो। गढ़वाल की भूमि देवताओं का तीर्थ स्थान है जहां पर कि देश-विदेश से तीर्थ यात्री पधारते हैं यहां पर प्रत्येक देवी देवताओं के मन्दिर स्थिति हैं। गढ़वाल की भूमि हरी-भरी है। पानी के हर जगह स्त्रोत हैं जिनका जल हमेशा शीतल रहता है। गढ़वाल की भूमि प्रत्येक तरह से प्रदुषण से रहिंत है प्राचीन काल से ही गढ़वाल अपने भौगालिक विष्टिता के लिए प्रसिद्ध रहा है, प्राचीन काल से यह क्षेत्र ऋषि मुनियों व तपस्वीयों का अधिवास रहा है। जनश्रुति आज भी उनकी स्मृति रखे हुए हैं, इनमें भारद्वाज, वशिष्ठ, अगस्त्य, कण्व, जमदाग्नि आदि मुख्य हैं। आचार्य वशिष्ठ का आश्रम हिमालय में था जिसे अर्जुन क्रीतवीर्य ने जला डाला था। व्यास जी ने 18 पुरण यहीं पूरे किये थे। शंकराचार्य जी ने बद्रीवन में 16 भाष्य वेदों पर लिखे थे। बुद्धदेव ने घर से निकलकर इन्हीं पर्वतों के जंगलों में भ्रमणकर तत्व ज्ञान की प्राप्ती की थी। इसी से केदारखण्ड भूमि में सहस्त्रों ऋषि आश्रम होने का वर्णन 'केदारखण्ड' नामक भूगोल में लिखा है।

पर्वत

यों तो हिमालय प्रदेश हरिद्वार तक माना जाता है। परंतु यहां अभिप्राय हिमालय

की उन चोटियों से है जो गढ़वाल में सबसे ऊँची और प्रतिष्ठित मानी जाती हैं। गढ़वाल में पूर्व से पश्चिम को हिमालय की सहस्त्रों छोटी बड़ी चोटियाँ विद्यमान हैं, उनमें से कुछ उंत्तुग चोटियाँ हैं जो अपनी ऊँचाई व प्रधानता के कारण वर्णन करने योग्य समझी गई हैं और उनका वर्णन इस प्रकार है - हेमकुंड, निषध, हरिवर्ष और हिरण्यशुंश आदि पर्वत भी गढ़वाल के उत्तरी सीमा पर विद्यमान हैं। मत्स्यपुरण में स्पष्टत: कहा गया है कि हेमकुंड पर्वत हिमालय के उत्तर से दक्षिण की ओर फैला है। मंदाकिनी और अह्वाणी गंधमादन पर्वत से होकर प्रभावित होती है। यह पर्वत गढ़वाल के बद्रीनाथ क्षेत्र में स्थित है। गंधमादन के समान ही मंदराचल भी गढ़वाल में ही स्थित है। यामुन पर्वत आधुनिक यमनोत्री का कांठा प्रतीत होता है यह वैदिक काल में यामुन अंजन के लिए प्रसिद्ध था। इसी पर्वत के पास त्रिकुद नामक पर्वत भी है। मैनाक पर्वत बद्रीनाथ का निकटवर्ती क्षेत्र माना जाता है रामायण में कहा गया है कि मैनाक का मार्ग क्रोंस (क्रोंच) पर्वत से होकर जाता है। अन्य प्रचलित पर्वत हैं - (1) त्रिशुली या नन्दा देवी कांठा (2) श्रीकण्ठ चोटी (3) बन्दरपुँच्छ (4) सतोपथ या सुमेरू पर्वत (5) स्वर्गरोहिणी (6) बद्रीनाथ का चौखम्बा आदि।

नदियाँ

गढ़वाल में पर्वतों की तरह अनेक एंतिहासिक नदियाँ भी हैं। जिनका उल्लेख प्राचीन साहित्यों में अनेक रूपों में हुआ है। गढ़वाल में गंगा, यमुना, अलकनन्दा, मन्दाकिनी, धौली, पिण्डंर, नयार, भलंगना, तमसीं प्रभृति अनेक नदियाँ सहस्त्रों छोटे बड़े नालों के अतिरिक्त हैं। परंतु इनमें से सबसे मुख्य नदियाँ गंगा व यमुना मानी जाती है। भिलंगना व भगीरथी टिहरी गढ़वाल की नदियाँ हैं। गढ़वाल में भगीरथी तथा जाह्नवी दोनों एक ही नदी हैं। जाह्नवी भगीरथी की सहायक नदी है जो बाद में उसी से मिल जाती है। जाह्नवी को लोग जाड़ गंगा कहकर पुकारते हैं। गंगा व यमुना को मुख्य नदियाँ इसलिए भी माना जाता है, क्योंकि भारतवर्ष में ये दो नदियाँ सर्वोच्च व पावन मानी जाती हैं शेष अन्य समस्त गढ़वाल के नदी-नालों को अपने में सम्मिलित करती हुई ये नदियाँ ही गढ़वाल की सीमा से बाहर निकलती हैं।

"गढ़वाल में ऋतुयें"

गढ़वाल के लोग वर्ष को तीन भागों में विभक्त करते हैं। अर्थात्

'वस्काल' (चर्तुमास) चार महिने यानी आषाढ़, श्रावण, भाद्रपद, असौज अर्थात 13 जून से 12 अक्तूबर तक। शीतकाल चार महिने कार्तिक, मार्गशीर्ष, पौष, माद्य अर्थात् 13 अक्तूबर से 12 फरवरी तक। रूड़ी या खड़सौ चार महिलने फाल्गुन, चैत्र, वैशाख अर्थात् 13 फरवरी से 12 जून तक। लेकिन उक्त ऋतुओं में से गढ़वाल के लोग वसन्त ऋतु को अधिक महत्व देते हैं क्योंकि वसन्त ऋतु में लड़कियाँ अपनी ससुराल से अपने मायके में जाती हैं तथा पूरे महिने अपने मायके में व्यतीत करती हैं पर्वतीय लोक जीवन में अनेक ऐसी परंपराओं ने जन्म लिया जो प्रकृति और मानव के सम्बन्ध सूत्रों का परिचय देते हैं। इन्हीं के कारण गढ़वाल में अनेक प्रकार के त्यौहारों ने जन्म लिया जैसे वैशाख के महिने में अनेक प्रकार के मेले (थौल) लगते हैं। जिसमें कि गढ़वाली लोग अपने रीति-रिवाज के अनुसार हर्ष व उल्लास मनाते हैं तथा अपने सम्बधियों से मिलते हैं। इसी कारण इन मेलों का उद्‌भव हुआ। हर फूल के प्रसव पर उत्सव व त्यौहार मनाने की यह आत्मीयता और उल्लासपूर्ण भावना ही ऋतु-पर्वों और ऋतु गीतों को जन्म देती है।

मध्य हिमालय में सर्वाधिक प्रचलित ऋतु पर्वों में वे पर्व ही मुख्य रूप स आते हैं जो वसन्त, वर्षा, शरद आदि ऋतुओं से सम्बन्धित हैं।

''गढ़वाल की वनस्पति एवं पशु पक्षी''

गढ़वाल की भूमि पर अनेक प्रकार के पेड़ पौधे होते हैं जिनमें चीड़ (कुलई) देवदार, बांज, बंरांश हैं। इन पेड़ों का अपना अपना महत्व है। चीड़ व देवदार इमारती लकड़ियाँ हैं तथा बाँज व बुरांश से गढ़वाल में जानवरों को पत्तिनुमा घास प्राप्त होता है। तथा इनके हँसियाँ व दराँतियों के हैंडल भी बनाये जाते हैं जो मज़बूत होने के कारण सालों साल चल जाते हैं। कृषक हल बनाने में भी इनका इस्तेमाल करते हैं गढ़वाल के गाँवों में आपको ज्यादातर पेड़ भिमल, डैंकण, खड़ीक, तोण व फलों में आम, अगरूद आड़ू, खुमानी, नारंगी, सेब, मौसमी, केला, चकुतरा, बड़ा निम्बू, जेमरू आदि मिलेंगे। इन पेड़ों के कारण गाँव की शोभा बढ़ती है। पहाड़ों में घने-घने जंगल भी हैं। जिन पर पशु-पक्षियों का बसेरा होता है। इन घने जंगलों में बाघ, रीछ शेर, खरगोश, चीता, हाथी, हिरन, काखड़ जंगली मुर्गी, जंगली सुअर आदि जानवर पाये जाते हैं। गांव के अन्दर आपको सुन्दर बाग-बगीचे भी देखने को मिलेंगे। जिनमें फलों व फूलों के पेड़ लगे रहते हैं जिनसे गांव की सुंदरता बढ़ती है। गाव में कई तरह के पक्षी भी होते हैं जैसे,

कबूतर (मल्यौ), बाज, घूघती, चील, सोनपरी, कठफौड़ा, तितर, बटेर तथा अन्य प्रकार की छोटी-छोटी चिड़ियां होती हैं जैसे घेन्दूड़ी, गूफेन्दणी आदि। इस प्रकार से ये पशु पक्षी इन पेड़ पौधों पर ही निर्भर रहते हैं।

फसलें

गढ़वाल में जमीन की बनावट ढालू है। नदियों के तटों में कहीं-कहीं सबसे अच्छी फसल के लिए गिने जाते हैं गढ़वाल में कृषकों के पास ऐसी भूमि नहीं है। जैसे देश के कृषकों के पास बड़े लम्बे चौड़े रकवे हैं। गढ़वाल में अस्सी प्रतिशत ऐसे कृषक हैं जिनके पास अपने कुटुम्ब को दो तीन महीने तक पालने के लिए प्रर्याप्त है। लेकिन शेष काल वे नौकरी मजदूरी से व वनस्पति अथवा शाक पर व्यतीत करते हैं। गढ़वाल में प्राय: दो प्रकार की खेती होती है, रबी व खरीफ। लेकिन कहीं कहीं अच्छी व उपजाऊ जमीन के कारण तीन फसलें भी हो जाती हैं कुछ भागों में जो हिमलाय के बिल्कुल नजदीक हैं, में एक ही फसल हो पाती है कारण वहां गहुत शीत होता है। गढ़वाल में रबी की फसल की अपेक्षा खरीफ की फसल अच्छी मात्रा में होती है। रबी की फसल में केवल गेहूँ, जौ, मटर, मसूर ये चार प्रकार के अन्न होते हैं लेकिन खरीफ में धान, उड़द, मक्की, मूंग, मार्सा (मारसू) मडुवा (कोदा), झंगोरा, गहत, सरसों, तोडिया सूंठा (सून्टा) तोर (साबूत अरहर) वेथू इत्यादि बारह प्रकार की अन्न पैदा होते हैं। गढ़वाल में कन्दवर्ग में पिंडालू, कुचाई, तल्ड, गेंणी, आलू होते हैं। टिहरी में चम्बा के पास लांखें मन आलू होते हैं जिनका व्यापार देहरादून या ऋषिकेश की मण्डियों से किया जाता है। कहावत है कि पहाड़ी आलू अभी मण्डी में नहीं आया क्योंकि यह मिठास से परिपूर्ण होता है। गढ़वाल के ऊपरी भागों में कैनूरी जीरा, अखरोट, आड़ू, चुल्लु तथा कहीं-कहीं पर सेब बहुतायात में पाये जाते हैं। रीठा और भरदार पट्टी में भांग की खेती होती है जिनके बीजों का तेल निकाला जाता है तथा उसकी छाल का कपड़ा पहनते हैं। इस कपड़े का नाम भंगेला या त्यूंखा कहते हैं। सीढ़ीनुमा खेत होने के कारण व पत्थरीली जमीन होने के कारण यहां अन्न के पैदावार कम मात्रा में होती है जो कि यहां के निवासियों के लिए प्रर्याप्त नहीं है इसलिए गढ़वाल का निवासी केवल भूमि पर ही निर्भर नहीं रहता उसे अपना व अपने परिवार के निर्वाह के लिए बाहर निकलना पड़ता है।

व्यवसाय

गढ़वाल के लोगों का व्यवसाय खेती व पशु-पालन है। गढ़वाल के लोग मुख्य रूप से खेती करते हैं अत्यन्त परिश्रम के पश्चात् भी अन्न पूर्ण नहीं होता। खेती का कार्य समाप्त करने के पश्चात आदमी लोग पशुओं का व्यापार करते हैं। व्यापार के लिए वे बकरियों, भैंसों तथा भेड़ों को पालते हैं जिनको वे एक स्थान से दूसरे स्थान पर ले जाते हैं तथा उनकी बिक्री करने के पश्चात् अपने गांव वास लौट जाते हैं। तथा खेती व मेहनत मजदूरी में लग जाते हैं। आजकल लोग अपनी खेती में पैदा किये हुए दालें जैसे भट्ट (सोयाबीन) तोर, मारसू आदि भी खूब मात्रा में बेच रहे हैं, या तो वे इन दालों व अनाजों के रूपयों में बेचते हैं या बदले में नमक या चावल लेते हैं लेकिन यह कहना उचित होगा कि गढ़वाल का आदमी बड़ा ही भोला है क्योंकि जो अनाज कुछ गिने चुने लोगों को बेचता है वे अनाज के बदले में कम कीमत देते हैं व बदलें में कम चावल व नमक देते हैं जब कि उनके द्वारा बेचा गया अनाज मण्डियों में अधिक कीमत पर जाता है। कहा जाता है कि धन से ही धन कमाया जाता है इसलिए गढ़वाल में जो गिने चुने साहूकार हैं उनका पूरा प्रभुत्व है कारण उनकी पहुँच बड़ी-बड़ी जगहों पर है व उनके पास साधन हैं वे माल को इधर से उधर ले जाने में समर्थ्य हैं ग्रामीण व्यक्ति सोचता है कि अगर वह अपने अनाज को मण्डी में ले जाएगा तो वहां के लिए मोटर इत्यादि का खर्च व अकेले वहन नहीं कर पायेगा इसलिए वह उन्हीं के हाथों बेच देता है। फिर गढ़वालियों में उद्योगशीलता का अभाव पाया जाता है। गढ़वाल की अपेक्षा गढ़वाल के पड़ोसी कुमायूं में अच्छे उद्योग धंधे हैं। इस प्रकार ये यह भी देखने को मिला है कि गढ़वाल का नागरिक अब नौकरी पेशे में भी आ गया है तथा वहां पर जो लोग विशेषकर भेटिया, मार्च्छिर्या जाति तथा बाहर का व्यक्ति अपने व्यवसाय को फैला रहा है। तथा गढ़वाल का व्यक्ति केवल पशुपालन खेती तथा अपने परिवार की जरूरतों तक ही सीमित है।

''गढ़वाल के लोगों में शिक्षा''

गढ़वाल में आज से 10 या 15 वर्ष पहले कक्षा आठवीं तक के ही विद्यालय होते थे। लोग बड़ी-गड़ी कठिनाईयों का सामना करते हुए बड़ी कठिनाई से आठवीं कक्षा पास करते थे तथा नौकरी पेशा के लिए शहरों में चले जाते हैं गढ़वाल में आर्थिक अभाव के कारण लोग अपने बच्चों को विद्यालय

में पढ़ने हेतु नहीं भेज सकते थे। उनके बच्चे अपनढ़ ही रहते थे खासतौर पर लड़कियों को पढ़ाने से वंचित रखते थे उनको विद्यालय के दर्शन भी नहीं कराये जाते थे उनसे हमेशा घर व बाहर का काम कराया जाता था। आजकल गढ़वाल में कक्षा बारहवीं (इंटर) तक के विद्यालय कहीं-कहीं पर हो गये हैं लेकिन अधिकतर गांवों में दसवीं तक ही विद्यालय हैं। उसके पश्चात् वे टिहरी बाजार या अन्य शहरों में पढ़ने के लिए चले जाते हैं दूर दराज होने के कारण लड़कियां आगे की पढ़ाई से वंचित रह जाती हैं। टिहरी बाजार में क्षात्रावास (कन्याओं के लिए) भी उपलब्ध है लेकिन घर से दूर होने के कारण छात्राओं के मां-बाप उन्हें नहीं भेजते। टिहरी बाजार में दूर-दूर से पैदल आना पड़ता है तथा शाम को फिर घर वापस जाना पड़ता है। अब तो गढ़वाल में लगभग सभी लोग अपने बच्चों को पढ़ाते हैं चाहे वह लड़का हो या लड़की। लेकिन दुर्भाग्यवश कुछ बच्चे अपनी पढ़ाई को सुचारू रूप नहीं दे पाते क्योंकि उनके माता-पिता की आर्थिक स्थिति कमजोर होती है और इस कारण उनके बच्चों को मेहनत मजदूरी करने के लिए मजबूर होना पड़ता है। गढ़वाल में लड़कियों को अधिकतर 10वीं या 12वीं तक ही पढ़ाया जाता हे तथा उसके बाद उनका विवाह संपन्न कर दिया जाता है। भगवान की नियति तो देखों कि इतना पढ़ने लिखने के पश्चात् भी लड़कियों को ससुराल में घास काटना पड़ता है।

गढ़वाल के लोगों का रहनसहन एवं खानपान

गढ़वालियों में रहन-सहन व खान पान अन्य लोगों की तरह से सामान्य है। लेकिन खान-पान में शहरों व कस्बों की भांति नहीं है। दाल, भात, खीर आदि सिक्तन्न के खाने में विशेष भेद पाया जाता है। रोटी, पूरी, प्रसाद (हलवा) का भेद केवल अछूत जाति को छोड़कर अन्य वर्णों में नहीं है। सिक्तान्न भोजन अर्थात् दाल भात आदि सरोला ब्राह्मण के हाथ से पका हुआ चौके के भीतर सब लोग खा लेते हैं लेकिन कुछ क्षत्रियों व ब्राह्मणों की ऐसी भी जातियां हैं जो सरोला (ब्राह्मण) के हाथ का बना हुआ भोजन नहीं खाते। गंगाड़ी ब्राह्मण की बीच दाल भात नातेदारी में चलता है तथा अछूत जाति सबका पकाया हुआ भोजन खा लेती है। इनमें चौके का प्रचलन नहीं है। अछूतों का छूआ हुआ जल या तरल पदार्थ ही शहद तेल आदि को छोड़कर अन्य प्रकार का भोजन राजपूत अथवा ब्राह्मण लोग नहीं करते। इनसे उच्च श्रेणी के लोग वैवाहिक सम्बन्ध भी नहीं बना सकते। गढ़वाल में दो जातियां हैं एक डोम (अूछत जाति)

तथा दूसरी बिटअ इस जाति में सब जातियों सम्मिलित हैं गढ़वाल में ब्राह्मण जाति मांस का भक्षण करती है जिस प्रकार अन्य जातियां करती हैं यहां तक कि देखा गया है कि ये लोग मदिरा का भी सेवन करते हैं। गढ़वाल के लोग धार्मिक प्रवृति के भी होते हैं। मसलन प्रत्येक वर्ष वे पाण्डवों को नचाते हैं उनका कहना है कि इससे गांव में दुर्भिक्ष व प्रेतादि का प्रकोप नहीं होता है। गढ़वाल के लोगों का रहन सहन भी एक प्रकार से अभिशाप प्रतीत होता है क्योंकि साधारणतया लोग कठिनाईयों का ही सामना करते हैं सुबह उठकर कार्य में मसगुल हो जाना तथा जब तक बिस्तर में सोने के लिए न आये जाये तब तक कठिन परिश्रम करना। गढ़वाल में मांस खाना व आखेट करना गढ़वाल के लोगों का स्वाभाविक धर्म है। गढ़वाल के लोगों का रहन-सहन बिल्कुल साधारण है। स्त्रियां जंगल में लकड़ी या घास काटने चली जाती है तथा गीत लगाकर (गाकर) लकड़ियां व घास काटने के साथ-साथ समय व्यतीत करती हैं। गढ़वाली लोग सादगी व सच्चाई के लिए प्रसिद्ध हैं।

"सामाजिक जीवन एवं रीति-रिवाज"

गढ़वालियों का समाजिक व रीति-रिवाज जीवन एक समान व एक रूप से विद्यमान नहीं हैं। गढ़वाल के रीति-रिवाज प्राचीन निवासियों खसिया व डोम जाति का अपने ढंग से व ब्राह्मणों व क्षत्रियों का अपने ढंग से पाया जाता था। गढ़वाल में वास्तव में लौकिक रिवाजों की खिचड़ी पकी हुई है। तथा धार्मिक रिवाज बिल्कुल पृथकता रखते हैं जैसे धर्म शास्त्र ने आठ प्रकार के विवाहों का प्रतिपादन किया है अर्थात् ब्रह्मम दैव, आर्ष, प्राजापत्य, आसुर, पैशाच, गान्धर्व और राक्षस। गढ़वाल के ब्राह्मणां व क्षत्रियों में केवल ब्रह्म विवाह की रीति से विवाह होते हैं तथा सुवर्णो से विवाह होता है, विवाह में वाक्यदान, संकल्प, पणिग्रहण सप्तपदी, होम इत्यादि वैदिक रीति से होते हैं लेकिन खसियों में खस-राजपूतों में, खस ब्राह्मणों में विवाह संस्था केवल आसुरी रीति पर है उनके बीच हजारों रुपयों का कन्या शुल्क देकर विवाह हाते हैं। डोम जाति में ब्याही हुई लड़कियां अथवा विधवा स्त्री सद्भा अवस्था में पति पत्नि की राजी पर विधवा होने पर अपने पूर्व पति या पति का घर छोड़कर अन्य व्यक्ति से विवाह कर सकती हैं। उनके बीच भाई की विधवा को घर में रखने और उससे सन्तति पैदा करने का भी रिवाज प्रकट रूप से है। ब्राह्मणों व क्षत्रियों में नामकर्म, जातकर्म, अन्नप्रासन, उपनयन संस्कार वेदविहित होने का रिवाज है।

लेकिन अब ये रिवाज केवल रिवाजी तौर पर रह गये हैं। पहले गढ़वाल में यह भी रिवाज था कि केवल ब्राह्मण व क्षत्रिया ही यज्ञोपतिव धारण कर सकते थे लेकिन अब खसिया व खस ब्राह्मण शिक्षित होने के कारण अपने बच्चों का नाम क्षत्रियों व राजपूतों के नामों की तरह रखने लग गये हैं जिससे कि वे राजपूत कहलाये जायें। इसी कारण अब उन्होंने भी यज्ञोपतिव धारण करना आरंभ कर दिया है। इस प्रकार हम देखते हैं कि गढ़वाल में रीति-रिवाज समान रूप से विद्यमान नहीं हैं जो कि गढ़वाल के लिए एक अभिशाप है।

"त्यौहार"

गढ़वाल में भी अन्य शहरों की भांति अनेक प्रकार के त्यौहार मनाये जाते हैं लेकिन दीपावली का त्यौहार बड़े धूमधाम से मनाया जाता है, यह त्यौहार अमावस्या की रात्रि को कार्तिक माह में आता है जनश्रुति है कि भगवान राम सीता जी व लक्ष्मण के साथ चौदह वर्ष के वनवास के पश्चात् अपनी नगरी अयोध्या वापस लौट कर आये थे। अमावस्या की रात्रि घनघोर अंधेरे से लिप्त होती है इसलिए लोग रामजी के आगमन में दीप जलाते हैं तथा रोशनी करते हैं गढ़वाल में भी दीपावली का त्यौहार अपनी रीति से मनाया जाता है। गढ़वाल के लोग दीपावली के दिन पूड़ी तथा चावल से बनी हुई पापड़ी (पापड़) बनाते हैं तथा एक दूसरे के घर में देते हैं। तथा रात को लोग चीड़ के पेड़ की लकड़ियों का छोटा सा गट्ठर (थैला) बनाते हैं जिसे जलाकर वे गांव से थोड़ी दूर जाकर सामूहिक मैदान में खेलते व नाचते हैं तथा वापस आकर गांव के सामूहिक (पंचायत) घर में रातभर नाचते हैं। यह जताने के लिए कि हम लोग रामजी के वापस लौटने की खुशी में नाच गा रहे हैं। दीपावली के साथ-साथ अन्य त्यौहार भी मनाये जाते हैं जैसे होली, रक्षा बन्धन, जन्म अष्टमी, पंचमी तथा थौल (मेले) बड़े ही अच्छे हैं लेकिन दीपावली, अष्टमी, पंजमी, शिवरात्री तथा थौल मेले आदि प्राचीन काल से ही मनाये जाते हैं। अष्टमी के समय गांव गांव में जौ कि हरियाली बोई जाती है तथा गांव के लोग यथासंभव आर्थिक सहयोग देकर इस पर्व को पूर्ण होने में सहयोग करते हैं। पंचमी के दिन लोग गंगा स्मान करते हैं तथा व्रत रखते हैं। शिवरात्री के दिन लोग व्रत रखते हैं तथा कोटेश्वर (शिवजी का लिंग) जाकर शिवजी को फूल दूध अपर्ण करते हैं गढ़वाल में मेलों का भी प्रचलन है जो कि वैशाख के महीने में मनाये जाते हैं प्रत्येक गते यानी हिन्दी का तिथि को ये थौल जगह-जगह पर होते हैं। थौलू (मेलों) में लड़कियां व

संबंधी आपस में बड़े प्रेम से मिलते हैं इस प्रकार से गढ़वाल के लोग लगभग प्रत्येक त्यौहार को मनाते हैं।

"गढ़वाल में विवाह व उसके निमय"

जब लड़के का या लड़की का विवाह होता है तो विवाह के एक महीने पहले से ही तैयारियां प्रारंभ हो जाती हैं। बाजार से चावल, आटा, दाल व शादी (विवाह) का अन्य सामान इक्ट्ठा करते हैं शादी के लिए जब 5 या 6 दिन शेष रह जाते हैं तो लड़के वाले लड़की वालों के यहां सापट्टा लिखवाने जाते हैं जिसमें कि तय होता है कि अमुक दिन कितने बाराती आयेंगे तथा उसी दिन लड़की को हार (तिमाण्या) पहनाया जाता है कि आज से लड़की दुल्हन हो गई है। उसके पश्चात् विवाह के एक दिन पहले शाम को पकोड़े, आरसे (एक प्रकार की मिठाई) आदि बनाये जाते हैं तथा बारात में जाने वाले को निमंत्रण दिया जाता है तथा दिन के खाने के लिए भी पूरे ग्राम को निमंत्रण दिया जाता है। पहले आदमी लोग पंक्तिबद्ध होकर खाना खाते हैं जिनको कि ब्राह्मण (सरौला) खिलाता है जिस दौरान ब्राह्मण खाना बांट रहा होता है इस दौरान कोई भी व्यक्ति बीच में अपनी जगह से उठ नहीं सकता जब तक कि सबने भरपेट भोजन नहीं कर लिया हो। उसके पश्चात् महिलाओं का नम्बर आता हे वे भी उक्त प्रकार से ही भोजन करती हैं। दुल्हे के साथ-साथ उसकी पालकी व घोड़ा भी सजाया जाता है। पालकी पर पीले रंग का खोल चढ़ाया जाता है। उसमें चमकीले फूल व रंगबिरंगे गुब्बारे लगाये जाते हैं। ढोल व नगारे बजाये जाते हैं। ढोल नगारों की ध्वनी को सुनकर बाराती भी अपनी-अपनी पोशाकों में सजधजकर बारात में जाने के लिए वहां पर एकत्रित हो जाते हैं ढोल नगारा व मुश्काबाजा (एक प्रकार का वाद्य यन्त्र) बजने लग जाता है जिनको सुनकर पुरूष नाचने लगते हैं। रास्तेभर नाचते-नाचते आखरीकार लड़की वालों के घर के नजदीक पहुंचते हैं जहां पर वे और भी जोश व उल्लास के साथ नाचते हैं लड़की वालों की तरफ से भी लड़की वाले दासों को लेकर उनके स्वागत के लिए खोली तक आते हैं जहां पर दोनों तरफ की राम-रामी होती है। इसके पश्चात् वे आंगन में आ जाते हैं जहाँ पर उनका स्वागत कुछ सुशिक्षित लड़कियां हाथ में माला लिये हुए करती है तथा दुल्हे की पूजा करते हैं। तत्पश्चात् उसके गले में माला शुशोभित करती हैं इसके बाद सभी बारातियों को दरी या तिरपाल में बैठाते हैं व दुल्हे के लिए बीच में आसन बिछाया जाता है। सर्वप्रथम, बैठक के बाद चाय व नमकीन पेश किये

जाते हैं चाय नमकीन के पश्चात् सिगरेट, बीड़ी व तम्बाखू का प्रबंध किया जाता है। वहीं पर ही दुल्हे की पूजा की जाती है। सारी प्रक्रियायें बड़े ही सुचरू व व्यवस्थित ढंग से की जाती हैं। उसके पश्चात् बारातियों, गांव के लोगों को व दासों (डाम) को खाना खिलाया जाता है जो कि गांव के ही आदमी खिलाते हैं जिन लोगों को रात्री में सोना होता है उनके लिए सोने का पूरा प्रबंध किया जाता है और जिन लोगों को मनोरंजन करना होता है वे या तो ताश खेलते हैं या दासों से मण्डाण लगवाते हैं फेरों का लग्न भी रात्रि में ही होता है, जिस समय फेरे होते है उस समय मांगलगीत गाये जाते हैं। फेरों के समय लड़की आगे होती है। लड़की छः फेरो तक तो बड़े ही आराम से चलती है तथा जैसे ही सातवां फेरा होता है तो कुछ तीव्र गति से चलती है इस दौरान लड़की की सहेलियां दुल्हे से अनेक प्रकार की चुंहले करती हैं। फेरों के समाप्त होते ही दुल्हन कमरे में चली जाती है और जब दुल्हा अंदर जाने की कोशिश करता है तो सहेलियों द्वारा उससे पैसे मांगे जाते हैं कारण कि फेरे संपूर्ण होने के पश्चात् अब दुल्हन उनसे अलग हो गयी है यह उनका साथ छुटाने का दंड है। जब दुल्हा मुंहमांगी रकम पेश करता है तभी उसे अंदर जाने दिया जाता है। दान का समय लगभग दस बजे प्रारंभ हो जाता है। पहले गाय का दान होता है। गाय के दान की प्रक्रिया में दुल्हन के माता-पिता, भाई, चाचा चाची व अन्य शितेदार गाय के चारों ओर परिक्रमा करते हैं उसके पश्चात् दुल्हन के माता-पिता दुल्हे व दुल्हन को दान स्वरूप रुपये भेंट करते हैं उसके पश्चात् लड़की के संबधिगण दान देते हैं उसके बाद ग्रामवासी दान देते हैं। दान समाप्त होने के पश्चात् सब लोगों को खाना खिलाया जाता है। तथा बारात दुल्हे के घर वापस जाने के लिए तैयार की जाती है। लड़की के लिए डोली तैयार की जाती है जिस पर की लाल रंग की खोली चढ़ाई जाती है व उसके चारों सिरों पर चांदी के छत्तर भी लगाये जाते हैं ब फूल व गुब्बारों से उसे शुशोभित किया जाता है। ढोल व नंगारा बजने लगता है जो कि यह संकेत करता है सारे बाराती चलने को तैयार हो जायें। इस दौरान लड़की अपने माता-पिता व सगे-संबधियों से मिलती है तथा रूदन करती है। लड़की को डोली में बैठाया जाता है जिसको को डोल्यार (कहांर) उठाते हैं लेकिन आजकल दुल्हन के भाई ही बहन की डोली को उसके नये घर पर छोड़कर आते हैं लड़के वालों के यहां पहुंचकर दुल्हा व दुल्हन की पूजा होती है और वहीं पूजा में ही दुल्हा के मुकुट इत्यादि उतारे जाते हैं तथा सुबह होते ही दुल्हन को पानी के सोते के पास ले जाया जाता है जहां स्त्रोते की पूजा होती है। उसके

पश्चात् दोपहर का खाना खाकर दुल्हा दुल्हन व उसके भाई दुल्हन के मायके में वापस आ जाते हैं वहां पर दो तीन दिन रहकर जिसको पल्युण कहा जाता है के पूरा होने पर वापस आ जाते हैं। कुछ दिन ससुराल में व्यतीती करने के पश्चात् दुल्हन फिर मायके आ जाती है और फिर वापस ससुराल। व ससुराल में ही अपना जीवन यापन करती है।

"गढ़वाल में स्त्री का जीवन एवं कठिनाईयां"

गढ़वाल के पारिवारिक जीवन के केन्द्र में नारी है। गढ़वाल के लोकगीतों में नारी सवत्र दुःखी और पीड़ित दिखाई देती है उन गीतों में एक युक्ति मिलती है कि बारह बरस का लड़का रण में तलवार संभालता है तो गढ़वाल में बारह बरस की लड़की अपना घरबार संभालती है। बारहवें वर्ष घरवार संभालने की शिक्षा गढ़वाल की लड़की को उसके जन्म के बारहवें बरस से ही दी जाने लगती। फलतः उसका सारा जीवन उसके परिवार की सेवा तथा अन्य प्रकार के परिश्रमों के लिए अर्पित हो जाता है तथा उसका समस्त जीवन काम करके ही समाप्त हो जाता है, परंतु भौगोलिक कारणों के कारण पहाड़ों पर अधिक परिश्रम नहीं फलता जिस कारण पुरूष को अजीविका के लिए घर से बाहर निकलना पड़ता है और पहाड़ में नारी का समर्पित जीवन को अभाव व विरह से भरा होता है अकेले की यापन करना पड़ता है, जिस पर क्रूर सास का शासन उसके सिर पर इस प्रकार टूट पड़ता है कि बेचारी बहू के लिए केवल कंदन मात्र ही बचा रह जाता है और जीवन से सारे सरस स्त्रोत सहसा सूख जाते है नारी को सुबह उठकर सर्वप्रथम चाय बनानी है तत्पश्चात् गढेरे या पाणी के धारे में से पानी लाना है जो कि कहीं-कहीं तो कोसां दूर है, पानी लाने के तुरंत पश्चात् उसे जानवरों का गोबर भी साफ करना है उसके पश्चात् नाश्ता बनाकर व करके जंगल व खेतों में काम करने या पशुओं के लिए घास लाने के लिए जाना पड़ता है। यही उसका सदैव से चली आ रही प्रथा है जो आज भी इसी प्रकार जीवित है। इस प्रकार से हम देखते हैं कि गढ़वाल की महिलाओं को कितना परिश्रम व कष्ट करने पड़ते हैं जिसका निदान अत्यन्त ही कठिन है।

"गढ़वाल की स्त्री का ससुराल में जीवन"

गढ़वाल की लड़की की जिंदगी भी एक अजीबो बरीब जिंदगी है क्योंकि जब तक लड़की का विवाह नहीं हो जाता वह अपने माता-पिता भाई

बहन व सगे संबंधियों के साथ जीवन बड़े ही सुचारू रूप से व्यतीत करती है लेकिन विवाह होने के पश्चात् उसे अपरिचित समाज व लोगों के बीच में जाना पड़ता है जो कि उसके लिए एकदम नया है। गढ़वाल की लड़की का ससुराल में जीवन व्यतीत करने का सर्वप्रथम कर्तव्य है परिश्रम जो कि उसके मा, भाभीयों से ग्रहण की होती है। गढ़वाल के लोगों का जीवन जब खेती से नहीं निकल पाता तो वे गांव से शहरों की ओर पलायन करते है तथा उनकी स्त्रीयां गांव में ही रहकर खेंतों में मेहनत करती है तथा घास व कलड़ काटती हैं। स्त्रीयों की पूरी जिन्दगी इसी मेहनत की उधेड़बुन में व अपनी पति के इंतजार में निकल जाती है। फिर ससुराल में वह ऊँची आवाज में तथा दूसरे व्यक्तियों से भी खुलकर नहीं बोल सकती क्योंकि डर ये लगा रहता है कि कहीं उसके बारे में कोई गलत न सोचे। ऊपर से घर में सासू का रूतबा व कड़वी बोली। सुबह चार बजे प्रातः उठकर भैसों को घास डालना, उनका गोबर साफ करना, दो तीन कोस दूर से पानी लाना तब चाय बनाना व एक-एक व्यक्ति को उठाकर बिस्तरे में चाय देना तथा साथ ही साथ नाश्ता भी तैयार करना आदि यह तो उसके प्रातः की दिनचर्या है जब सबको नाश्ता करा लिया तो उसके बाद अपनी दाथूड़ी (दरांती) उठाना व घास के लिए चल देना। जंगल से घास लेकर जब थकीहारी आयी तो घर में पानी नहीं बन्ठा उठाया और चल दी पानी को। खाना खाया व फिर जंगल या खेत में इस तरह से उसकी जिन्दगी बिना आराम के घसीटती जाती है और उसे इस जिंदगी में पता ही नहीं चलता कि वह बढ़ी कब हों गयी। मायके कि याद आ रही है लेकिन जिम्मेवारियों का बोझ सिर पर है जो कभी हल्का या खत्म ही नहीं होता। पति शहर गया हुआ है उसकी याद आ रही है लेकिन मजबूरियां है तो जंगल में जाकर पति याद में गाकर अपने मन को बहला रही है यही है जिन्दगी।

''पति एवं पत्नि के संबंध''

पति के पत्नि के साथ अच्छे संबंध हैं लेकिन कुछ इंसान ऐसे भी हैं कि पत्नि को पांव की जूती समझते हैं वे केवल यह सोचते हैं कि स्त्री तो केवल काम करने के लिए बनी हुई है। यद्यपि गढ़वाल का आदमी भी कर्मठ व कुशल होता है लेकिन स्त्रीयों का काम आदमियों से ज्यादा कठिन है वह प्रातः काल उठकर अपना प्रत्येक कार्य करती है तथा अपने पति को चाय वगैरह पलंग पर ही देती है तथा सारे दिन थकी हारी शाम को घर आकर चूल्हा वगैरह करती

है अगर भोजन स्वादिष्ट या मनपसंद नहीं बना हुआ है तो संपूर्ण दोष अपनी पत्नि पर मड़ता है और यहां तक की उसको पीड़ित भी कर देता है लेकिन बेचारी असहाय क्या कहे चुपचाप सारी कठिनाईयों को सहन करती हुई उसी पति के सेवासुश्रवा में बीताती है। कहीं-कहीं पर तो यह भी देखा गया है कि अगर घर में पुत्र रत्न की प्राप्ति नहीं होती तो सारा दोष औरत पर ही मढ़ दिया जाता है तथा पति दूसरा विवाह कर लेता है और अगर मौका लगा तो उसे प्रताड़ित किया जाता है जिससे वह दु:खी होकर गृह त्याग भी कर देती है या आत्महत्या के लिए बाध्य हो जाती है। यह सब तब संभव होता है क्योंकि गढ़वाल में शिक्षित वर्ग की कमी है और ऐसा घिघौना अपराध करने वाले प्राचीन विचारों के होते हैं लेकिन यह कहना उचित नहीं होगा कि गढ़वाल में पति के संबंध माधुर्य नहीं हैं क्योंकि प्रत्येक इंसान एक ही विचार के नहीं होते। यह भी देखने में आता है कि पति अपनी पत्नि के साथ ही प्रात: उठकर उसके कार्य में हाथ बंटाता है। आजकल के पति पत्नि के संबंध माधूर्य हैं कारण उनके पति उनसे दूर रहते हैं क्योंकि लगभग 10 प्रतिशित गढ़वाल का व्यक्ति अजीविका अर्जित करने के लिए बाहर होते हैं और जब वापस घर जाते हैं तो काफी दिन व्यतीत हो जाते हैं और यही दूरी उनके संबंधों को माधूर्य बनाते हैं तो हमने देखा कि गढ़वाल में पति के संबंध आज ठीक हैं। व कुछ ही दिन साथ रहते हैं तथा सोचते हैं कि फिर हमें अलग तो होना ही है सो क्यों आपस में झगड़ा किया जाए।

GLOSSARY

Aarti — A ceremony performed in worship of a *deity* whereby a dish holding a lamp burning *ghee* is moved in a series of circles in front of the idol

Adhikar — Right

Ashaad — June/July

Asooj — September/October

Andolan — Movement

Baan-Snan — The ceremonial bath of turmeric and sandal wood paste given to the bride before the marriage ceremony

Badris — The seats of Vishnu

Baju-Band geet — Songs sung in a dialogue manner across the hills by women while cutting grass in the forest

Banj — The Oak tree

Barahmasa — Songs describing each of the months of the year

Basi — Stale

Bazaar — Market place

Bhadon — August/September

Bhagywati — The fortunate one

Bhanwara — Bumble bee

Bhoomidaan — The gift of land

Bidai — Farewell

Birahi Ganga — A small stream joining the river Ganga

Bulak — Nose-ring worn on the lower part of the nose which covers the lips

Burans — The Rhododendron tree

Buwari — Daughter-in-law

Chait — March/April

Churakram — Ceremony performed for the first shaving of the hair of the child

Chakki — Stone Grinder

Daan — Gift, Offering

Darati — Sickle
Devar — Husband's younger brother
Dev Bhumi — The land of Gods
Devlok — The abode of Gods
Dhaguli — Bracelets
Dharam — Religion
Dholi dancers — Traditional dancers belonging to the lower castes, who play the drums.
Drub — A kind of green grass

Ganesh Puja — The first ritual performed during the marriage ceremony in Garhwal
Ghagra — Skirt
Gharat — Water mill
Ghasiyari — Woman who cuts grass
Gingyal — Long wooden stick for grinding grain
Gobar — Cow-dung
Gotroucchar — Ceremony where the bridegroom is asked to tell his *gotre*

Hamdardi — Sympathy
Hanseeli — Necklace
Hazaar — One thousand
Heeradaan — Gift of diamonds
Hul-chalana — Ploughing the field
Hurkiyas — Traditional dancers belonging to the lower caste, who play the instrument called Hurka

Jagar — Religious songs
Jhangora — A coarse grain like ragi
Jija — Sister's husband

Kanya-daan — The giving away of the daughter by the father as a gift
Kanya-bikri — Selling the daughter in exchange for money
Karam — Action
Kartavya — Duty
Kartik — October/November
Kedars — The seats of Shiva
Kheer — Rice pudding

Khuder geet	—	Emotional songs
Koda	—	A coarse grain, grown in high altitudes
Kohra	—	Fog
Kund	—	Pond
Kunwari	—	Virgin
Lehenga	—	Skirt
Lipai	—	To wash over with mud
Maang	—	Parting in the hair
Magh	—	January/February
Mahajan	—	Money lender
Makarsankrant	—	Festival to mark the entry of the Sun or Planet into a new sign of the zodiac; celebrated on 14 January.
Mama	—	Mother's brother
Manbabura	—	Black bulbul
Mangal geet	—	Songs of celebration, sung on auspicious occasions
Mangalacharins	—	Women who sing mangalgeet, belonging to the lower caste
Manduwa	—	A coarse grain
Mela	—	Fair
Mistry	—	Carpenter
Moti-daan	—	Gifts of pearls
Murki	—	Ear-ring
Nai	—	Barber
Namkaran	—	Naming ceremony
Nath	—	Nose ring
Nayika	—	Heroine
Oujis	—	Traditional narrative singers, belonging to the lower caste
Okhli	—	Stone grinder
Panghat	—	Natural spring
Patrol	—	Forest guard
Phagun	—	February/March
Prayag	—	Confluence

Poos	—	December/January
Rada-Bada	—	Ceremony in which money is given by bridegroom's father to the bride's father in exchange for the daughter
Ritu geet	—	Songs of the season
Roop	—	Beauty
Sawan	—	July/August
Sali	—	Wife's younger sister
Saptapadi	—	Seven steps taken around the sacred fire during the marriage ceremony
Sasural	—	In-laws home
Satyagrah	—	Non-violent movement or protest
Shivir	—	Camp
Sindoor	—	Vermilion powder, put in the parting of the hair as a symbol of marriage
Suhagin	—	Married woman whose husband is alive
Tai	—	Father's elder brother's wife
Tigra	—	Twisted woollen cord worn on a loose shirt by men in Garhwal
Tirathsthanas	—	Pilgrimage centres
Vatsalya	—	Motherly love
Viraha	—	Longing

REFERENCES

Appadurai, Arjun, Frank J. Korom & Margaret Mills (eds.), 1991, *Gender, Genre and Power in South Asian Expressive Traditions.* Philadelphia: University of Pennsylvania Press

Ask, Karin, 1994, "Veiled Experience:Exploring female practices of Seclusion", in P. Hervik & K. Hastrup (eds.), *Social Experience and Anthropological Knowledge*, London and New York, Routledge.

Bahulkar, Mohan Lal, 1964, *Garhwal Lok Sahitya Ka Vivechanatmak Adhyan*, Prayag : Hindi Sahitya Sammelan.

Barua, Hem, 1963, *Folk Songs of India,* New Delhi : Indian Council for Cultural Relations.

Bhargava, N., 1972, "*Content Analysis of Folk Song sung by Rural Women in a selected village*", An unpublished dissertation, New Delhi : Lady Irwin College.

Bhatnagar, M., 1988, "Indian Folksongs take a turn", *Folklore*, Vol.29(9): 203-204.

Bhatnagar, M., 1989, "In Folklore Daughter is Dear But Also Unwanted", *Folklore*,Vol.30(3) : 64-67.

Biswas Hemango (ed.), 1967, *Folk Music and Folklore: An Anthology*, Vol.1, Calcutta : Folk Music and Folklore Research Institute and Sangeet Natak Academy.

Blackburn, Stuart & A.K. Ramanujan, 1986, "Introduction", in Stuart H. Blackburn and A. K. Ramanujan (eds.) *Another Harmony : New Essays on the Folklore of India*. New Delhi : Oxford University Press.

Bond,Ruskin, 1988, *Beautiful Garhwal, Heaven in Himalayas*. Dehradun: EBD Educational Pvt. Ltd.

Chatak,Govind, 1973, *Garhwali Lokgeet:Ek Sanskritik Adhyayan*,Delhi : Vidyarthi Prakashan,

Choondal, C., 1970, *Christian Folk Songs*. Kerala Folklore Academy.

Claus, Peter J. & Frank J Korom, 1991, *Folkloristics and— Indian Folklore —A Handbook*, Udipi : International Folkloristics.

Coomaraswamy, A.K., 1936, "The nature of folklore and popular art, *Quarterly Journal of the Mythic Society*, 27: 1-12.

Davis, John, 1994, "Events and processes, marriages in Libya, 1932-79",in P. Hervik & K. Hastrup (eds.) *Social Experience and Anthropological Knowledge*. London and New York : Routledge.

Deva, Indra, 1989, *Folk Culture and Peasant Society in India.,* New Delhi : Rawat Publications.

Diaz de Rada, Angelo & Cruces Francisco, 1994, "Some problems to do with analytic language of practice", in P. Hervik & K. Kastrup (eds.), *op.cit.*

Dilwali, Ashok & Pushpesh Pant, 1987, *The Garhwal Himalayas:Ramparts of Heaven.* New Delhi : Lustic Press.

Egnor, T.Margaret, 1986, "Internal Iconicity in Pariyar 'Crying Songs'", in Stuart Blackburn & A. K. Ramanujan (eds.) *op.cit.*

Elwin Verrier & Shamrao Hivale, 1944, *Folk Songs of the Maikal Hills*, Bombay : Oxford University Press.

Finnegan, Ruth, 1992, *Oral Traditions and the Verbal Arts — A Guide to Research Practice*, London and New York : Routledge.

Fiumara, G.C., 1990, *The Other Side of Language — A Philosophy of Listening*, London : Routledge.

Friedman, Maurice; S.C. Malik,and Pat Boni, 1995, *Maurice Friedman at IGNCA — An Intercultural Dialogue and the Human Image*. New Delhi : IGNCA and D.K. Print World.

Gingrich, Andre, 1994, "Time, Ritual and Social Experience". In P. Hervik and K. Kastrup, (eds.) *op.cit.*

Gold, Ann Grodzins, 1994, "Gender, Violence and Power: Rajasthan Stones of Shakti", in Nita Kumar (ed.) *Women as Subjects, South Asian Histories*. New Delhi : Stree, Book Review Literary Trust.

Grima, Benedicte, 1991, "The Role of Suffering in Women's Performance of Paxto", in Arjun Appadurai, Frank J. Korom and Margaret Mills (eds.), 1991, *op.cit.*

Gupta, Sankar, S.& Upadhyaya,K.D, 1964, *Studies in Indian Folk Culture*.

Calcutta : Indian publications.

Henige, D., 1982, *Oral Historiography*, London : Harlow.

Hervik, Peter & Kirsten Kastrup (eds.), 1994, *Social Experience and Anthropological Knowledge*. London & New York : Routledge.

Hervik, Peter , 1994, "Shared reasoning in the Field: Reflexivity beyond the author". In P. Hervik and K. Kastrup (eds.) *op.cit.*

Islam, Mazharul, 1985, "Social Change and Folklore". *In The Pulse of the People : In the Context of Indic Folklore.* New Delhi : Concept Publishing Company.

Jasimuddin, 1967, "The Decline of Folksongs". In Hemango Biswas (ed.). *op.cit.*

Kakar, Sudhir, 1988, "Feminine Identity in India". In Rehana Ghandially (ed.) *Women in Indian Society, A Reader.* New Delhi : Sage Publications.

Kakkar Sukhvinder, 1986, "*Women as Portrayed in Folk Songs, A Participatory Study in Village Kirari of Delhi*," an unpublished dissertation. New Delhi : Lady Irwin College.

Katarya, Gita & Anjali Capila, 1987, "Women as Portrayed in Folk Songs: Attempts to Create Alternatiavesa". *Man in India*, Vol.67, 2.

Kempny, Marian & Burszta, J. Wojciech, 1994, "On the Relevance of Commonsense for Anthropological Knowledge". In P. Hervik and K. Kastrup (eds.) *op.cit.*

Kohn,Tamara, 1994, "Incomers and Fieldworkers:Study of Social Experience", in P. Hervik and K. Kastrup (eds.) *op.cit.*

Kumar, Nita (ed.), 1994, *Women as Subjects, South Asian Histories*. New Delhi : Stree, Book Review Literary Trust.

Mahapatra, P., 1967, "Folk songs: Problems of Collection and Editing", in Hemango Biswas,*op.cit.*

Mahahajan, Anil, 1991, "An Anthropological Encounter with the Social Reality: A Dialogue with the Self", in Zamora,Mario D. & Bjorn B. Erring, (eds.) *Fieldwork in Cultural Anthropology,* New Delhi : Reliance.

Malik, S.C., 1968, *Indian Civilization : The Formative Period,* Shimla :

IIAS. (reprint 1987), New Delhi : Motilal Banrasidas.

Malik, S.C., 1989, *Modern Civilization : A Crisis of Fragmentation,* New Delhi, Abhinav.

Malik, S.C., 1995, *Reconceptualising the Sciences and Humanities : An Integral Approach.* New Delhi : Nehru Memorial Museum and Library and Manohar.

Naithani, R.C., 1968, "Water : A Social Problem", in Ram Rahul (ed.) *Social Work in the Himalayas.* University of Delhi : Delhi School of Social Work.

Nanda, Neeru, 1990, "Who is destroying the Himalayan Forest",in N.K. Rustomji and Charles Ramble (eds.) *Himalayan, Environment and Culture.* New Delhi : IIAS, Shimla and Indus.

Nautyal, Kusum, 1992, *Garhwali Nari : Ek Lokgeetatmak Pehchan.* Delhi : Bharati Bhasa Prakashan.

Nautyal, Shivanand, 1975, *Garhwali Lokmanas.* Ghaziabad, U.P. : Amit Prakashan.

Negi, S.S., 1990, *A Handbook of the Himalayas.* New Delhi : Indus.

Negi, S.S., 1994, *Garhwal — The Land and the People,* New Delhi : Indus.

Okely, Judith, 1994, "Vicarious and Sensory Knowledge of Chronology and Change". In P. Hervik and K. Kastrup (eds.) ,*op.cit.*

Raheja, Gloria Goodwin, 1994, "Women's Speech Genres, Kinship and Contradiction", in Nita Kumar (ed.) *Women as Subjects, South Asian Histories.* New Delhi : Stree, Book Review Library Trust.

Ramaswamy, Vijaya, 1994, "Women and the Domestic in Tamil Folk Songs". In *Man in India,* 74, 1.

Ramanujan, A.K., 1991, "Towards a Counter system; Women's tales". In Appadurai, Arjun, Frank J. Korom and Margaret Mills (eds.) *op.cit.*

Riviere, Peter. 1989. "New Trends in British Social Anthropology", *Cadernoes do Noroeste* 2, 2-3 : 7-24 : In Ruth Finnegan, *op.cit.*

Rudie, Ingrid, 1994, "Making Sense of New Experience". In P. Hervik and K. Hastrup (eds.) *op.cit.*

Sax, William, 1994, "Gender and Politics in Garhwal". In Nita Kumar, (ed.) *op. cit.*

Seth, Mridula and Anjali Capila, 1988, *Studies in Communication,* Dept. of Community Resource Management & Extension, Lady Irwin College, New Delhi. Funded by UNICEF.

Shiva, Vandana, 1988, *Staying Alive — Women, Ecology and Survival in India*, New Delhi : Kali for Women.

Singh, Jitendra, 1986, "Ecological bearing in the religious milieu of the Garhwal Himalayas," in Vidyarthi, *op. cit.*

Skolimowski, Henryk 1994, *The Participatory Mind — A new theory of knowledge and of the universe*, Penguin.

Sondhi, K. L., 1991, *Beyond Mass Communication : A New Strategy for Planning and Development*, B. R. Publishing, Delhi.

Srivastava, S. L., 1974, *Folk Culture and Oral Tradition (Comparative Study in Eastern U. P. and Rajasthan*), Abhinav, New Delhi.

Trawick, Margaret E., 1991, "Wandering Lost: A Landless Labourer's Sense of Place and Self", in Appadurai, *op. cit.*

Upadhyaya, K. D., 1964, "Folklore and folk music of U. P.", in Biswas, *op. cit.*

Vaidya, K. L., 1977, *Cultural Heritage of the Himalayas*, National, New Delhi.

Vansina, Jan, 1961, *Oral Tradition: A Study in Historical Methodology*, translated by H.M. Wright, Aldine, Chicago.

Vatsyayan, Kapila, 1976, *Traditional Indian Folk Dance,* New Delhi, Indian Book Co.

Vidyarthi, L. P. & Jha, Makhan, 1986, *Ecology, Economy and Religion of the Himalayas*, Orient, New Delhi.

Vohra, Gautam, 1995, *The Central Himalayas : Socio-economic profile of Garhwal and Kumaon*, Haranand, New Delhi.

Widlok, Thomas, 1994, "Space and the 'other': Social Experience and ethnography in the Kalahari desert", in Hervik, *op. cit.*

INDEX